Adobe® Illustrator® 10

Virtual Classroom

About the Author

David Karlins is a web designer, author, and teacher who uses Adobe Illustrator in his commercial, theatrical, music production, and other web site projects. David teaches web design at San Francisco State's Multimedia Studies Center.

Other recent web design and graphics books by David Karlins include *FrontPage 2002 Virtual Classroom* (Osborne), *The Complete Idiot's Guide to Dreamweaver* (Alpha), *The Complete Idiot's Guide to Flash* (Alpha), *Teach Yourself CorelDRAW in 24 Hours* (Sams), and *FrontPage Bible* (co-author/HMI).

Hook up with David at his web site: www.ppinet.com.

ABOUT THE CONTRIBUTING ILLUSTRATOR

Mahjabeen Butt is a web designer, illustrator, and digital artist based in San Francisco. Her portfolio URL is www.afridweb.com. She currently works as a multimedia developer for Ideum (www.ideum.com).

ABOUT THE TECHNICAL EDITOR

Carrie Gatlin is a web developer, writer, and multimedia instructor in San Francisco. Over the course of her career, she has served as the principal web producer for the Webby Awards and has authored technical features on a wide variety of topics, from web color theory to programming techniques.

Adobe® Illustrator® 10

VIRTUAL CLASSROOM

David Karlins

 OSBORNE

New York   Chicago   San Francisco
Lisbon   London   Madrid   Mexico City
Milan   New Delhi   San Juan
Seoul   Singapore   Sydney   Toronto

McGraw-Hill/Osborne
2600 Tenth Street
Berkeley, California 94710
U.S.A.

To arrange bulk purchase discounts for sales promotions, premiums, or fund-raisers, please contact **McGraw-Hill**/Osborne at the above address. For information on translations or book distributors outside the U.S.A., please see the International Contact Information on the next page of this book.

Adobe® Illustrator® 10 Virtual Classroom

Brainsville.com™
The better way to learn.

1 2 3 4 5 6 7 8 9 0 QPD QPD 0 1 9 8 7 6 5 4 3 2

Book p/n 0-07-222340-5 and CD p/n 0-07-222341-3
parts of
ISBN 0-07-222339-1

Publisher
Brandon A. Nordin

Vice President & Associate Publisher
Scott Rogers

Acquisitions Editor
Margie McAneny

Project Manager
Jenn Tust

Acquisitions Coordinator
Tana Diminyatz

Technical Editor
Carrie Gatlin

Illustrators
Mahjabeen Butt
Lyssa Sieben-Wald
Michael Mueller

Design & Production
epic

Cover Design
Ted Holladay

This book was composed with QuarkXPress™.

INTERNATIONAL CONTACT INFORMATION

AUSTRALIA
McGraw-Hill Book Company Australia Pty. Ltd.
TEL +61-2-9417-9899
FAX +61-2-9417-5687
http://www.mcgraw-hill.com.au
books-it_sydney@mcgraw-hill.com

CANADA
McGraw-Hill Ryerson Ltd.
TEL +905-430-5000
FAX +905-430-5020
http://www.mcgrawhill.ca

**GREECE, MIDDLE EAST,
NORTHERN AFRICA**
McGraw-Hill Hellas
TEL +30-1-656-0990-3-4
FAX +30-1-654-5525

MEXICO (Also serving Latin America)
McGraw-Hill Interamericana Editores S.A. de C.V.
TEL +525-117-1583
FAX +525-117-1589
http://www.mcgraw-hill.com.mx
fernando_castellanos@mcgraw-hill.com

SINGAPORE (Serving Asia)
McGraw-Hill Book Company
TEL +65-863-1580
FAX +65-862-3354
http://www.mcgraw-hill.com.sg
mghasia@mcgraw-hill.com

SOUTH AFRICA
McGraw-Hill South Africa
TEL +27-11-622-7512
FAX +27-11-622-9045
robyn_swanepoel@mcgraw-hill.com

**UNITED KINGDOM & EUROPE
(Excluding Southern Europe)**
McGraw-Hill Publishing Company
TEL +44-1-628-502500
FAX +44-1-628-770224
http://www.mcgraw-hill.co.uk
computing_neurope@mcgraw-hill.com

ALL OTHER INQUIRIES Contact:
Osborne/McGraw-Hill
TEL +1-510-549-6600
FAX +1-510-883-7600
http://www.osborne.com
omg_international@mcgraw-hill.com

Dedication

Dedicated to my mom, Rhoda Karlins, who imbued me with an appreciation for the world of art.

Acknowledgments

Thanks to everyone who contributed to this book, starting with the helpful suggestions, questions, and insights of my web design students.

Special thanks to Illustrator guru, teacher, and author T. Michael Clark for his technical expertise and advice on productivity and design techniques. And to Mahjabeen "Bina" Butt for contributing to the artwork used as models in the book.

More than any other "series" of computer books that I've written for, the Virtual Classroom authors, editors, video production folks, and publicity people work together as a responsive, innovative team. Thanks to all of them, past and present, including Roger Stewart, Margie McAneny, Gretchen Campbell, Jenn Tust, Tana Diminyatz, Eric Houts, Carrie Gatlin, the art and cover designers, and the video guys at Brainsville.com.

Contents

Introduction

WHO WILL ENJOY THIS BOOK?

You will! There comes a time in the life of every budding young (and old!) graphic designer when he or she needs to design artwork using Adobe Illustrator—the most impressive drawing package available. But translating the vision in your head to Illustrator can be intimidating.

With this book, I've set out to demystify the power of Illustrator by focusing on the most important tools and features, and illustrating them with helpful projects. Throughout the book I'll explain how to integrate your Illustrator artwork with real-world design and production projects. Since I'm not tied to Adobe, I can share candid appraisals of how Illustrator works together with both Adobe's suite of design applications, as well as graphic design packages from Macromedia and others.

By the time you finish the lessons and videos packaged with this book, I'm confident that you'll feel at ease as you translate your artistic vision into Illustrator.

WHAT MAKES THIS A VIRTUAL CLASSROOM?

The accompanying CD makes this book a *virtual classroom*. Instead of just reading about Adobe Illustrator, you can watch and listen as I discuss the different topics examined in each chapter while helpful visuals appear on screen, demonstrating various features and techniques.

It's important to note that the CD is not a visual repetition of the book—not everything discussed in the book is covered on the CD, and some topics broached on the CD are covered in more detail there than in the book. The goal for the CD is to give you the experience of sitting in on one of my classes, allowing me to elaborate on certain topics that can be better expressed and explained in a full-color, moving medium. Topics in the book that wouldn't be any better explained through sound, color, and motion are not found on the CD, whereas topics that couldn't be effectively explained through text and black-and-white images *are* found on the CD.

You can learn a great deal from the book without ever watching the CD. I hope, however, that you'll read the book *and* watch the CD to enhance what you've absorbed through your reading. This approach is the closest match to hands-on classroom training experience, because I typically discuss a topic and then show it to or demonstrate it for the class, inviting the students to work along with me on their computers so that the skills become part of each student's personal experience.

HOW THIS BOOK WORKS

Of course you know how a book *works*: you open it and start reading, turning pages as you go. Not too difficult, right? This book, however, has some useful features that you should be aware of:

▶ **Figures and Illustrations** Figures are referred to by number in the text and those numbers appear next to the figures themselves to help you associate them. When I think you will be helped by looking at a picture of what I'm describing in the text, you'll see "...as shown in Figure..." or "see Figure..."

and a reference to a particular figure by its number. Illustrations are not numbered, but the illustration appears directly below or next to the text that refers to it.

▶ **Tips and Sidebars** Whenever I thought of something that I'd present as a quick aside during class, I turned it into a tip. Tips relate to the main topic in the nearby text, but are extra bits of helpful information rather than entire topics unto themselves. Sidebars delve a little deeper, discussing larger topics that relate to nearby text.

▶ **CD references** At the end of chapters containing topics covered on the CD, an "On the Virtual Classroom CD-ROM" notation appears, directing you to the specific CD lesson that relates to the chapter you've just read.

I hope you enjoy the book and the attached videos. You'll find additional Illustrator, graphics, and web design resources at my Web site: www.ppinet.com. I invite you to use those resources, and to contact me at the site with specific questions, insights, suggestions, and constructive criticisms.

ILLUSTRATOR 10 VIRTUAL CLASSROOM CD

This CD contains an exciting new kind of video-based instruction to help you learn Illustrator 10 faster. We believe this learning tool is a unique development in the area of computer-based training. The author actually talks to you, right from your computer screen, demonstrating topics he wrote about in the book. Moving "screen-cams" and slides accompany his presentation, reinforcing what you're learning.

The technology and design of the presentation were developed by Brainsville.com. The content on the CD-ROM was developed by McGraw-Hill/Osborne, Robert Fuller, and Brainsville.com. Patents (pending), copyright, and trademark protections apply to this technology and the names *Brainsville* and Brainsville.com.

Please read the following directions for usage of the CD-ROM, to ensure that the lessons play as smoothly as possible.

GETTING STARTED

The CD-ROM is optimized to run under Windows 95/98/ME/NT/2000 or a Mac, using the QuickTime player version 5 (or later), from Apple. If you don't have the

QuickTime 5 player installed, you must install it, either by downloading it from the Internet at http://www.quicktime.com, or running the Setup program from the CD-ROM. If you install from the Web, it's fine to use the free version of the QuickTime player. You don't need to purchase the full version. If you can't install the QuickTime player, or you prefer to use Windows Media Player, we have provided the lessons in that format as well, primarily as a backup plan. See the Troubleshooting section for details.

> **NOTE** In order to play this video, be sure to install QuickTime player version 5, which is included on this CD.

To install the QuickTime player from the CD-ROM follow these steps:

On a Windows PC

1. Insert the CD-ROM in the drive.
2. Use Explorer or My Computer to browse to the CD-ROM.
3. Open the QuickTime folder.
4. Open the Windows folder.
5. Double-click on the QuickTime Installer program there.
6. Follow the setup instructions on screen.

On a Mac

1. Insert the CD-ROM in the drive.
2. Open the QuickTime folder.
3. Open the Mac folder.
4. Run the QuickTime installer file there.

RUNNING THE CD IN WINDOWS 95/98/ME/NT/2000/XP

Minimum Requirements

▶ QuickTime 5 player

▶ Pentium II P300 (or equivalent)

▶ 64MB of RAM

▶ 8X CD-ROM

▶ Windows 95, Windows 98, Windows NT 4.0
(with at least Service Pack 4), Windows ME,
Windows 2000, or Windows XP

▶ 16-bit sound card and speakers

> **NOTE** If you are having trouble running the CD using a Windows XP machine, see the Troubleshooting section later in this chapter.

Illustrator 10 Virtual Classroom CD-ROM can run
directly from the CD (running the videos from the
hard drive for better performance is explained in the "Improving Playback" section below) and should start automatically on a PC when you insert the CD in the
drive. If the program does not start automatically, your system may not be set up
to automatically detect CDs. To change this, you can do the following (but read
the next section first):

1. Choose Settings, Control Panel, and click the System icon.

2. Click the Device Manager tab in the System Properties dialog box.

3. Double-click the Disk Drives icon and locate your CD-ROM drive.

4. Double-click the CD-ROM drive icon and then click the Settings tab in the
   CD-ROM Properties dialog box. Make sure the "Auto insert notification" box
   is checked. This specifies that Windows will be notified when you insert a compact disc into the drive.

If you don't care about the auto-start setting for your CD-ROM, and don't mind
the manual approach, you can start the lessons manually, this way:

1. Insert the CD-ROM.

2. Double-click the My Computer icon on your Windows desktop.

3. Open the CD-ROM folder.

4. Double-click the startnow.exe icon in the folder.

5. Follow instructions on the screen to start.

RUNNING THE CD ON A MAC

Minimum Requirements

▶ A PowerPC processor–based Macintosh computer

▶ At least 64MB of RAM

▶ Mac OS 7.5.5 or later including the latest version of OS X

To run the CD:

1. Insert the CD-ROM.
2. Double-click on the file INlesson to start the introduction.

THE OPENING SCREEN

When the program autostarts on a PC, you'll see a small window in the middle of your screen. Simply click the indicated link to begin your lessons. This will launch the QuickTime player and start the introductory lesson.

On some computers, after the lesson loads you must click the Play button to begin. The Play button is the big round button with an arrow on it at the bottom center of the QuickTime player window. It looks like the play button on a VCR. You can click on the links in the lower left region of the presentation window to jump to a given lesson.

The QuickTime player will completely fill a screen that is running at 800x600 resolution. (This is the minimum resolution required to play the lessons.) For screens with higher resolution, you can adjust the position of the player on screen, as you like.

If you are online, you can click on the Brainsville.com logo under the index marks to jump directly to the Brainsville.com web site for information about additional video lessons from Brainsville.com.

IMPROVING PLAYBACK

Your Virtual Classroom CD-ROM employs some cutting-edge technologies, requiring that your computer be pretty fast to run the lessons smoothly. Many variables determine a computer's video performance, so we can't give you specific requirements for running the lessons. CPU speed, internal bus speed, amount of RAM, CD-ROM drive transfer rate, video display performance, CD-ROM cache settings, and other variables will determine how well the lessons will play. Our advice is to simply try the CD. The disk has been tested on laptops and desktops of various speeds, and in general, we have determined that you'll need at least a Pentium II-class computer running in excess of 300MHz for decent performance. (If you're doing serious web-design work, it's likely your machine is at least this fast.)

CLOSE OTHER PROGRAMS

For best performance, make sure you are not running other programs in the background while viewing the CD-based lessons. If you want to have the program you're learning (in this case, Illustrator) open so you can switch to it to try new techniques as you learn them, that is perhaps the one exception. Rendering the video on your screen takes a lot of computing power, and background programs such as automatic e-mail checking, web-site updating, or Active Desktop applets (such as scrolling stock tickers) can tax the CPU to the point of slowing the videos.

ADJUST THE SCREEN COLOR DEPTH
TO SPEED UP PERFORMANCE

It's possible the author's lips will be out of synch with his or her voice, just like web-based videos often look. There are a couple of solutions. Start with this one. Lowering the color depth to 16-bit color makes a world of difference with many computers, laptops included. Rarely do people need 24-bit or 32-bit color for their work anyway, and it makes scrolling your screen (in any program) that much slower when running in those higher color depths. Try this (on a PC):

1. Right-click on the desktop and choose Properties.
2. Click the Settings tab.
3. In the Colors section, open the drop-down list box and choose a lower setting. If you are currently running at 24-bit (True Color) color, for example, try 16-bit (High Color). Don't use 256 colors, since video will appear very funky if you do.
4. Click OK to close the box. With most computers these days, you don't have to restart the computer after making this change. The video should run more smoothly now, since your computer's CPU doesn't have to work as hard to paint the video pictures on your screen.

On a Mac, use the Control Panels, then Monitors, to adjust the color depth. On OS X changes are made in System Preferences, Displays. Choose Thousands.

If adjusting the color depth didn't help the synch problem, see the section about copying the CD's files to the hard disk.

TURN OFF SCREEN SAVERS, SCREEN BLANKERS, AND STANDBY OPTIONS

When lessons are playing you're not likely to interact with the keyboard or mouse. Because of this, your computer screen might blank, and in some cases (such as with laptops) the computer might even go into a standby mode. You'll want to prevent these annoyances by turning off your screen saver and by checking the power options settings to ensure they don't kick in while you're viewing the lessons. You make settings for both of these parameters from the Control Panel. (You can, if you prefer, just press the SPACEBAR or the SHIFT key to wake up the screen if it blanks.) For PCs (only):

1. Open Control Panel, choose Display, and click on the Screen Saver tab. Choose "None" for the screen saver.

2. Open Control Panel, choose Power Management, and set System Standby, Turn Off Monitor, and Turn Off Hard Disks to Never. Then click Save As and save this power setting as "Brainsville Courses." You can return your power settings to their previous state if you like, after you are finished viewing the lessons. Just use the Power Schemes drop-down list and choose one of the factory-supplied settings, such as Home/Office Desk.

COPY THE CD FILES TO THE HARD DISK TO SPEED UP PERFORMANCE

The CD-ROM drive will whir quite a bit when running the lessons from the CD. If your computer or CD-ROM drive is a bit slow, it's possible the author's lips will be out of synch with his or her voice, just like web-based videos often look. The video might freeze or slow down occasionally, though the audio will typically keep going along just fine. If you don't like the CD constantly whirring, or you are annoyed by out-of-synch video, you may be able to solve either or both problems by copying the CD-ROM's contents to your hard disk and running the lessons from there. To do so on a PC or Mac:

1. Check to see that you have at least 650MB free space on your hard disk.

2. Create a new folder on your hard disk (the name doesn't matter) and copy all the contents of the CD-ROM to the new folder (you must preserve the subfolder names and folder organization as it is on the CD-ROM).

3. Once that is done, you can start the program by opening the new folder and double-clicking on the file startnow.exe (on a PC) or Inlesson (on a Mac). This will automatically start the lessons and run them from the hard disk.

4. (Optional in Windows) For convenience, you can create a shortcut to the startnow.exe file and place it on your desktop. You will then be able to start the program by clicking on the shortcut.

Update your QuickTime player

The QuickTime software is updated frequently and posted on the Apple QuickTime web site, www.quicktime.com. You can update your software by clicking Update Existing Software, from the Help menu in the QuickTime player. We strongly suggest you do this from time to time.

Make sure your CD-ROM drive is set for optimum performance

CD-ROM drives on IBM PCs can be set to transfer data using the DMA (Direct Memory Access) mode, assuming the drive supports this faster mode. If you are experiencing slow performance and out-of-synch problems, check this setting. These steps are for Windows 98 and Windows ME.

1. Open Control Panel and choose System.

2. Click on the Device Manager tab.

3. Click on the + sign to the left of the CD-ROM drive.

4. Right-click on the CD-ROM drive.

5. Choose Properties.

6. Click the Settings tab.

7. Look to see if the DMA check box is turned on (has a check mark in it).

If selected, this increases the CD-ROM drive access speed. Some drives do not support this option. If the DMA check box remains selected after you restart Windows, then this option is supported by the device.

In Windows 2000, the approach is a little different. You access the drive's settings via Device Manager as above, but click on IDE/ATAPI Controllers. Right-click the IDE channel that your CD-ROM drive is on, choose Properties, and make the settings as appropriate. (Choose the device number, 0 or 1, and check the settings. Typically it's set to DMA If Available, which is fine. It's not recommended that you change these settings unless you know what you are doing.

TROUBLESHOOTING

This section offers solutions to common problems. Check www.quicktime.com for much more information about the QuickTime player, which is the software the Virtual Classroom CDs use to play.

THE CD WILL NOT RUN

If you have followed the previous instructions and the program will not work, you may have a defective drive or a defective CD. Be sure the CD is inserted properly in the drive. (Test the drive with other CDs, to see if they run.)

YOU ARE RUNNING WINDOWS XP AND THE LESSONS WON'T START

Due to strange interactions between Windows XP and QuickTime 5, QuickTime movies may not run when the link on the splash screen is clicked on. This appears to have to do with the .MOV file association not being made correctly during installation of QuickTime. Here is the workaround to get things going:

1. After installing QuickTime (which I assume you have done), run QuickTime Player (from the Start button).
2. In the QuickTime Player window, click File/Open Movie.
3. Browse to the CD-ROM drive using the resulting dialog box.
4. Open the movie called INlesson.mov.
5. The introductory lesson should now play. Now you can open other lessons by clicking on the navigation menu within the lessons.

THE SCREENCAM MOVIE IN A LESSON HANGS

If the author continues to talk, but the accompanying screencam seems to be stuck, just click on the lesson index in the lower left region of the QuickTime window to begin your specific lesson again. If this doesn't help, close the QuickTime window, then start the Virtual Classroom again.

Volume is too low or is totally silent

1. Check your system volume first. Click on the little speaker icon next to the clock, down in the lower right-hand corner of the screen. A little slider pops up. Adjust the slider, and make sure the Mute check box is not checked.

2. Next, if you have external speakers on your computer, make sure your speakers are turned on, plugged in, wired up properly, and the volume control on the speakers themselves is turned up.

3. Note that the QuickTime player also has a volume control setting. The setting is a slider control in the lower left of the QuickTime Player window.

4. The next place to look if you're still having trouble, is in the Windows volume controls. Double-click on the little speaker by the clock, and it will bring up the Windows Volume Control sliders. Make sure the slider for "Wave" is not muted, and it's positioned near the top.

BACKUP LESSONS This CD includes alternate files for all of the lessons, in the Windows Media format, for playing in the Windows Media Player. We've supplied these extra files in case you have trouble running the lessons in the QuickTime player. These files, though of a somewhat lower-quality appearance than the QuickTime files, may still be useful if you have trouble running the QuickTime files. Note also that the navigation links that appear beneath the author's face will not work in the Windows Media Player files. This is due to limitations in the Windows Media player.

To view the backup lessons:

Windows users can click on the Windows Media Files link in the normal startup screen for this CD. (If the startup screen didn't appear when you inserted the CD, double-click the startnow.exe icon.) Use the resulting browser window for starting your lessons. When a lesson ends, return to the browser window and click on the next lesson you want to run.

Mac users can double-click the HTML file called WMfiles.html. Use the resulting browser window for starting your lessons. When a lesson ends, return to the browser window and click on the next lesson you want to run.

(Continued)

BACKUP LESSONS *(Continued)*

In Media Player, we suggest you set the skin to Classic, then switch to Compact Mode and then set the view to 100%. The picture will be much clearer that way.

As an alternative approach to running the Windows Media files, you can simply use Windows Explorer or the Mac Finder to navigate to the Windows Media folder on the CD. Then open the Windows Media folder and double-click on the lesson name you want to see. For example, 01lesson.wmv is lesson 1.

To view the Windows Media files, you will need the Windows Media player. (This player is available for both the PC and Mac platforms.) It is likely to be installed on your Windows PC already. If you're on a Mac, or if you don't have the latest Windows Media player (you'll need version 6.4 or later), you can download the latest Windows Media Player for free from www.microsoft.com/windowsmedia.

FOR TECHNICAL SUPPORT

▶ Phone Hudson Software at (800) 217-0059

▶ Visit www.quicktime.com

▶ Visit www.brainsville.com

© 2002 The McGraw-Hill Companies

© 2002 Brainsville.com Patents pending

A Quick Tour of Illustrator 10

Adobe Illustrator is an almost magical tool for

generating artwork for print and web projects. There's simply

no other tool that allows you the kind of control over lines and

curves, fills, and color effects. The power of Illustrator comes

from the fact that it is a *vector*-based drawing tool. And while

vectors give Illustrator its muscle, versatility, and subtlety, most

artists find vectors rather unintuitive at first.

THE LOGIC OF ILLUSTRATOR'S CURVES

What are vectors? *Webster's Dictionary* offers a helpful, synthesized definition: "a quantity that has magnitude and direction" (Zane Publishing, Inc., and Merriam-Webster, Incorporated, 2000).

To break this down a bit, vector magnitude incorporates elements like length, outline color, outline thickness, and fills. Vector direction means that they go from point *a* to point *b,* although not necessarily in a straight line.

Vector art is best understood in contrast to *bitmap* graphics, the more prevalent way of creating and saving digital artwork. Bitmap (also called raster) artwork maps tiny bits on a printer or monitor. Bitmaps are composed of large numbers of tiny dots (pixels). Each individual pixel in a bitmap image is generated individually, and stores information like color, brightness, transparency, and so on.

VECTORS AND BITMAPS

From an efficiency standpoint, vector art is much better than bitmaps. Instead of each file having to store data for huge numbers of bitmaps, illustrations are saved in a format that simply keeps track of each *path* (line) in the illustration, and the properties associated with that path. As a result, especially for large illustrations, Illustrator's vector files are generally smaller than a similar illustration saved to a bitmap format.

Vector art is also *scalable.* The drawing you create in Illustrator can be printed on a matchbook cover, a business card, a large banner, and a billboard over Times Square without losing any quality or increasing significantly in file size. By comparison, bitmap images lose quality and/or bloat way out in file size as an image size is increased. Figure 1-1 shows an image at its original size, and then enlarged five times as both a vector and a bitmap image.

Bitmap images are better for editing photographs, where the ability to edit an image pixel by pixel creates more freedom for intricate fine-tuning of the image appearance. Vector images are better for working with lines and curves, including customizing text, technical illustrations, animation, and artwork that simulates drawings created with pens, brushes, and other drawing tools (ranging from spraypaint to calligraphic pens).

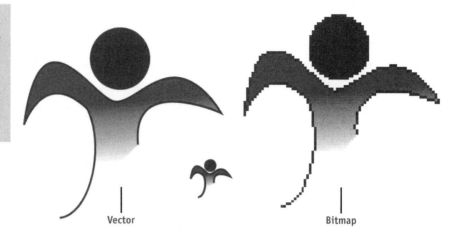

FIGURE 1-1
The bitmap image loses quality as it is enlarged, while the vector image retains the smoothness of the original curves without increasing in file size.

Vector

Bitmap

Many complex illustrations mix both bitmap and vector art. Illustrator can incorporate bitmaps into illustrations, and provides some rudimentary editing features for bitmaps. But in general, you (or a collaborator) will create bitmaps in a program like Adobe Photoshop and bring them into Illustrator in a basically finished state.

VECTORS IN PRINT AND WEB DESIGN

What happens to illustrations after you create them in Illustrator? Leaving aside those you create for fun and flush down the drain by exiting without saving, your Illustrator artwork will either appear digitally on someone's monitor, or in some form of hardcopy (book, magazine, brochure, billboard, etc.).

Illustrator drawings can be easily integrated into desktop publishing programs like Adobe PageMaker, Adobe InDesign, and QuarkXPress. These programs, and others, support Illustrator's native AI file format, and even more programs support Illustrator's EPS file format that preserves the features of your illustration for export.

Presenting Illustrator artwork on the Web is a bit more of a challenge because mainstream browser support for images is limited to bitmap file formats like JPEG and GIF. However, Illustrator provides extremely powerful and easy-to-use export-to-web tools that make it easy to convert your Illustrator vectors to web-compatible bitmaps.

Over the last two or three years, vector images have found a home on the Web, largely due to the success of Macromedia Flash. The Flash Player is, according to some studies, installed on most web browsers, and it allows the display of vector images on the Web. In addition, Adobe in particular is promoting the Scalable Vector Graphics (SVG) format that integrates with XML, a more powerful page-description language that has the potential to be adopted widely on the Web.

In short, the vector images you create in Illustrator are likely to be shipped off to another program to be integrated into a publication, a movie, a web site, or some other larger presentation. Adobe, with some justification, pitches their suite of graphic, web design, page layout, and animation applications as a seamless environment. Not being on the Adobe payroll, I can confide to you that Illustrator integrates quite nicely with non-Adobe products as well.

What's New in Illustrator 10?

Illustrator 10 is an evolutionary enhancement of version 9. It's more stable, runs better in the new operating systems from Steve and Bill (OS X and Windows XP, respectively), and includes some cool new features.

My favorite new feature is object-based slicing. Illustrator veterans and artists familiar with creating web illustrations are familiar with slicing images to improve download time and provide easier web page layout. But *object-based slicing* allows you to easily transform any selected object into a slice. Further, each slice can be exported to the Web with its own graphic format settings, so part of an illustration can be exported as a GIF image, part as a JPEG, and—if you need to—you can even export sections of an illustration as SVG or Flash Player files.

Other nice, new features include a bunch of fun distortion tools the folks at Adobe are billing as *liquefying* tools because they "melt" sections of an image and apply effects that spin, warp, and otherwise flow lines and curves. *Symbols*—reusable graphic objects—are a new and efficient way to place multiple copies of a single object throughout an illustration, with options for revising all instances of that symbol throughout the file.

Some of the enhancements in version 10 are aimed at very high-level image production processes, and are beyond the scope of this book. Among those is dynamic data-driven graphics, a tool for rationalizing the production of large numbers of similar graphics.

All that said, if you're using an older version of Illustrator, I think you'll find this book and the accompanying instructional videos quite useful. And, when you bump into a new feature you just *have* to have, you can run out (or go online) and upgrade to version 10.

CREATING AN ILLUSTRATOR DOCUMENT

When you first launch Illustrator, a blank screen appears. The screen will display whichever palettes were showing when you exited your last session.

To create a new document, choose File | New, or press COMMAND/CTRL-N. The New Document dialog box opens, allowing you to define the size and color system for your illustration. The New Document dialog box reflects the settings you last used to define your document, so yours might well look different than mine, shown here.

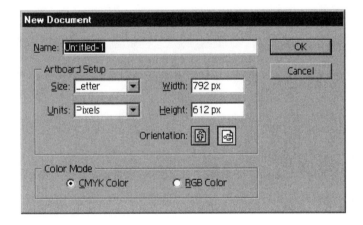

If you wish, you can simply accept the existing settings in the New Document dialog box. In that case, you can change document settings later by choosing File | Document Setup. But in general, you'll want to define document settings in advance that correspond to the type and size of artwork you are creating. I'll walk you through the process of defining new document properties next.

CREATING A NEW DOCUMENT

The New Document dialog box presents you with three decisions. You need to assign a filename to your illustration, you need to set up the workspace for your illustration (called the *artboard*), and you need to decide which set of colors to use in your illustration.

Assigning a name in the New Document dialog box does not save your file. But when you choose File | Save from the Illustrator menu, the document name you assign will be the default filename.

The size of the artboard and the color palette you select should reflect how you plan to produce your illustration. You should define an artboard size that corresponds to the size of your final output, and a color palette that will be used when your illustration is produced.

SETTING UP THE ARTBOARD

The artboard defines the size of the area of the workspace that will be produced when you print your illustration. Figure 1-2 shows the artboard, along with the scratch area outside the artboard.

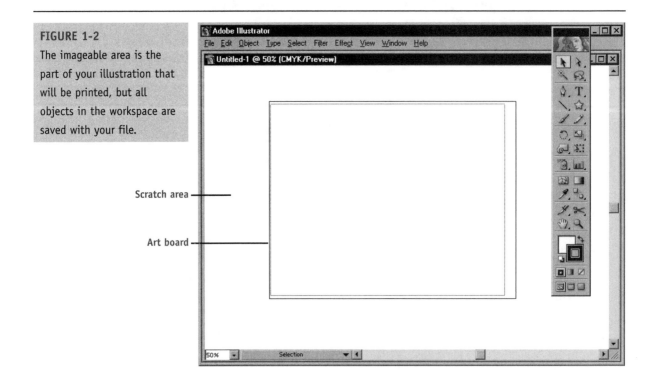

FIGURE 1-2
The imageable area is the part of your illustration that will be printed, but all objects in the workspace are saved with your file.

Scratch area

Art board

The artboard is also important when you are preparing illustrations for the Web. You can size the artboard to 800x600 pixels, or other widths typical of the size of web browsers.

To Define THE SIZE OF THE ARTBOARD

1 In the Artboard Setup area of the New Document dialog box, select a unit of measurement for your artboard from the Units drop-down list. Typically, you will chose pixels for images headed for the Web, and inches, picas, points, millimeters, or centimeters for illustrations destined for printed output.

2 Use the Size drop-down list to choose from one of the preset output sizes, or choose Custom from the Size drop-down list and use the Width and Height boxes in the dialog box to define a size not listed.

3 Use the Orientation buttons to toggle between portrait and landscape orientation for your artboard. The "sideways" icon (looks like a horizontal piece of paper) represents landscape orientation.

> **NOTE** If you decide you made a wrong choice while setting up your new document, you can change document settings at any time. Change file size by choosing File | Document Setup. The Document Setup dialog box opens, which allows you to change the size of your artboard. Or, choose Document | Color Mode to open a pop-out menu that allows you to toggle between the CMYK (printed color) or RGB (web or monitor output color). The CMYK and RGB color schemes are explained in the next section.

DEFINING COLORS

The New Document dialog box offers two options for defining colors: cyan-magenta-yellow-black (CMYK) and red-green-blue (RGB). We'll explore colors in Illustrator throughout this book; we'll look carefully at printed color output in Chapter 14, and examine web coloring in Chapter 15. But it is helpful to understand a few basic points about these options when you begin to work on your illustration.

RGB is a method of defining colors displayed on monitors. And, as the name implies, these colors are generated by combining various levels of the colors red, green, and blue.

In the CMYK color scheme, cyan is a shade of greenish blue, magenta is a purplish red, yellow is yellow, of course, and black is represented with a *K* so as not to be confused with blue. These colors are applied in layers during four-color printing to produce a wide array of colors.

There are many variations on these options. For example, a set of 216 RGB colors are supported by all (or mostly all) operating systems, and they are commonly known as *web-safe* RGB colors. Again, we'll explore all this in Chapter 12, but when you create a new document, you will generally want to choose CMYK for printed output and RGB for monitor or web output.

Once you have selected a document name, artboard setup, and color mode, you can click OK to close the New Document dialog box, and open your new file.

Navigating Palettes

Illustrator features are found both in the menu structure and in floating sets of tools called *palettes.* In many cases, the features found on the menu and in palettes intersect—that is, you can access a feature from either a menu or a palette.

Palettes are displayed by selecting them from the unintuitively named Window menu. As you select a palette, it appears on your screen. You can close a palette by deselecting it from the Window menu.

The Tool palette, referred to as the toolbox, is a special palette in that it holds dozens of tools. The toolbox provides a third way to access Illustrator features. In Chapter 2, I'll walk you through the features in the toolbox.

Most palettes (with the exception of the toolbox) have pop-out menus, accessed by clicking the right-pointing triangle in the top-right corner of the palette.

The toolbox, palettes, and menus offer a somewhat Byzantine set of options for finding Illustrator features. Throughout this book, I'll show you the easiest ways to access the features you need.

Creating New Objects in a Document

After you create a new document, you can use one of Illustrator's tools—like the Pencil tool, the Pen tool, a shape tool, a paintbrush, or type—to add new objects to your page.

If you want to do a quick experiment at this point, try the Rectangle tool. Select the tool in the toolbox. (If your toolbox is not visible, choose Window | Tools.) Then click and drag anywhere in the workspace to draw a rectangle, as shown here.

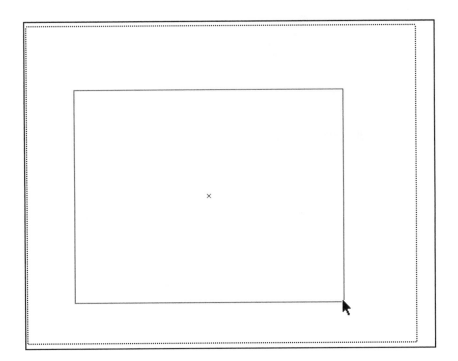

After you create objects in your document, save your work.

CUSTOMIZING PREFERENCES

With nine sets of customizable preferences, Adobe almost lets you design your own custom version of Illustrator. I won't detail every customizable option here. In many cases, I'll note preference options throughout the book where they are relevant to the feature being explored. But you will want to be aware of some preferences as you start out in Illustrator.

To access the whole set of preferences, choose Edit | Preferences in Mac OS 9 and Windows, or Illustrator | Preferences in Mac OS X, and choose from one of the sets of definable options, as shown next.

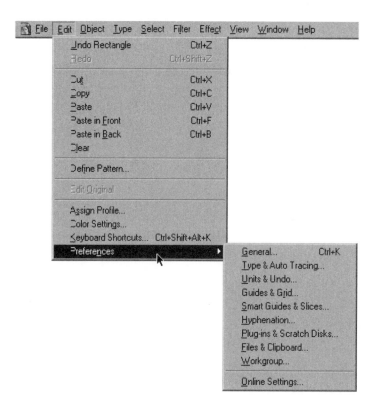

Once you open the Preferences dialog box, a drop-down menu at the top of the dialog box allows you to switch between any of the nine sets of preferences, as shown here.

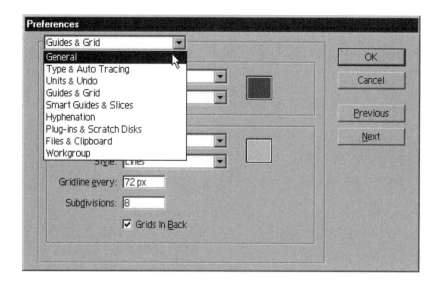

The following list summarizes the customizing features available in each set of preferences:

▶ **General** These preferences include options as remote (to non-Japanese users) as enabling Japanese crop marks, to more widely used features like ToolTips. The Keyboard Increment setting defines how much you move a selected object when you click a direction arrow on your keyboard. You'll probably want to leave all the General settings at their default state unless you recognize one you know you want to change.

▶ **Type & Auto Tracing** These preferences define how type is laid out on a page. I'll explain these features in Chapter 9. The Auto Tracing preferences define how the Auto Trace tool works when it converts imported bitmaps to vectors. Auto Trace Tolerance values can range from 1–10, and determine how carefully the Auto Trace tool adheres to the shape of the object being traced. Lower values trace more accurately, while higher values smooth out irregularities in the outline of the traced bitmap. Auto Trace Gap settings define how closely an imported bitmap image will be traced when converted to a vector, with smaller values resulting in more accurate traces. The range is from 0–2.

▶ **Units & Undo** These preferences define units of measurement for objects in Illustrator and how many Undo levels you want to enable. I'll refer back to the Units options throughout the book as we prepare illustrations for printed copy (where units like points, inches, or centimeters are appropriate) and the Web (where objects are measured in pixels). The more Undo levels you enable, the more memory Illustrator will consume from your system resources.

▶ **Guides & Grid** These preferences define how customized guides and regularly spaced alignment grids appear in Illustrator. I'll show you how to take advantage of guides and grids in Chapter 4.

▶ **Smart Guides & Slices** These preferences control which information is displayed when you enable Smart Guides from the View menu. Slices are explained in Chapter 15 when I show you how to prepare illustrations for the Web.

▶ **Hyphenation** These preferences allow you to choose a language dictionary from which to apply hyphenation to text.

▶ **Plug-Ins & Scratch Disks** These preferences allow you to define a folder with any plug-in programs you might have that are compatible with Illustrator. The Scratch Disks preference has two drop-down menus, Primary and Secondary, which define where Illustrator will store temporary files while the program is running. Pick fixed disks (not CD-R/W, Zip, or floppy disks).

▶ **Files & Clipboard** These preferences define how files are saved, and how objects are saved through the clipboard. Leave the Clipboard setting at AICB because it supports more features than PDF. The Files setting differs depending on your operating system. Mac users can append extensions (like AI) to files, which makes them more accessible to PC users. The Update Links drop-down menu defines how linked images within a file are updated, and I'll explain that in Chapter 12 when I show you how to import bitmaps (and other files) into Illustrator documents.

▶ **Workgroup** These preferences are used with files that are shared over a server.

One more customizable element of the Illustrator environment is the display in the status bar at the bottom of the Illustrator window.

At the far left of the status bar, the zoom percentage pop-up menu allows you to define zoom levels. To the right of the Zoom menu is a customizable display. By default, the status bar displays your selected tool. This can be changed to display date and time, free memory, the remaining number of undos, or the document color profile.

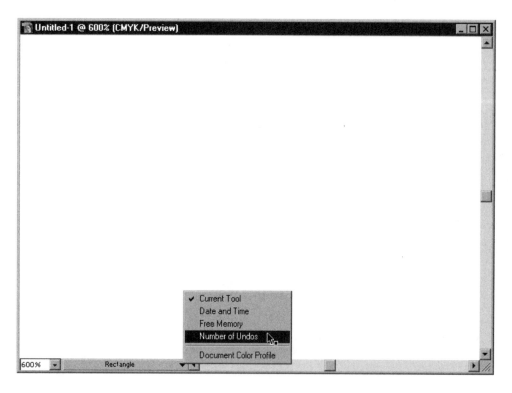

SUMMARY

Adobe Illustrator is a vector graphics program. Vector graphics are defined by paths (lines). In contrast, bitmap graphics programs like Photoshop create graphics that are edited and saved by controlling the appearance of individual pixels (dots) in an illustration. Vector images have the advantage of being small in file size, and scalable.

You can define document features like output format (print or web) and size (billboard, brochure, 800-pixel-wide computer monitor, etc.) when you create a new document. Or you can define these properties later.

You access Illustrator features from menus, palettes, and the toolbox. You create new Illustrator objects by using tools in the toolbox.

Navigating Illustrator's Interface

The Illustrator interface can be a bit overwhelming.

Like an artist working with paint or another medium, you'll be more productive and creative if you organize Illustrator's interface so that the tools you need are easy to find and use.

The nice thing about the Illustrator environment is that you can easily adapt it to your needs. Whether you're designing a billboard, a business card, or a web site, you can customize Illustrator to provide a drawing area and a set of accessible tools that fit your project.

Most of the features available in Illustrator are organized into the toolbox, or into one of the numerous available palettes. Many of these Illustrator features are available from both sources, so you can often accomplish a task in two ways.

In the course of this book, I'll introduce you to tools, menu options, and palettes as needed. But I thought it would be helpful to organize a listing of all the tools in one place—and this is it. As I introduce you to tools, I'll briefly illustrate how some of the more useful ones work.

You might find it helpful to carefully read through this chapter and explore how to control the Illustrator environment step by step. If you do that, you'll learn your way around Illustrator and get a quick introduction to its main features.

On the other hand, you might rush ahead to start on your project, and retreat back to this chapter when you can't figure out how to define required elements of your work environment. Or you might well do both! I've organized this chapter so you can use it either way.

USING THE TOOLBOX

Much of the power of Illustrator is stored in the 76(!) tools in the toolbox. In addition, the color and screen buttons at the bottom of the toolbox let you quickly assign (or remove) colors from objects, and you can easily toggle between different views of your workspace.

Unfortunately, the majority of the Illustrator tools are initially hidden. You see them only when you click on a tool pop-out (indicated by a small triangle in the lower-left corner of the tool).

All this can be a bit overwhelming until you learn your way around the toolbox. You will eventually get comfortable finding needed tools, but I wanted to provide a clear, easy map to the toolbox right away and explain very briefly what each tool does. Figure 2-1 shows the Illustrator toolbox with pop-outs.

FIGURE 2-1

The toolbox (top) with tool pop-outs (below).

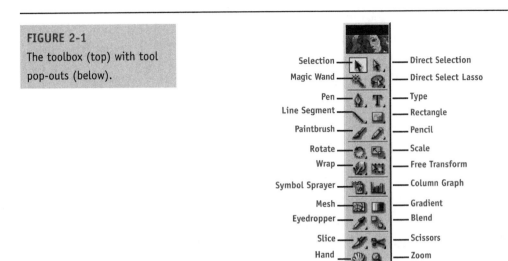

Selection — Direct Selection
Magic Wand — Direct Select Lasso
Pen — Type
Line Segment — Rectangle
Paintbrush — Pencil
Rotate — Scale
Wrap — Free Transform
Symbol Sprayer — Column Graph
Mesh — Gradient
Eyedropper — Blend
Slice — Scissors
Hand — Zoom

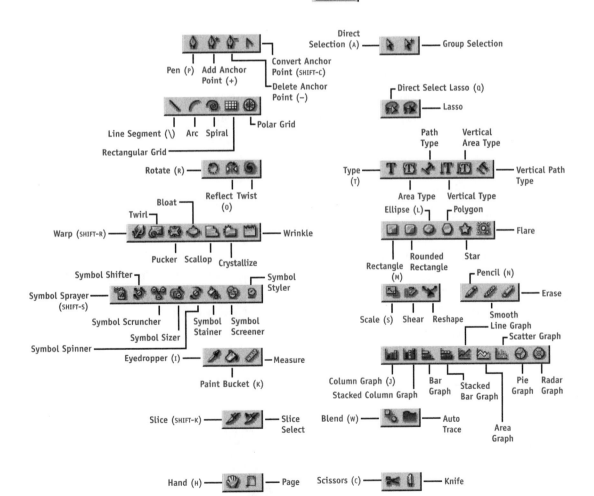

Pen (P) Add Anchor Point (+) Convert Anchor Point (SHIFT-C) Delete Anchor Point (–)

Direct Selection (A) — Group Selection

Line Segment (\) Arc Spiral Polar Grid
Rectangular Grid

Direct Select Lasso (Q) — Lasso

Rotate (R) Reflect Twist (O)

Path Type   Vertical Area Type
Type (T) — Vertical Path Type
Area Type   Vertical Type

Warp (SHIFT-R) Twirl Bloat Pucker Scallop Crystallize Wrinkle

Ellipse (L)   Polygon
Rectangle (M) Rounded Rectangle Star Flare

Symbol Shifter Symbol Styler
Symbol Sprayer (SHIFT-S)
Symbol Scruncher Symbol Stainer Symbol Screener
Symbol Sizer
Symbol Spinner

Pencil (N) — Erase
Smooth

Scale (S) Shear Reshape

Eyedropper (I) — Measure
Paint Bucket (K)

Line Graph Scatter Graph
Column Graph (J) Bar Graph Pie Graph Radar Graph
Stacked Column Graph Stacked Bar Graph

Slice (SHIFT-K) — Slice Select

Blend (W) — Auto Trace Area Graph

Hand (H) — Page

Scissors (C) — Knife

The buttons at the bottom of the toolbox help you quickly assign colors to the fill or stroke (outline) of objects. Other buttons make it easy to select from standard or full-screen views. I'll explain how they work in the section "Using the Selection Tools" a bit later in this chapter, but first, I'll identify the buttons in Figure 2-2.

CONTROLLING TOOLBOX DISPLAY

The toolbox is so useful that you're likely to display it all the time when you work in Illustrator. If for some reason you've "lost" your toolbox, choose Window | Tools to display it. As you work on an illustration, you can move the toolbox out of the way by clicking and dragging the blue bar at the top of the toolbox.

FINDING TOOLS

One way to search for tools is to hover over a tool. The tool name displays, along with the shortcut key in parentheses, if there is one. The illustration on the right shows the Selection tool (and its shortcut key, v) identified with a Tool Tip.

Some tools have shortcut keys, as identified in Figure 2-1. And I'll list them again in the course of this chapter when I explain what each tool does. Nobody memorizes all the shortcut keys, but if you use some tools frequently, you'll soon get comfortable accessing them with a quick keystroke.

As I warned you in the beginning of this chapter, the really crazy thing about the toolbox is that most of the tools aren't visible! They display only

> **NOTE** You can turn Tool Tips on (or off) by choosing Edit | Preferences | General, and selecting (or deselecting) the Show Tool Tips check box.

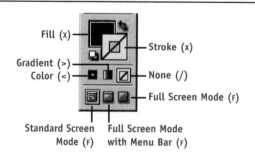

FIGURE 2-2
The color and screen buttons in the toolbox

Fill (x)
Stroke (x)
Gradient (>)
Color (<)
None (/)
Full Screen Mode (F)
Standard Screen Mode (F)
Full Screen Mode with Menu Bar (F)

when you click on a tool pop-out. Tool pop-outs are distinguished in the toolbox by a tiny triangle in the lower-right corner of the tool.

When you click and hold down the mouse button on a tool pop-out, a set of additional tools displays. You select a tool from the pop-out. Or, if you will be frequently using the set of tools found on a pop-out, you can remove a pop-out by clicking the Tearoff button at the end of each pop-out, as shown here.

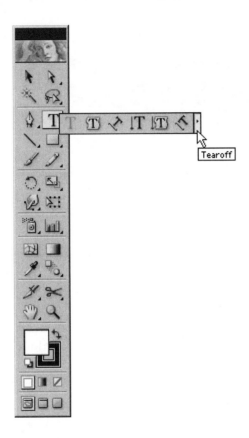

TOURING ILLUSTRATOR'S TOOLS

This section introduces you to Illustrator's tools and provides you with a quick preview of how to accomplish some of the most useful drawing and editing techniques in Illustrator. Along the way, I'll show you how to select objects and elements of objects, how to draw lines, shapes, and curves, how to edit drawings, and how to select and move objects. Ready? Here goes...

USING ADOBE ONLINE

The Adobe Online tool isn't exactly a *tool,* but it does link you to the Adobe web site, where you can download updated files when the folks at Adobe fine-tune Illustrator 10.

> **NOTE** You must be connected to the Internet to access Adobe Online.

To access Adobe Online, click the drawing on the top of the toolbox. The Adobe Online dialog box appears, as shown here.

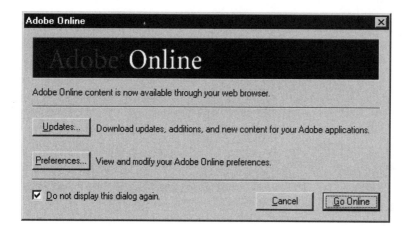

The Preferences options are also available by choosing Edit | Preferences | Online. You can tell Illustrator to automatically check for program updates every day, week, or month. And it allows you to define whether to show download progress while files are streaming into your hard disk.

The Updates button displays a list of available downloads. If you click the Updates button, the Adobe Product Updates dialog box opens. There, you can use the Choose button to define a location for the downloaded files.

> **TIP** You can also access Adobe Online and download new updates by choosing Help | Adobe Online.

USING THE SELECTION TOOLS

Before you can manipulate an object in Illustrator, you need to select it. You must select an object to move it, to scale (resize) it, to delete it, to edit it, or to apply features like effects and filters.

All those features are covered in different chapters in this book, but here, I'll show you some of the fine points of selecting all or part of objects (paths).

You use the following tools (listed with shortcut keys where applicable) to select objects in Illustrator: the Selection tool (V), the Direct Selection tool (A), the Group Selection tool, the Direct Select Lasso tool (Q), the Lasso tool, and the Magic Wand tool (Y).

That's a lot of selection tool options! And each selection tool works differently, allowing you to do different things with the path you select. The selection tools basically break down into two different types: ones that allow you to *move* or assign properties to selected objects (or to delete or copy them), and ones that allow you to *edit* individual paths and anchor points. You use the Selection, Group Selection, Lasso, and Magic Wand tools to *select* entire objects (or groups of objects). You generally use the Direct Selection and Direct Select Lasso tools to *edit* the outline of an object.

SELECTING ENTIRE OBJECTS

The Selection tool selects an entire path (object). Or, you can click and drag to draw a marquee and select several objects, as the following illustration shows.

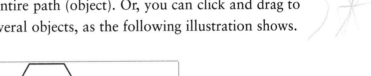

After you select an object (or objects) with the Selection tool, you can move the object by simply clicking and dragging. You can delete objects by pressing DELETE or BACKSPACE. (Select Edit | Undo if you do this by mistake.)

As you hover over parts of an object, Smart Guides identifies whether you are selecting a path or an anchor point.

The Group Selection tool is useful when you have used grouping to organize many objects into groups. You'll explore grouping in Chapter 5, and I'll discuss the Group Selection tool more there.

> **SEE ALSO** For an explanation of paths and other selectable elements of an object like anchor points, see Chapter 1.

> **NOTE** You'll have a much easier time familiarizing yourself with selection tools if you turn on Smart Guides (choose View | Smart Guides). With Smart Guides on, Illustrator provides helpful tips as you hover over objects.

The Lasso tool is similar to the Selection tool, except that you can click and drag to select irregularly shaped sets of objects, as shown here.

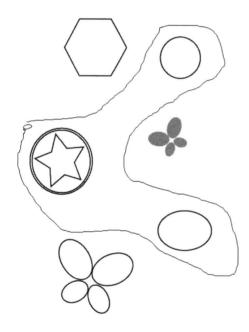

Once you have selected a bunch of objects with the Lasso tool, you can switch to the Selection tool, and drag the selected group of objects to a different location on the screen.

Finally, the Magic Wand tool selects all objects with the same color fill in an open file. Use it, for example, when you have dozens of red roses dispersed throughout an illustration and you want to select them all.

> **TIP** Holding down OPTION-ALT as you drag selected objects creates a *duplicate* of the selection you are moving.

SELECTION TOOLS THAT EDIT OBJECTS VS. SELECTION TOOLS THAT EDIT ANCHOR POINTS AND PATHS

You use the Direct Selection and Direct Select Lasso tools to select specific anchor points or paths when you want to move those specific anchor points or paths. In other words, use these tools when you want to modify the outline of a path.

To quickly see for yourself how these two types of tools work, you can draw a rectangle by choosing the Rectangle tool, as shown here, and clicking and dragging from the upper-left corner to the lower-right corner to define the rectangle size.

Use the Selection tool to select the entire rectangle by clicking on the edge, or if your rectangle has a fill, by clicking in the fill.

With your rectangle selected, click and drag to move it, as shown next.

> **NOTE** If clicking in the fill area of your rectangle doesn't work to select the object, select Edit | Preferences | General, and make sure the Use Area Select check box is selected.

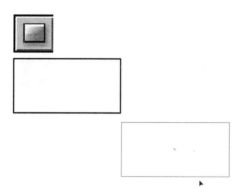

Now, try the Direct Selection tool. With the Direct Selection tool selected, click outside the rectangle first to deselect it. Then, click the upper-left corner of the rectangle. With just the anchor point selected, click and drag to move the anchor point, as shown here.

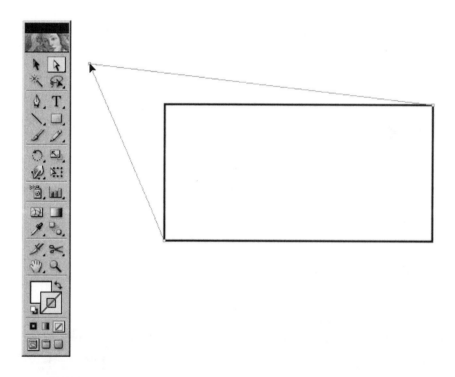

If you practice using the different selection tools to select and move objects or to select anchor points and paths and edit them, you'll become comfortable with one of the most essential skills you need to create and work with objects in Illustrator.

ESSENTIAL BASIC PROCESS

EXPLORING THE PEN TOOL POP-OUT

In some ways, the Pen tool (P) is the essential tool in Illustrator. You use it to generate lines and curves, and to give you vast control over them.

Because the Pen tool is both powerful and somewhat counterintuitive (tricky), I'll devote a whole chapter to it (Chapter 6). Here, I'll briefly introduce the tool, show you how it works, and explain the supplemental tools in the Pen tool pop-out.

The Pen tool generates objects with two basic elements: anchor points and lines. The lines can be curved or straight, and the anchor points associated with them control the curve properties of the line to which they are attached.

The tools in the Pen tool pop-out—Add Anchor Point (+), Delete Anchor Point (−), and Convert Anchor Point (SHIFT-C)—all modify anchor points and lines generated by the Pen tool. The easiest way to grasp this concept is to try it, so follow these steps to explore the tools.

To Draw AND TRANSFORM CURVES USING THE PEN TOOL

1 Click the Pen tool to select it. Click once anywhere on the artboard. Don't click and drag, just click.

2 Point and click on another location on the artboard. Nice work! You just generated a line using the Pen tool. The line has anchor points, as shown here.

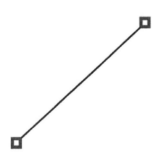

3 To finish your line, click the Selection tool (or any other tool).

4 Next, try a curved line. This is trickier, but I'll use a simple example. With the Pen tool selected, click and drag down about an inch anywhere on the artboard, as shown on the right.

5 After you draw the first line segment, release the mouse button. Then, click and drag another segment from the bottom of the first segment, about two inches to the right, as shown here. Then click the Selection tool to finish your curve.

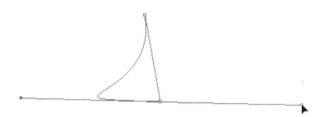

In the previous exercise, you created the two basic types of lines (also known as paths) and anchor points: straight and curved. These points act differently when you edit them. If you use the Direct Selection tool to drag on a corner or straight anchor point, it moves. But if you click a smooth point with the Direct Selection tool, you can either move that anchor point, or you can adjust the curve by moving the associated direction lines that appear when the anchor point is selected.

You use the Add Anchor Point tool, Delete Anchor Point tool, and Convert Anchor Point tool to add, delete, or modify the type of anchor point. You'll learn how to use these tools in Chapter 6.

> **NOTE** A couple clues about things that happen as you draw: If you click and drag along a horizontal or vertical axis or along a 45 degree angle, Smart Guides will appear, identifying the angle at which you are drawing. Also, by default, Illustrator adds a fill to your curve. If your settings have been changed, your curve may display without a fill.

EDITING AND FORMATTING WITH THE TYPE TOOL POP-OUT

Illustrator can create, edit, format, align, lay out in columns, and yes, even spell check text. In fact, some people use Illustrator as their word processor!

That's OK, but the real power of Illustrator's type tools lies in their ability to mold text around and inside of objects, as shown here.

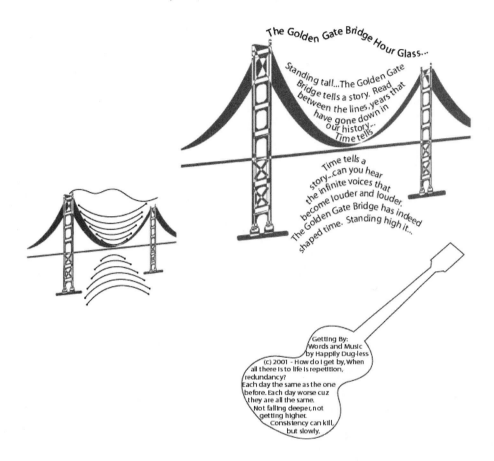

You'll explore the Type tool (T) and its pop-out cousins—the Area Type tool, the Path Type tool, the Vertical Type tool, the Vertical Area Type tool, and the Vertical Path Type tool—in Chapter 8. So if you want to create objects with aligned and filled text like I've shown you here, jump right to Chapter 8.

DRAWING TOOLS IN THE LINE TOOL POP-OUT

Although the Pen tool provides infinite control over the shape of your drawing, Illustrator also includes a set of easy-to-use tools for drawing common curves: the Line Segment tool (\), the Arc tool, the Spiral tool, the Rectangular Grid tool, and the Polar Grid tool. Each of these tools is demonstrated in the illustration on the right, and they are covered in detail in Chapter 3.

Accessing Shapes in the Rectangle Tool Pop-Out

Like the tools in the Line tool pop-out, the tools in the Rectangle tool family draw prefab shapes, as shown on the right.

The Rectangle tool pop-out comprises the Rectangle tool (M), the Rounded Rectangle tool, the Ellipse tool (L), the Polygon tool, the Star tool, and the Flare tool. I'll cover all these tools in Chapter 3.

Using the Paintbrush Tool

The Paintbrush tool (B) draws freehand lines that look like traditional brush strokes, like the ones here.

I'll demonstrate how to use the Paintbrush tool in Chapter 3.

Draw, Smooth, and Erase: Using the Pencil Tool Pop-Out

The Pencil tool (N) provides an easy way to draw freehand lines—without the complexity (or power) of the Pen tool. Accompanying the Pencil tool in its pop-out are the Smooth tool and the Erase tool. You use the Erase tool to erase sections of a curve.

The Smooth tool is pretty cool; you can use it to smooth out kinks in the curves you draw with the pencil, as shown here.

ROTATION TOOLS IN THE ROTATE TOOL POP-OUT

The Rotate tool pop-out includes not only the Rotate tool (R), but also the Reflect tool (O) and the Twist tool.

The Rotate tool spins a selected object around a selected point. The Reflect tool acts like a mirror, creating an opposite object. And the (new) Twist tool acts like you placed an object on a record player and cranked up the speed, as shown here.

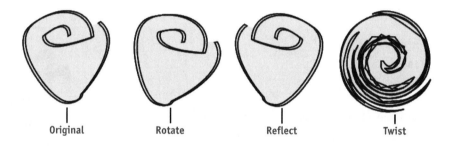

Original   Rotate   Reflect   Twist

SIZING AND SKEWING: THE SCALE TOOL POP-OUT

The Scale tool (S) resizes an object, the Shear tool skews (distorts) a selected object, and the Reshape tool provides some interesting ways to smooth out a curve or alter an object, while keeping the object's basic shape intact. The next illustration shows the effects of all three tools, and they are explored in detail in Chapter 5.

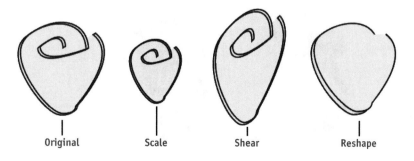

Original   Scale   Shear   Reshape

Using the Warp Tool and the Warp Tool Pop-Out

The seven tools in the Warp tool pop-out are new to Illustrator 10, and have been dubbed the *Liquefy* tools by the publicists at Adobe—so-called because they "liquefy" fixed objects into putty-like malleability. The tools are the Warp tool (SHIFT-R), the Twirl tool, the Pucker tool, the Bloat tool, the Scallop tool, the Crystallize tool, and the Wrinkle tool. Each of them applies a separate and wild distortion to a selected curve. Click and drag on any part of a selected object to experiment with these effects. If you don't like the change, choose Edit | Undo to restore the original artwork.

Apply one of the tools in the Warp tool pop-out by first selecting an object, and then clicking different parts of the object with one of the Warp tool pop-outs. In Figure 2-3, I used all seven of these tools to distort the drawing on the left into the one on the right.

Easy Object Editing with the Free Transform Tool

The Free Transform tool (E) is kind of a combination tool. When you select an object and then click the Free Transform tool, a marquee with handles appears around the selected object.

You can use the handles on this marquee to rotate (as shown in the illustration on the right), resize, reflect, or shear the object.

FIGURE 2-3
The Warp, Twirl, Pucker, Bloat, Scallop, Crystallize, and Wrinkle tools are applied to different parts of the drawing on the right.

GOING WILD WITH THE SYMBOL SPRAYER TOOL POP-OUT

You use the Symbol Sprayer tool (SHIFT-S) to reproduce many copies of a symbol selected from the Symbols palette. I'll explain how palettes work in the section "Managing Palettes" later in this chapter, but if you want to try this out now, choose Window | Symbols to display the Symbols palette, click one of the symbols in the palette, and then click and drag with the Symbol Sprayer tool to "shoot" symbols onto the page as if you were spraying them with a spraycan. The result will look something like this.

You can use the Symbol Shifter, Symbol Scruncher, Symbol Sizer, Symbol Spinner, Symbol Stainer, Symbol Screener, and Symbol Styler tools to distort sets of symbols created using the Symbol Sprayer tool. To experiment with any or all of these tools, select an object sprayed out of the Symbol Sprayer tool, and then choose a tool from the Symbol Sprayer tool pop-out and click away.

> **TIP** Select Edit | Undo to undo sprayer effects—or any other action in Illustrator.

GRAPHING? USE THE COLUMN GRAPH TOOL POP-OUT

If you need to create and format charts and graphs, you can use Illustrator's set of graphing tools in the Column Graph tool pop-out: the Column Graph tool (J), the Stacked Column Graph tool, the Bar Graph tool, the Stacked Bar Graph tool, the Line Graph tool, the Area Graph tool, the Scatter Graph tool, the Pie Graph tool, and the Radar Graph tool.

When you select any of the graphing tools and draw a marquee on the artboard, a spreadsheet grid appears, as shown in Figure 2-4. You can enter data in this spreadsheet or import data from a text file. Tools on the graph spreadsheet allow you to import data, transpose rows and columns, switch the x and y (vertical and horizontal) axes, define cell styles, revert (undo) an entry, or apply an entry.

Illustrator performs a lot of tasks well, but for full-featured spreadsheet and charting, you'll probably want to use a spreadsheet program.

CREATING HIGHLIGHTS WITH THE MESH TOOL

Illustrator's Mesh tool (U) gives you total control over the placement of highlighting within an object fill. I'll cover this feature in detail in Chapter 7, but the next illustration gives you a basic sense of how the tool works.

Here's the quick version of how to use this tool: Select an object with a fill, and use the Mesh tool to create anchor points (as shown in the illustration on the next page).

FIGURE 2-4
The tools in the graphing spreadsheet allow you to create chart data right in Illustrator.

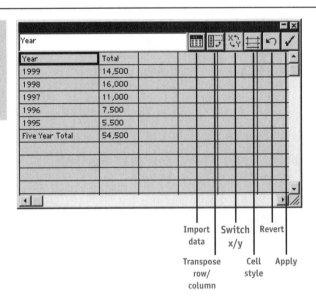

Then, click within a fill to create an anchor point for the mesh fill. Finally, click a color in the Color palette. For the whole story on using the Color palette, see Chapter 7.

USING THE GRADIENT TOOL

Gradient fills create fills that merge colors. I'll explain how to create gradient fills in Chapter 9. The Gradient tool (G) allows you to control the flow of defined gradients within an object, as shown here.

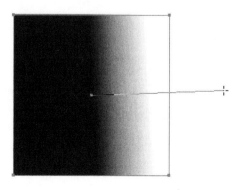

SELECTING COLORS WITH THE EYEDROPPER TOOL POP-OUT

You use the Eyedropper tool (I) and the Paint Bucket tool (K) to assign colors to selected objects. I'll walk you through this process in Chapter 4, but the short version is that you use the Eyedropper tool to grab colors from objects on the screen, while you use the Paint Bucket tool to assign to an object the defined fill color (shown in the fill swatch at the bottom of the toolbox).

The Measure tool is on the Eyedropper tool pop-out, but it has nothing to do with coloring. This tool is used to literally *measure* an object. Click and drag with this tool, and the dimensions you select will display in the Info palette that appears on screen.

BLEND AND AUTO TRACE: THE BLEND TOOL POP-OUT

Use the Blend tool (W) to create a set of objects that transition from one object to another. The Blend tool allows you to decide how quickly and smoothly you want to define a blend. You can even add a curve to define the direction of your blend, as shown here.

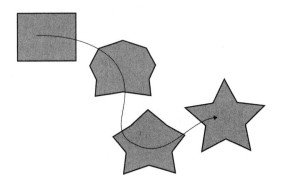

I'll explain how all this works in Chapter 9.

Use the Auto Trace tool to convert a placed object from a bitmap object into a vector-based drawing, allowing you to take advantage of all of Illustrator's effects and editing features. I'll break this down in more detail in Chapter 3, but the next illustration provides a quickie visual aid of how to use this tool.

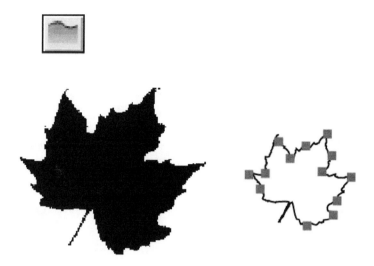

PREPARING GRAPHICS FOR THE WEB WITH THE SLICE TOOL POP-OUT

You use the Slice tool (SHIFT-K) to break large illustrations into many puzzle-type pieces. It's used for large images destined for the Web to control download time. Click and drag on selected objects with the Slice tool to divide them into smaller images.

After you have sliced up an image, you can use the Slice Selection tool—found in the Slice tool pop-out—to move the lines that define the individual slices.

CUTTING OBJECTS WITH THE SCISSORS TOOL POP-OUT

You use the Scissors tool (C) to snip a path into two paths that can be moved, edited, or deleted separately. Just click anywhere on a curve to split it.

You use the Knife tool to split a path or objects (including fills) into two objects. Use it when you need to cut a shape in half, for instance. Just click and draw as if you were slicing a pie to split an object in two.

USING THE HAND AND PAGE TOOLS

Use the Hand tool (H) to click and drag on the artboard to move it around within the visible window. Use the Page tool to define complex page printing (discussed in Chapter 13).

Zooming In and Out

Select the Zoom tool (z) and click a spot on the artboard to zoom in on that spot. Press OPTION-ALT and click to zoom out. Or, use the Zoom tool to draw a marquee around an area on the artboard, and zoom in to have that selected area fill the viewing window.

Another way to control magnification levels is to use the Zoom pop-up list found in the lower-left corner of the Illustrator window—inside the program status bar. You can use this list to choose from many levels of magnification, or you can choose the Fit On Screen option to select a zoom level that displays all objects on your artboard.

Selecting Colors with the Fill and Stroke Buttons

Located at the bottom of the toolbox, the Fill button (upper left) and Stroke button (lower right) define the color of the fill and stroke (outline) of a selected object. Press X to toggle between them.

When you select the Fill or Stroke button, the Color palette appears (if it wasn't already displayed) with the currently selected set of colors visible. As you hover over the color bar at the bottom of the palette, the cursor becomes an eyedropper, as shown here.

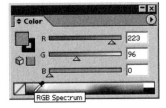

Selected fill and stroke colors are applied when you create a new curve or object. The selected fill and stroke can also be applied using the Color button at the bottom of the toolbox. You can apply the default gradient fill by clicking the Gradient button, and assign no fill or no stroke by clicking the None button.

Defining Your View with the Screen buttons

Located at the very bottom of the toolbox are the Standard Screen Mode button, the Full Screen Mode With Menu Bar button, and the Full Screen Mode button. These three tools allow you to display the normal (preview) screen, a full-screen view without windows but with a menu, or a full-screen view. Pressing F on your keyboard toggles between them.

Managing Palettes

Depending on how and what you count, Illustrator includes about two dozen palettes. I won't do a quick tour of each of them in this chapter because you won't use them all, and I'll introduce you to them throughout the book as you need them.

However, you'll use some palettes often. The most frequently used palette is the Color palette, which appears when you click the Stroke or Fill button in the toolbox.

Choose a palette by selecting the Window menu and clicking any of the available palettes.

Many palettes first appear *docked,* that is, linked to other palettes. For example, in the next illustration, the Appearance, Navigator, and Info palettes are docked.

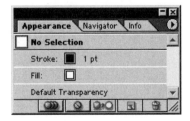

You can select a palette from a docked set by clicking on the tab for the palette you wish to use. You can undock a palette by clicking and dragging the tab, to pull the palette out of a docked set. Or you can drag a palette onto another palette (or set of docked palettes) to dock it.

Every palette has a palette menu that provides additional options for the features and tools on that palette. Palette menus are accessed by clicking on the small right-pointing triangle in the top right corner of each palette, as shown next.

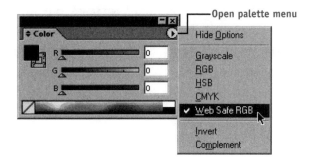

SUMMARY

You access Illustrator's most commonly used features through the toolbox and the palettes.

In this chapter, you took a quick tour of dozens of the main Illustrator features found in the toolbox. You'll return to many of these tools in the other chapters. You'll want to keep this chapter bookmarked so you can find tools in a hurry when needed.

You also learned to display and control Illustrator's array of palettes. You'll be exploring many of these palettes as you work your way through this book.

3

Drawing
Illustrations

In Illustrator, you create and edit drawings by

defining anchor points and the paths between them. Before

you start drawing lines and curves, it will be helpful to be

introduced to the basic way paths and anchors work.

PATHS AND ANCHORS

In a sense, much of this book (and much of Illustrator) is all about points and paths, and throughout this book, you'll learn different ways of creating and manipulating them. The Pencil, Line Segment, Curve, Spiral, Rectangular Grid, and Polar Grid tools that you'll explore in this chapter are essentially different ways to generate various kinds of paths and anchors.

An *anchor* (or anchor point) is the end of a line segment, and it controls the curvature (if any) and end location of that line segment. You can edit objects by selecting and moving an anchor point with the Direct Selection tool.

anchor

Anchor points that define curved nodes in a line are called *smooth points*. When you use the Direct Selection tool to click a path between curved anchor points, *handles* appear connected to each curved anchor. Clicking and dragging on these handles changes the angle of the curve, as shown in Figure 3-1.

FIGURE 3-1
Curved path anchors have handles that control the curvature of the path.

Editing smooth points can be quite complex. I'll demonstrate techniques for doing this in detail in Chapter 7. But the short story is that by clicking and dragging anchor points, you can change the angle of the curve, and by lengthening or shortening the handle, you can alter the size of the curve.

Now that you understand the basic components of lines in Illustrator, let's start drawing!

DRAWING WITH THE PENCIL TOOL

The Pencil tool is a convenient, simple way to draw freehand lines in Illustrator. Of course it doesn't replace a real pencil. When you want to create a complex illustration, you'll often want to create artwork on paper first, and scan your artwork into Illustrator. I'll walk you through that process later in this chapter in the section "Tracing an Imported Bitmap." But the Pencil tool provides a flexible way to draw by using your mouse or drawing pad.

> **TIP** As you experiment with the line drawing tools in this chapter, you'll want to create curves and lines that are visible, but that do not include a fill color. To define a visible stroke color, click the Stroke tool, and then click a color in the Color palette that appears. (Black is good for experimenting with drawing.) Click the Fill tool, and click the None tool in the toolbox or the Color palette to avoid assigning a color fill to your drawings. You'll learn more about defining stroke and fill properties in Chapter 4.

As you draw curves with the Pencil tool (skip ahead to the Line Segment tool if you want a straight line), Illustrator generates curves. You can ask Illustrator to smooth those curves out (to varying degrees) as you draw. Or, you can use a special tool in the Illustrator tool pop-out, the Smooth tool, to soften your curves after you draw with the Pencil tool.

The Pencil tool is actually two tools in one. You can use it to draw curves, and you can also use it to edit curves. I'll show you how to use it both ways in the following sections.

DEFINING PENCIL TOOL PREFERENCES

Before you start sketching away with the Pencil tool, double-click the tool to open the Pencil Tool Preferences dialog box, shown next.

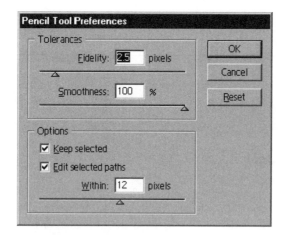

Use the Fidelity slider to define how many anchor points to generate as you draw. The fidelity value tells the program how faithful it should be (in pixels) to the user's actual mouse movements. A low fidelity value, for instance, tells Illustrator to stay very close to the mouse movements. This strategy can create more angular curves. A high fidelity value allows Illustrator more freedom to stray from the path you draw to create a smoother curve. A low value generates more anchor points, while a high fidelity value creates a smoother line.

The Smoothness slider works in a similar fashion: a high setting evens out your drawing. In Figure 3-2, I drew the same illustration three times. The first drawing has a fidelity setting of 20 pixels—too much to accurately capture my onscreen drawing. The third drawing has a smoothness setting of 90 percent—too much to preserve the drawing. The middle drawing was done with the default fidelity setting and a smoothness setting of 50 percent.

In the Options area of the Pencil Tool Preferences dialog box, selecting the Keep Selected check box means that after you draw a curve with the Pencil tool, the anchor points will all be selected. This feature is useful if you expect to edit your anchor points after you draw with the Pencil tool.

Selecting the Edit Selected Paths check box enables the Pencil tool to function like an editing tool, changing the size and direction of selected paths. This feature can be a little disorienting because it's sometimes hard to tell whether your Pencil tool is in a state where it will add to a drawing or edit it. If you find that the Pencil tool is a little too schizo for you, you can disable the Edit Selected Paths feature.

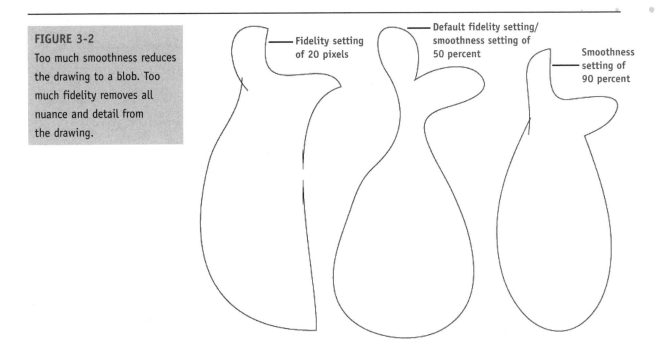

FIGURE 3-2
Too much smoothness reduces the drawing to a blob. Too much fidelity removes all nuance and detail from the drawing.

Fidelity setting of 20 pixels

Default fidelity setting/ smoothness setting of 50 percent

Smoothness setting of 90 percent

If you enable this feature, the Within Pixels slider allows you to define how close to a curve you need to be before the Pencil tool converts to editing mode.

I'll walk you through the process of using the Pencil tool as an editing tool in the next section.

EDITING DRAWINGS WITH THE PENCIL TOOL

All three of the tools in the Pencil tool pop-out are used to edit curves. You can use the Pencil tool itself to not only draw curves, but to modify existing curves. The Smooth tool irons out zigs and zags, making your curves flow more smoothly. And the Erase tool works like a pencil eraser to eliminate part of a curve.

NOTE Once you create a drawing with the Pencil tool, there are many ways to edit that drawing. You'll explore resizing and reshaping drawings in detail in Chapter 5, along with rotating and other techniques for modifying an illustration. See Chapter 7 for a detailed discussion of editing curves.

SMOOTHING A LINE

The Smooth Tool Preferences dialog box works much like the Pencil Tool Preferences dialog box. You open it by double-clicking the Smooth tool (in the

Pencil tool pop-out). Higher fidelity value settings remove more anchor points, while higher smooth values apply more sweeping changes to the curve. Clicking the Reset button in the dialog box returns to Illustrator's default settings. When you have finished defining Smooth tool preferences, click OK.

> **TIP** Want to *unsmooth* a line? Choose Effect | Distort And Transform, and then experiment with using the Roughen, Twist, or Zig Zag effects to add wrinkles, twists, and zig zags to a curve.

To use the Smooth tool, first double-click the Smooth tool and define the degree of fidelity and smoothing you want to use.

Then, use the Selection (or Lasso) tool to select the curve to be smoothed.

Finally, click and drag with the Smooth tool along the path to which you want to apply smoothing, as shown here.

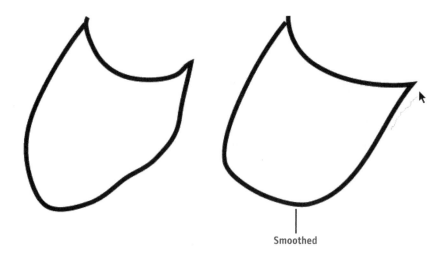

Smoothed

ERASING A LINE

The Eraser tool deletes selected sections of a curve. It's not the most precise way to edit lines, but it's handy for quick and dirty drawings.

To Erase A SECTION OF A LINE

1 Select a curve using the Selection tool or Lasso tool.

2 With the object selected, click the Erase tool (in the Pencil tool pop-out).

3 Click and drag with the Erase tool along the selected curve to erase a section of the curve.

The Erase tool is versatile. You can use it on any curve, and in any place within a curve. If you want to make a clean cut in a line, click and drag across the line as if cutting with a knife.

EDITING A CURVE WITH THE PENCIL TOOL

As I mentioned earlier, the Pencil tool is both a drawing and an editing tool. If you use the Pencil tool to draw on or next to an existing path, you normally create a new path.

> **TIP** As with many of the Illustrator tools, you can convert the display of the Eraser cursor from the Eraser icon to cross hairs by pressing CAPS LOCK on your Mac or PC keyboard. This approach sometimes makes it easier to identify exactly where you are erasing.

If you want to use the Pencil tool to edit a curve, first select that path (line) with a selection tool. Select the Pencil tool again, and then click and drag on a curve to change that curve, as shown here.

anchor

DRAWING STRAIGHT LINES AND CURVES

NOTE If you're looking for tools to draw rectangles, ovals, stars, and polygons, check out Chapter 4.

Illustrator's Line Segment tool pop-out provides a set of tools for drawing lines, arcs, spirals, rectangular grids, and polar grids.

Each of the tools in the Line Segment tool pop-out can be used two ways: you can interactively click and drag to create an object, or you can select the tool, click once on the artboard, and then define the parameters of the object in a dialog box like the one shown here (for spirals).

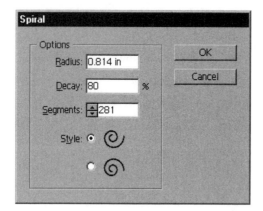

The Arc, Rectangular Grid, and Polar Grid tools include four clickable corner buttons in the upper-left side of the dialog box. These clickable corners determine where you want to start your object. You can define the insertion point to start the drawing at the top left, top right, bottom left, or bottom right of the object you generate.

DRAWING STRAIGHT LINES

To draw a line, select the Line Segment tool, then click and drag. Hold down SHIFT as you draw to constrain your line to 45 degree angles.

If you hold down OPTION/ALT as you click and drag, you will draw your line symmetrically, around a central radius. You can combine these features—holding down OPTION/ALT as you draw—to create lines that expand from a center point and are at increments of 45 degrees, as shown next.

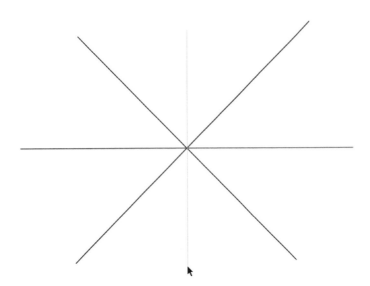

DRAWING ARCS, SPIRALS, RECTANGULAR GRIDS, AND POLAR GRIDS

You can draw a symmetrical arc, spiral, rectangular grid, or polar grid by simply selecting any of these tools and clicking and dragging.

I find that it's easier to draw an arc interactively on the artboard than it is to generate one from a dialog box. Just click and drag to approximate the length, direction, and curvature of your arc. When you release the mouse button, your arc is complete. You can always rotate, resize, or reshape a curve using tools like the Free Transform tool. I'll walk you through that process in Chapter 5. You can help yourself draw symmetrical curves by holding down SHIFT to constrain arcs to increments of 45 degrees, or holding down OPTION-ALT to draw an arc starting from a center point.

Since spirals, rectangular grids, and polar grids can be rather complex sets of curves, it's often easier to use the click-and-define technique for generating these shapes. First select a tool, and then click on the artboard. An associated dialog box appears, allowing you to define the exact configuration of the resulting object.

The Spiral tool options allow you to define the radius (distance from the center to the edge), decay (degree of spiraling), and the number of segments. A decay angle of anything less than 50 produces something more like a curve than a spiral. A decay angle close to 100 percent creates a very tight spiral, as shown in Figure 3-3.

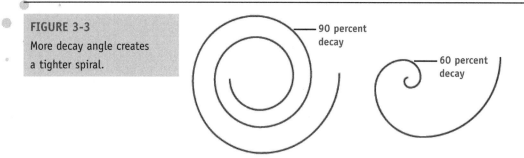

FIGURE 3-3

More decay angle creates a tighter spiral.

90 percent decay

60 percent decay

The number of segments defines how many times the spiral winds around, with each wind containing four segments. As you increase the segment number, it creates more winds in the center of the spiral. A small number of segments creates a choppy-looking curve, while a large number creates a smoother curve.

Rectangular grids are defined by their size, the number of horizontal dividers, and the number of vertical dividers. The Polar Grid dialog box defines the number of concentric dividers (rings) and radial dividers (pie slices), as shown here.

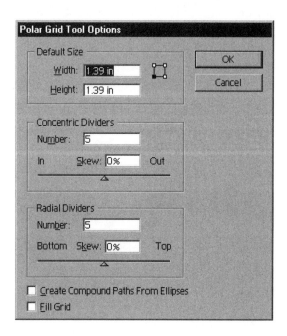

The Rectangular Grid and Polar Grid definition dialog boxes both have Skew sliders. These sliders warp your grid to make it asymmetrical—with dividers grouped more closely on the left or right, outside or inside, or top or bottom of an object, as shown here.

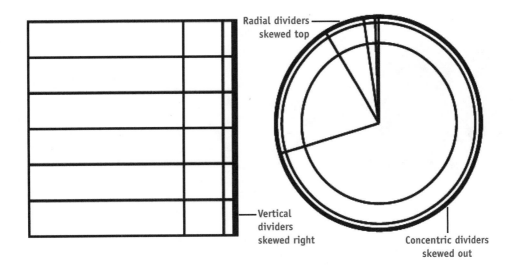

TRACING AN IMPORTED BITMAP

Many Illustrator drawings originate with sketches, photos, or other hardcopy illustrations. You can scan these images into Illustrator as bitmap images, but then you lose all the advantages and features of vector-image editing that I introduced you to in Chapter 1: bitmap images are too large, can't be resized well, and you can't apply Illustrator's full range of editing tools and effects to bitmaps.

However, you can convert an imported bitmap graphic into an Illustrator vector image. When you do, you have all the advantages of an Illustrator vector image. You can import a bitmap by choosing File | Place, and navigating to and selecting an image in any of almost two dozen bitmap formats (including JPEG, GIF, TIFF, and other popular bitmap file formats).

To Convert A PLACED (IMPORTED) BITMAP OBJECT INTO A VECTOR OBJECT

1 Select the Auto Trace tool from the Blend tool pop-out.

2 Click the edge of the placed bitmap image to convert it to a vector, as shown next.

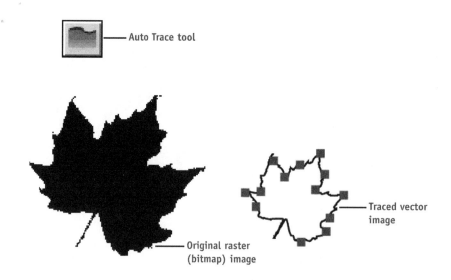

— Auto Trace tool

— Traced vector image

— Original raster (bitmap) image

3 To adjust the sensitivity and accuracy of the Auto Trace tool, choose Edit | Preferences | Type | Auto Tracing. The Preferences dialog box appears, as shown here.

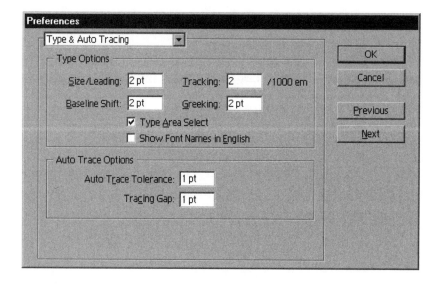

The Auto Trace Tolerance setting is defined on a scale of 1–10. A low value creates a more accurate trace, while a higher value creates smoother curves, but a less accurate reflection of the original bitmap.

The Tracing Gap setting is between 0 and 2. This setting defines how Illustrator handles breaks (or gaps) in the outline of a traced image. A setting of 1 converts only very small breaks in an outline into a solid line, while a setting of 2 (defined in pixels) converts larger breaks into a solid line.

DRAWING WITH PAINTBRUSHES

The Paintbrush tool draws using a defined shape as the brush. Simply select the Paintbrush tool, and draw like you would with the Pencil tool to create a curve. The default (plain) creates flowing, ribbon-like curves, like the ones in this illustration.

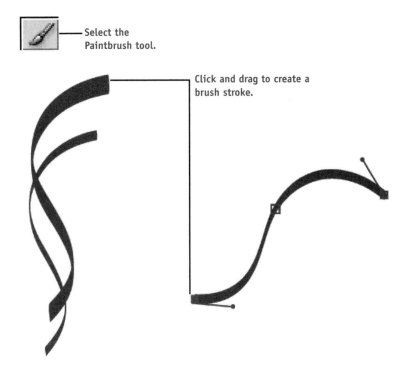

Select the Paintbrush tool.

Click and drag to create a brush stroke.

You can also use the Paintbrush tool to "paint" curved lines using all kinds of symbols and images. You can choose from a wide variety of brush types that come with Illustrator, or you can even create your own brush shapes.

CHANGING BRUSH STROKE SYMBOLS

To choose from Illustrator's gallery of available brushes, choose Window I Brushes (or press F5 on your Mac or PC keyboard) to display the Brushes palette.

Scroll down the Brushes palette, and click a symbol you wish to use as a brush shape, as shown here.

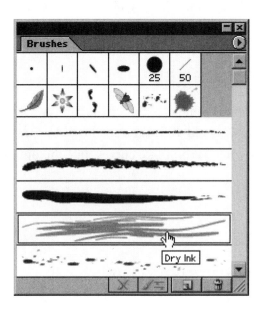

With a brush selected from the palette, you can use the Paintbrush tool to paint curves using the selected symbol.

To turn off a brush stroke (so it won't be painted when you use other drawing tools), click the Remove Brush Stroke button at the bottom of the Brushes palette. Each time you select the Paintbrush tool in the toolbox, you'll turn the selected brush stroke back on, and it will apply to any drawing tool.

USING ADDITIONAL BRUSH STROKES

You can add brushes to the Brushes palette by choosing Window | Brush Libraries, and choosing from one of the available sets of brushes. A new palette with brush symbols appears.

Clicking a symbol in the new Brush Library palette adds a symbol to your working Brush palette, as shown next.

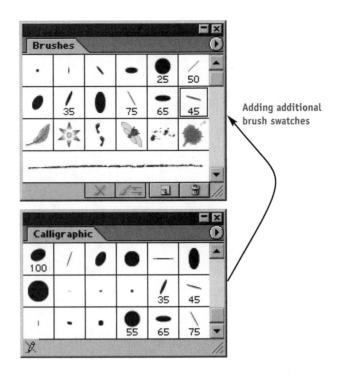

Adding additional
brush swatches

Once you add brush symbols to your regular Brush palette, you can use them like any other brush shape.

CREATING YOUR OWN BRUSH STROKE SHAPES

Creating your own custom strokes can be rather complex, and an exploration of all the possible brush-stroke options is beyond the scope of this book. But the following steps will lead you to create a simple, custom brush stroke.

To Define A CUSTOM BRUSH STROKE

1 Use the Pencil tool (or any of the tools you've explored in this or other chapters) and create a small, simple drawing.

2 If the Brush palette is not displayed, press F5.

3 Select the drawing using a selection tool.

4 With the drawing selected, click the New Brush button in the Brushes palette, as shown here.

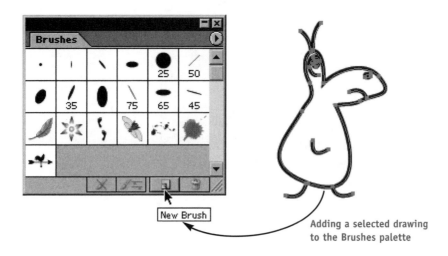

New Brush

Adding a selected drawing
to the Brushes palette

5 The New Brush dialog box appears. For shapes you will use simply as pen points, click the New Calligraphic radio button. For drawings like the one you created here, choose the New Scatter, Art, or Pattern Brush radio button. A good place to start experimenting is the Scatter Brush. Choose it now and click OK in the New Brush dialog box.

6 Most of the options in the Scatter Brush Options dialog box control how the image will be distorted when you draw curves using the symbol. Start with the defaults, and experiment with other settings.

7 Normally, the color assigned to a brush stroke will be that selected in the Color palette for strokes. If you want to assign tinting or other color attributes to the brush symbol, use the options in the Colorization area of the Scatter Brush Options dialog box. Click the Tips button in the Scatter Brush Options dialog box for more details on how to assign color attributes to a custom brush.

Once you create a custom brush, you can apply it with the Paintbrush tool (or other drawing tools).

SUMMARY

In this chapter, you learned to use basic drawing tools to create lines, curves, free-hand drawings, and preset shapes. You saw that Illustrator drawings are made up of anchor points and paths, and you learned how to edit curves by changing these points and paths.

Finally, you learned to use the Paintbrush tool, and to create custom brushes. In the next chapter, you'll learn to create shapes and assign fills to them.

 ON THE VIRTUAL CLASSROOM CD In Lesson 1, "A Custom Brush," I'll show you how to use simple drawing tools like the Pencil tool, the Arc tool, the Spiral tool, and the Polar Grid tool to create a drawing. Then I'll show you how to save an illustration as a brush stroke and apply it using the Paintbrush tool.

Filling and
Arranging Objects

One of the huge advantages of using Illustrator

to create drawings is that you can precisely and quickly define

strokes and fills for objects, line them up, and move them

behind or in front of each other.

In this chapter, I'll start by showing you how to create shapes using the various shape tools (like rectangles, ellipses, stars, and polygons). And then I'll show you how to apply customized strokes (outlines) and fills. Finally, you'll explore how to arrange objects in two and three dimensions.

WORKING WITH SHAPES, FILLS, AND STROKES

Many illustrations start with or are based on some common shapes like rectangles, ellipses (ovals), stars, and polygons. Sometimes shapes are used as a framework or background for an illustration, and sometimes—with a little enhancement—they *are* the illustration, as shown in Figure 4-1.

You can either interactively draw each of the shape tools in the Rectangle tool pop-out by clicking and dragging, or you can define them in a dialog box. In the following sections, I'll show you how to use each shape tool and turn you on to some tricks for using them effectively.

FIGURE 4-1
This figure is built around rectangles, ovals, a star, and polygons.

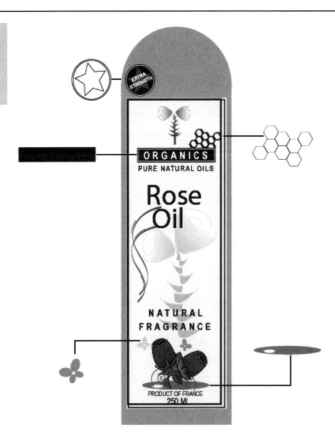

DRAWING RECTANGLES

To draw a rectangle, select the Rectangle tool, and then click and drag anywhere on the artboard. If you hold down SHIFT as you click and drag, you constrain the rectangle to a square. If you hold down OPTION/ALT as you click and drag, you define the rectangle not from the location from which you start to click and drag, but instead, that point becomes the center point for the rectangle.

The other way to define a rectangle is to select the Rectangle tool, and click anywhere on the artboard without clicking and dragging. The Rectangle dialog box appears, as shown in the following illustration.

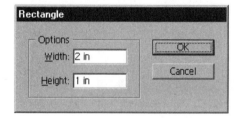

Enter a width and height in the dialog box to define the size precisely.

To draw a rounded rectangle, select the Rounded Rectangle tool from the Rectangle tool pop-out. Like with the regular Rectangle tool, you can either click and drag to interactively define the rounded rectangle, or you can click once to define the rounded rectangle in a dialog box.

The Rounded Rectangle dialog box (shown here) differs from the regular Rectangle dialog box only in that you can also define the size of the radius.

> **NOTE** If you want to change the units that appear in the shape dialog boxes, select Edit | Preferences | Units & Undo. In the Preferences dialog box, change the selected unit of measurement in the General drop-down list to pixels, points, inches, or one of the other measurement options.

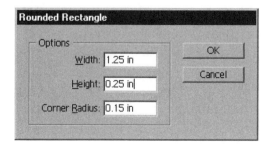

The size of the radius determines how much rounding to apply: larger values increase the rounding. Once you define a radius, it applies to each rounded rectangle you draw.

DRAWING ELLIPSES AND CIRCLES

To draw an ellipse (aka an oval), select the Ellipse tool, and then click and drag anywhere on the artboard. If you hold down SHIFT as you click and drag, you constrain the ellipse to a perfect circle. If you hold down OPTION/ALT as you click and drag, you define the circle from a center point.

The other way to define an ellipse is to select the Ellipse tool, and click anywhere on the artboard without clicking and dragging. The Ellipse dialog box appears, as shown next.

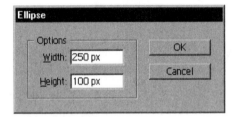

CREATING POLYGONS AND STARS

The Polygon and Star tools work like the other shape tools: you can interactively draw on the artboard, or click and define the polygon or star in a dialog box.

Because polygons and stars can have anywhere from three to 1000 points or sides, you'll probably want to define the number of points and sides in a dialog box before you start drawing. The way to do this is to select the tool, and click. Use the dialog box to define the number of sides or points you want, and then click OK. If necessary, delete the just-created star or polygon by pressing DELETE or BACKSPACE. Then draw away. The subsequent stars or polygons will have the number of points or sides you just assigned in the dialog box.

USING THE FLARE TOOL

I'll quickly note Illustrator's new Flare tool here because it's been added (for lack of a better place) to the Rectangle tool pop-out. The Flare tool doesn't draw a shape, like the rest of the tools in this pop-out; instead, it creates a far-out effect. I had trouble describing that, so I asked Illustrator's Product Manager Mordy Golding to explain what this tool does:

> "The Flare tool is used to add 'flair' (hee hee) to artwork. Not much more than that. Many designers want to add lens flarelike effects to artwork to make them look more realistic. The Flare tool allows designers to apply these effects easily."

The next illustration shows the Flare tool in action—here it's used to create an "eye" for the figure.

To interactively create a flare, start by selecting the Flare tool and then clicking and dragging to create the first part of the flared object. During this first click and drag, you'll define the radius of the flare. Then, click a second time on the artboard to create the eyeball part of the effect. Alternatively, you can click once, and use the Flare Tool Options dialog box to define the details of your flared object.

ARRANGING OBJECTS

Illustrator provides several options for aligning objects in two dimensions. You can view and activate built-in grid lines to align the tops, bottoms, or sides of objects.

You can create custom rulers to align objects without being constrained by preset grids. Or you can select sets of objects and align them horizontally or vertically.

Along with aligning objects in two dimensions, you can also move objects in front of or behind each other. If you plan to incorporate many layers in your illustration, you'll want to check out Illustrator's powerful layers features, which I cover in Chapter 11. But if you simply want to move one object in front of or behind another, I'll show you how to do that in the next section.

CONNECTING AND LOCATING OBJECTS

You can easily and accurately connect lines and align objects using Smart Guides. A simple way to align objects is to view grid lines, and activate the Snap-To-Grid feature that transforms these (nonprinting) lines into magnet-like alignment tools.

TAKING ADVANTAGE OF SMART GUIDES

Smart Guides makes it easy to move or copy existing objects while keeping them aligned horizontally, vertically, or even at a 45 degree angle. It is one of the quickest and easiest tools you can use in Illustrator, and one of the most helpful.

To use Smart Guides, open the View menu and make sure Smart Guides is selected. When you move an object with Smart Guides turned on, the guides indicate when your object has been moved horizontally, vertically, or at a 45 degree angle. If you hold down SHIFT as you drag, you constrain your move to 45 degree increments. Hold down OPTION-ALT as you drag a selected object, and you will copy it. To create the following illustration, I held down both SHIFT and OPTION-ALT to copy the star at a 45 degree angle.

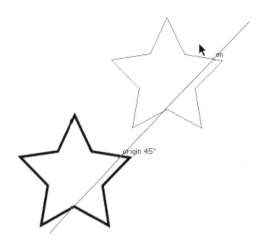

ALIGNING WITH RULERS AND GUIDES

Another technique for aligning and locating objects on the artboard is to display rulers or guides. Particularly if you zoom way in on an illustration, rulers can be helpful in sizing and locating objects.

To view rulers, select View | Show Rulers. Hide them by selecting View | Hide Rulers. To define the unit of measurement on the ruler, select Edit | Preferences | Units & Undo. The General drop-down list in the Units area of the Preferences dialog box defines the unit that is displayed on the ruler.

The easiest way to generate horizontal or vertical nonprinting guides on the artboard is to click and drag on either of the rulers, pulling a guide onto the artboard. These guides are locked, by default. So if you want to move or delete them, select View | Guides, and deselect Lock Guides. With guides unlocked, you can click and drag on them to move them, or select them and press DELETE to remove them.

You can perform most of the ruler functions better by using other techniques. For example, if you want to precisely size an object, you can view the Info palette while you resize with the Scale tool. I'll show you how to do that in detail in Chapter 5. If you want to locate an object at an exact spot, you can view the Info palette, and see exact x coordinates (horizontal from the left edge of the page) and y coordinates (vertical from the bottom of the page) as you move a selected object.

Similarly, you can use guides to align objects, but the Align palette, which I'll explain later in the "Using the Align Palette" section, is a more precise way to line up objects.

Still, I often find myself using rulers and guides as rough layout tools for arranging objects on a page because they're simple and easy to use, and they provide an approximate idea of the size and alignment of objects as you rough out an illustration. Perhaps in the next version of Illustrator, we'll see Snap-To-Guides enabled so that guides are more useful.

SNAPPING TO GRIDS

You can turn on an invisible set of horizontal and vertical lines called *grids,* and use these lines to easily align or size objects. Grid lines are especially useful for creating technical drawings, creating maps, designing floor plans, and creating other illustrations that tend to be regular in shape and rely closely on measurements.

To view grid lines, choose View | Show Grid. Hide the grid lines by choosing View | Hide Grid. Enable Snap-To-Grid by choosing View | Snap To Grid. Deselect Snap-To-Grid to turn off snapping.

To change the increments (or units of measurement) of the grid, choose Edit | Preferences | Guides | Grid. In the Preferences dialog box, use the Gridline Every box to define the spacing of grid lines, as shown here.

> **NOTE** The Preferences dialog box also allows you to change grid display from lines to dots, to change grid display color, or to move grid lines on top of (instead of behind) your displayed objects.

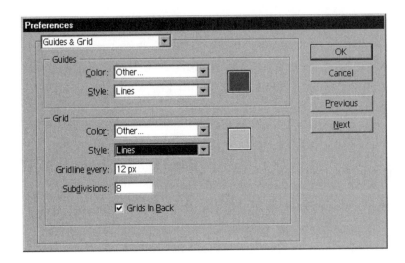

SNAPPING TO POINTS

Snapping to points is a handy trick for connecting two anchor points in the same or different curves. You can use this to close an open curve (make a curved object a contiguous outline).

Choose View | Snap To Point to enable Snap-To-Point. Then, select an anchor point (use the Direct Selection tool), and drag it to another anchor point. When the anchor points connect exactly, the mouse cursor changes from black to white, indicating that you have exactly connected the two points, as shown here.

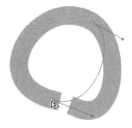

USING THE ALIGN PALETTE

You use the Align palette to align selected objects horizontally or vertically, or to assign even spacing between selected objects.

View the Align palette by choosing Window | Align. The six buttons in the top row of the palette align selected objects either horizontally or vertically. Selected objects can be aligned left, horizontally centered, aligned right, aligned top, vertically centered, or aligned along their bottoms. The bottom row of buttons distribute (space) objects using the top, vertical center, bottom, left, horizontal center, or right side of the selected objects.

Figure 4-2 illustrates using vertical and horizontal alignment, as well as vertical and horizontal distribution to evenly space objects, and align. Because the objects on the left side of the figure are right aligned, their right edges line up horizontally. Because the objects on top are vertically aligned using their bottoms, the bowls appear to be on the same vertical plane.

ARRANGING OBJECTS FRONT AND BACK

You can move any object or group of selected objects in front of or behind other objects on the artboard. For complex illustrations, this job is managed powerfully

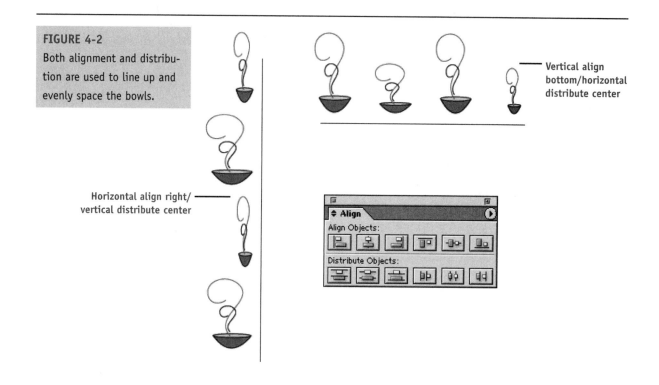

FIGURE 4-2
Both alignment and distribution are used to line up and evenly space the bowls.

Vertical align bottom/horizontal distribute center

Horizontal align right/ vertical distribute center

with layers, which I cover in Chapter 11. But for simple illustrations, you can move any selected objects forward or backward by choosing Object | Arrange, and then choosing Bring To Front, Bring Forward, Send Backward, or Send To Back.

Choosing Send Backward or Bring Forward moves the selected object(s) up or back one layer at a time. Choosing Send To Back or Bring To Front moves an object behind or in front of all objects on the artboard.

> **NOTE** You can hold down COMMAND-CLICK (Mac), or right-click (PC) any selected object(s), and then choose Arrange and one of the four arrange options from the context menu. The menu also displays keyboard shortcuts for moving objects forward and backward, but because they require three keystrokes, they're a bit unwieldy.

If you "lose" objects behind other objects and can't select them, switch to Outline view (View | Outline). Switch back to Preview view (View | Preview) to see objects as they will appear in your final output—in front of or behind each other.

DEFINING STROKES AND FILLS

The most basic way to assign stroke (outline) or fill colors to an object is to select the object, click the Fill or Stroke button at the bottom of the toolbox, and then click a color in the Color palette.

There are many other options (aren't there always in Illustrator?) for assigning colors to strokes or fills. And there are other stroke and fill attributes that you can define. In this section, I'll show you how to define thickness and different styles (like dashed) for strokes. And you'll learn how to assign to fills not only solid colors, but also custom-defined gradients (rainbow-like sets of transitioning colors).

You can also pick up a color from anywhere on your screen and apply it to selected objects using the Eyedropper tool. You'll explore that technique in this section as well.

DEFINING STROKE ATTRIBUTES

You define stroke thickness and style by using the Stroke palette. You can also use the Stroke palette to define how lines join (connect) with each other. Choose Window | Stroke (or press F10) to view the Stroke palette. (See Figure 4-3.)

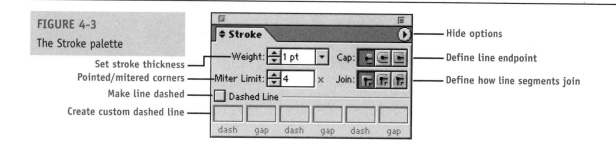

FIGURE 4-3
The Stroke palette

Set stroke thickness
Pointed/mitered corners
Make line dashed
Create custom dashed line

Hide options
Define line endpoint
Define how line segments join

To define the weight (thickness) of a selected line, choose a dimension from the Weight drop-down list. The units of measurement in the list are defined in the Preferences dialog box. (Choose Edit | Preferences | Units & Undo, and select a unit of measurement from the Stroke drop-down list in the Preferences dialog box.)

Line segments can end at the anchor point (butt style), be rounded (round style), or project past the anchor point (projecting). Choose line cap styles for a selected line segment by clicking one of the three cap buttons. All three cap styles are shown in this illustration.

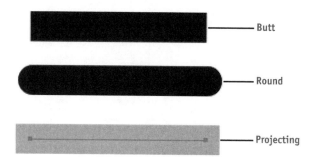

Butt

Round

Projecting

The three join buttons (Miter, Round, and Bevel) control how corner line segments connect. Rounded joins create curved corners, and beveled joins create a cut off corner instead of a sharp corner. You can limit mitered joins by choosing a value in the Miter Limit spin box. A high enough value will prevent beveling. All three types of joins are displayed in the next illustration.

Miter (limited)　　　　　Round　　　　　Bevel

You can assign dashed lines to selected line segments by clicking the Dashed Line check box. If you want to define custom dashed lines, you can use the Gap area(s) to define spacing between dashes.

ASSIGNING COLORS

Before you start assigning colors to objects in your illustration, you should know (or decide!) its target output medium. I'll discuss color printing and web output options in much more detail in Chapter 12, but the short version is this:

▶ If your output is destined for the Web, choose the Web Safe RGB color palette.

▶ If your output is destined for a professional color printing shop using four-color printing plates, choose the CYMK palette.

▶ If your output is destined for black-and-white output, choose the Grayscale palette.

To choose a color set, view the Color palette. (Select Window | Color, or press F6.) Use the Color palette menu to choose one of the color models, as shown here.

> **NOTE** If your output options aren't in this list (like, for instance, for spot color printing), you might want to jump to Chapter 12 now to explore how to set up appropriate color palettes and how to create custom swatch palettes.

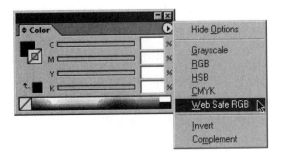

With a color model selected, you can assign a fill to any selected path (object). When you click the Fill button in the toolbox, the Color palette appears if it isn't visible already. As you move the cursor over the Color palette, the cursor becomes an eyedropper. Point and click on a color in the Color palette to assign that color to the selected object fill.

The last selected fill color appears in the Fill swatch in the toolbox, and you can assign it to selected objects by simply clicking directly on the Fill swatch.

You can "steal" colors from other fills by using the Eyedropper tool. I'll walk you through that process now.

To Select A COLOR USING THE EYEDROPPER

1 Using a selection tool (like *the* Selection tool), select the object to which you want to assign a new fill color.

2 Click the Eyedropper tool in the toolbox.

3 Move the Eyedropper tool mouse cursor over a section of the illustration from which you want to steal a fill color, and click. The color you point to will be assigned to the fill of the selected object.

The Paint Bucket tool works a little differently than the Eyedropper tool. It's used for quickly assigning the currently selected stroke and fill attributes to any curve. Just select the Paint Bucket tool (no objects need be selected first), and point and click on curves to assign the selected fill and stroke attributes.

MIXING UP GRADIENT FILLS

Gradient fills create transitions between two or more colors. The most basic gradient fills merge from one color to another. Gradient transitions can be linear (top to bottom or right to left) or radial (from the outside of an object to the inside).

Figure 4-4 illustrates both a linear and a radial gradient fill. As you can see, the gradient applied to the clouds creates a gradually disappearing edge to the clouds, while the radial fill applied to the figure creates a dark outline that transitions to a white center.

FIGURE 4-4

Linear (on top) and radial (on the bottom) gradient fills

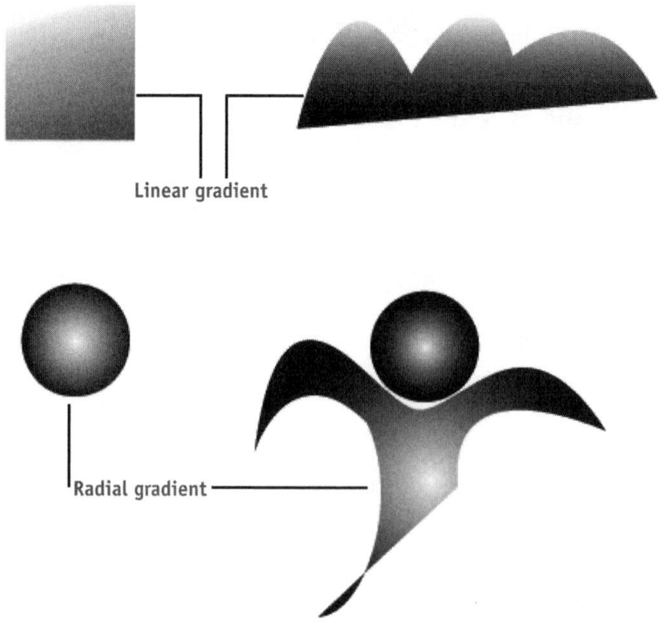

Linear gradient

Radial gradient

Gradient fills are one of the coolest Illustrator features. They add depth, subtlety, and either realism or surrealism to an illustration. But before you get too excited about applying them to your artwork, be warned that gradients don't do well on the Web. Why not? I'll discuss this in more detail in Chapter 12, but the basic reason is that the color model for browser-compatible web colors is limited to 216 colors. And that set of colors is not sufficient to maintain a smooth gradation between colors.

Furthermore, the low resolution of monitors (usually 72 or 96 dots per inch) as opposed to printing (even desktop printers typically print at 600 dots per inch) reduces the attractiveness of gradients. Instead of a seamless transition between colors, gradients on the Web usually appear as bands. In Chapter 14, I'll show you some tricks for maximizing the appearance of gradients on web sites, but in general, it's something you want to avoid.

USING PREFAB GRADIENTS

Illustrator comes with several preconfigured gradient fills. To view them, choose Window | Swatches. Depending on your previous docking or undocking activity, the Swatch palette may be docked with other palettes.

To view existing defined gradients, click the Show Gradient Swatches button on the bottom of the Swatches palette, as shown here.

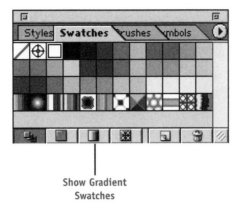

Show Gradient
Swatches

Once you view the existing gradients in the Swatches palette, you can assign any of them as the default fill simply by clicking on one of them. As you do, the selected gradient appears in the Gradient button in the toolbox.

Assign the selected gradient to a curve by selecting the curve, and then pointing to the gradient in the toolbox. Or use the Eyedropper tool to point to any gradient swatch, and apply that fill to any selected object(s).

> **NOTE** You can't assign gradients to paths or strokes the same way you can assign them to other objects. To apply a gradient to a stroke, first you have to convert the stroke to a filled object (select Object | Path | Outline Stroke) and then assign the gradient.

CREATING TWO-COLOR GRADIENTS

The preset gradients provide a nice selection, but the real fun is defining your own gradients. The basic routine for creating a two-color gradient involves selecting the two colors, defining how they will transition into each other, and defining a radial or linear fill.

The process for defining linear and radial fills is slightly different. With linear fills, you have to define a fill angle that determines whether your fill transitions from top to bottom, from right to left, or something in between.

To Define A LINEAR TWO-COLOR GRADIENT FILL

1 Open the Gradient palette by selecting Window | Gradient, by pressing F9, or by double-clicking the Gradient tool in the toolbox.

2 From the Gradient Type drop-down list, choose Linear.

3 Select Window | Color (or press F6) so that the Color palette is accessible: you'll need it to define colors for your gradient fill.

4 Click on the first (left) Gradient slider, as shown here.

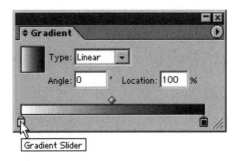

5 With the first Gradient slider selected, click a color in the Color palette. This assigns the first gradient fill color.

6 Click the second (right) Gradient slider, and select a second color from the Color palette. The fill is previewed in the bar that runs between the two Gradient sliders.

7 Slide the diamond-shaped midpoint to the right or left on the slider bar to change the rate at which the first color merges into the second color. As you do this, the Location percentage box in the Gradient palette will display a changing percentage, and the slider bar will preview the changes in your gradient fill.

> **TIP** Gradient angles are not previewed in the slider bar; you have to apply them to see how they look.

8 Use the Angle box in the Gradient palette to rotate the fill. A setting of –90 degrees (enter –90 in the Angle box) will tilt your fill so that the first color is at the top instead of on the left. A setting of 180 will switch the direction of your fill and move the right color to the left edge of the fill.

9 As you define your fill, it becomes the default fill in the Fill swatch in the toolbox. Use the Paint Bucket tool to apply it to any object on the artboard.

> **NOTE** Later in this section, I'll show you how to save a gradient fill as a swatch.

You can interactively change the angle of a gradient fill by selecting an object to which the fill has been applied, and then selecting the Gradient tool in the toolbox. Click and drag with the Gradient tool cursor to change the direction, start point, and endpoint of a gradient fill, as shown in Figure 4-5.

You define radial fills just like linear fills, except that you can't define an angle (because they go from inside an object to outside). If you want to explore complex radial fills, check out the discussion of gradient meshes in Chapter 7.

USING MULTICOLOR GRADIENTS

In most cases, you need only two colors to create a complex and subtle gradient fill. Sometimes, however, you might want to add additional colors (for example, if you were creating a rainbow fill). You can add additional color by clicking below the Gradient slider bar. Or, if you want to start with an existing color, hold down OPTION-ALT and drag an existing color to a new location on the Gradient slider bar.

Assign colors to additional sliders by selecting them and then clicking a color in the Color palette. Each color transition will have its own diamond-shaped midpoint slider that you can use to define the location angle for the fill. However, a single linear gradient fill can have only one angle setting—and that applies to the entire fill.

FIGURE 4-5
Defining a gradient fill interactively with the Gradient tool

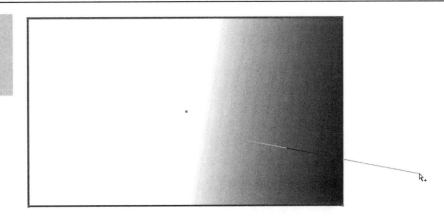

SAVING GRADIENTS AS SWATCHES

If you've gone to considerable work to create a custom gradient fill, you'll probably want to save it for future use. You do this by saving the gradient as a swatch in the Swatches palette.

To Save A GRADIENT FILL AS A SWATCH

1 Define a gradient fill. (See instructions earlier in this chapter in the section called "Creating Two-Color Gradients.")

2 With the gradient fill defined in the Gradient palette, open the Swatches palette.

3 From the Swatches palette menu, choose New Swatch. The New Swatch dialog box opens.

4 In the Swatch Name box of the New Swatch dialog box, type a descriptive name for your gradient fill.

5 Click OK. Your fill appears in the Swatches palette. View only gradient swatches by clicking the Show Gradient Swatches button on the bottom of the Swatches palette.

You can delete a swatch from the Swatches palette by selecting it and then choosing Delete Swatch from the Swatches palette menu. Swatches are saved as part of your open Illustrator file. When you save the file and reopen it, the swatches are available.

SUMMARY

In this chapter, you learned to use shapes like rectangles, ellipses, polygons, and stars. You also learned many different ways to connect and arrange objects in Illustrator: to connect anchor points in curves, to align and distribute (space) objects horizontally or vertically, and to move objects in front of or behind other objects.

Finally, you learned how to assign stroke attributes, as well as how to define and assign color fills. And you learned how to create and save gradient fills.

ON THE VIRTUAL CLASSROOM CD In Lesson 2, "Aligning and Gradients," I'll show you how to align objects vertically and horizontally, and how to automatically assign even spacing between objects. I'll also show you how to whip up and apply a gradient fill.

5

Sizing, Scaling, and Rotating

Illustrator offers multiple options for sizing,

reshaping, rotating, and flipping objects or groups of objects.

You can make changes through dialog boxes, or interactively by

clicking and dragging. You can use tools that allow you to easily

resize and rotate all at once, or you can use specific tools that

provide an intense amount of control over just how objects are

rotated, sized, flipped, and otherwise reshaped.

In this chapter, I'll start by introducing you to more versatile techniques for transforming objects. Later in the chapter, I'll show you how to use the Scale, Shear, Reshape, Rotate, Reflect, and Twist tools to finely tune changes to your drawn objects.

GROUPING OBJECTS

Before I show you how to modify objects, it will be helpful to examine how objects can be grouped together, and then moved or transformed together.

To group objects, first select them using a selection tool (like the Selection tool or the Lasso tool). Then choose Object | Group.

> **NOTE** The keyboard shortcut for grouping is COMMAND/CTRL-G. An alternate way to select several objects is to hold down SHIFT while clicking with the Selection tool.

Once objects are grouped, you can select the entire group by clicking within it with the Selection tool. With the entire set of grouped objects selected, you apply fill or stroke changes to the entire group. (See Chapter 4 for details on how to apply fill and stroke changes to objects.) In a similar way, the transforming tools covered in the rest of this chapter (like those that resize or rotate an object) generally apply to the whole selected group of objects.

If you want to change just one object within a group, you can ungroup the objects and then select an individual object within the group. That can get tedious, however, especially if you're frequently switching back and forth between changes to a bunch of grouped objects and changes to a single object (or a few objects) within the group.

The solution to this problem is to use the Group Selection tool found in the Selection tool pop-out. The Group Selection tool allows you to select any object(s) within a group. So, for example, if you wanted to change the fill color of just the roses in the grouped set of objects shown next, you could use the Group Selection tool, hold down SHIFT, and click on the two roses.

To more or less permanently ungroup a set of objects, select the group and choose Object | Ungroup (or use the shortcut keys COMMAND/CTRL-SHIFT-G).

Groups can themselves be grouped again. However, if you're going to get into multiple levels of grouping, you'll probably be better served by organizing sets

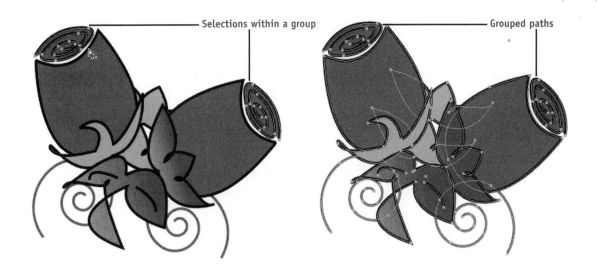

of objects into more powerful layers. I'll show you how to do this in Chapter 11. Be aware that each level of grouping has to be ungrouped in turn. So if you've grouped a group within a group, you'll have to choose Object | Ungroup more than once to ungroup all the objects.

CHANGING OBJECTS WITH A BOUNDING BOX

A *bounding box* is an imaginary nonprinting border around an object or group of objects. It enables some basic transformations, including resizing, reshaping, mirroring (flipping), and rotating objects.

Illustrator's object editing tools are powerful, detailed, and awesome for any kind of tweaking you wish to apply to an object or group of objects. I'll walk you through these tools later in this chapter, one by one. But sometimes you just want to quickly and (relatively) crudely resize, rotate, or flip an object or quickly experiment with all these changes to an object. I find the simplest way to transform objects is to use a bounding box.

To view bounding boxes around selected objects, choose View | Show Bounding Box (if this is not already selected). When you do, a bounding box with four (small, square) side anchor points and four corner anchor points appears, as shown in Figure 5-1.

FIGURE 5-1
The bounding box around this set of grouped objects provides easy access to basic transformation actions.

To move an object or group with the bounding box displayed, click on a path or fill within the bounding box, and click and drag to a new location on the artboard. Holding down ALT as you click and drag makes a copy of the object(s) at a new location. Turning on Smart Guides (View | Smart Guides or COMMAND/CTRL-U) activates Smart Guides features like helping you move along a 90 or 45 degree angle, or locating a path or anchor point as you move the object(s).

RESIZING AND RESHAPING WITH A BOUNDING BOX

To resize an object, click and drag on a side or corner anchor point while holding down SHIFT. Holding down SHIFT maintains the height-to-width (aspect) ratio of your object(s) as you resize.

In the following illustration, I'm resizing a group using a bounding box with the SHIFT key.

Resizing with the bounding box: holding down the SHIFT key
—— maintains height-to-width ratio.

If you want to resize without maintaining the height-to-width ratio of your object(s), click and drag a side anchor point to change height or width, or a corner anchor point to resize both height and width independently of each other. With this technique, you can make an object or group wider, narrower, shorter, or taller.

ROTATING AND FLIPPING WITH A BOUNDING BOX

Displaying a bounding box around selected objects also makes it easy to rotate or mirror (flip) these objects.

To rotate a selection, choose the Selection tool, and move your cursor near a corner or side anchor point. As you do, a rotation cursor appears, as shown here. Click and drag with the rotation cursor to rotate the selected object(s) around the center point of the selection.

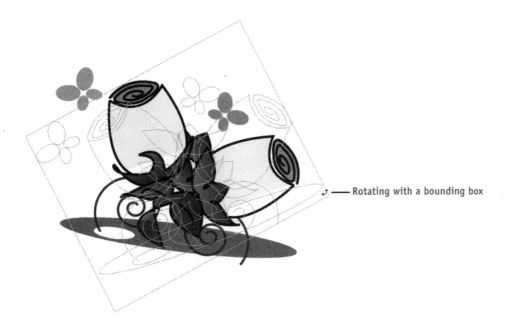

— Rotating with a bounding box

You can also use a bounding box to mirror (flip) an object horizontally or vertically. The routine for mirroring an object is similar to resizing, except that you drag an anchor point past the edge of the bounding box, creating a mirrored version of the object, as shown next.

NOTE If you want to rotate your object around an axis other than the center point, jump ahead to the "Rotating Objects with the Rotate Tool" section.

Mirroring horizontally
using a bounding box

If you hold down OPTION/ALT as you mirror an object with a bounding box, the mirroring pivots around the center point of the object. This holds the object in place as you mirror it horizontally, vertically, or even diagonally.

RESIZING AND RESHAPING WITH THE FREE TRANSFORM TOOL

Enabling a bounding box around selected objects has its merits: it makes rotation, sizing, and mirroring easy to accomplish. The downside is that you have to put up with a bounding box popping up on your screen whenever you select an object or group of objects. If the bounding box is getting in your way, choose View | Hide Bounding Box (or COMMAND/CTRL-SHIFT-B) to make it disappear.

The Free Transform tool applies a functioning bounding box to selected objects. Use it to rotate, resize, or mirror a selected object. When you select a different tool, the bounding box created by the Free Transform tool disappears.

If you are an artist or designer who is new to Illustrator or you don't need precision sizing and rotating, you will find the Free Transform tool easy to use, versatile, and intuitive. You can quickly resize a selected object using the Free Transform tool by clicking and dragging on a side or corner anchor point. Hold down SHIFT as you drag to maintain the height-to-width ratio as you resize the object.

To rotate a selected object with the Free Transform tool, hover over a corner or side anchor point, and click and drag to rotate clockwise or counterclockwise. The Free Transform tool rotates an object around its center.

You can easily mirror (flip) a selected object using the Free Transform tool by clicking and dragging on a side anchor point. To mirror the object horizontally, drag a right or left side anchor point over and past the other side anchor point. To mirror vertically, click and drag on the top anchor point and drag past the bottom anchor point.

For more precise control over sizing and rotating, you'll want to use the Scale and Rotate tools. These tools allow you to enter sizes or rotation angles digitally, and to rotate an object around any of the anchor points—not just the middle of the object.

RESIZING PRECISELY WITH THE SCALE TOOL

The Scale tool has a couple advantages over sizing freehand with a bounding box or the Free Transform tool. The Scale tool allows you to resize to an exact percentage—so for instance, you can resize an object to 50 percent to make it exactly half size. And you can use the Scale tool to resize an object from a defined point, as opposed to just scaling from a selected anchor point with the Free Transform tool.

To Resize AN OBJECT ANCHORED BY A DEFINED POINT

1 Select the object (using the Selection tool).

2 Choose the Scale tool.

3 With the Scale tool cursor, click a path or an anchor point (for example, a corner of a rectangle) to establish a point to which you will resize the object.

4 With the Scale tool still selected, click and drag from a different anchor point. The object will resize, but the original anchor point will not change its location, as shown here.

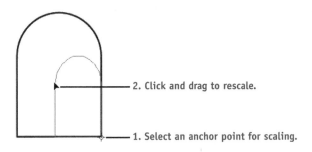

2. Click and drag to rescale.

1. Select an anchor point for scaling.

The Scale dialog box resizes digitally—no clicking and dragging required. It also allows you to control whether you want to rescale an object's stroke (outline) proportionally as you rescale the object. The next illustration shows an object rescaled with and without rescaling the associated stroke.

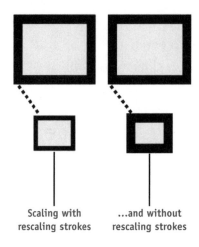

Scaling with
rescaling strokes

...and without
rescaling strokes

To Resize USING THE SCALE DIALOG BOX

1 Select any object(s).

2 With the object(s) selected, double-click the Scale tool. The Scale dialog box appears.

3 Use the Scale box in the Uniform section to enter a percentage if you want to resize the object while maintaining the same height-to-width ratio.

4 Use the Horizontal and Vertical boxes in the Non-Uniform section of the dialog box to enter different percentages if you want to resize the height and width independently.

5 Click the Preview check box to see the object interactively resize on the artboard as you enter values in the sizing boxes.

6 Click the Scale Strokes & Effects check box if you want to proportionally resize strokes and effects. (I explain how effects work in Chapter 10.)

7 Click the Objects check box to resize objects. You'll almost always want to select this option; otherwise, the object itself won't resize.

8 Click the Patterns check box to proportionally resize patterns within a shape. (I explain how patterns work in Chapter 10.) The Scale dialog box with all check box options selected is shown here.

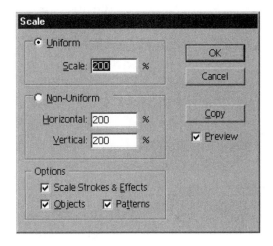

9 If you have the Preview check box checked, you can test out your settings on the artboard before you click OK or press ENTER. When your object is correctly resized, click OK (or press ENTER).

ROTATING OBJECTS WITH THE ROTATE TOOL

The Rotate tool rotates objects with the same kind of precision and control that the Scale tool uses. Like with the Scale tool, you can use an associated dialog box to define rotation to a precise angle. You can also define a rotation point that acts as a fulcrum as you interactively rotate an object.

To rotate a selected object (or set of objects) precisely with the dialog box, double-click the Rotate tool. The Rotate dialog box appears, as shown here.

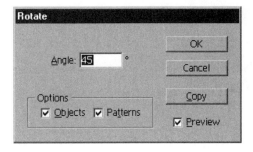

The value you enter in the Angle box of the dialog box defines the degree of rotation. The Copy button creates a second, rotated version of your selected object while leaving the original unchanged.

The Preview check box allows you to view changes on the artboard as you make them in the dialog box, before your press ENTER or click OK.

The Objects and Patterns check boxes allow you to elect to rotate objects and/or their fill patterns independently. I'll explain fill patterns in Chapter 10.

The Rotate tool also allows you to rotate around a selected anchor point in a selected object.

To Rotate AN OBJECT AROUND A SELECTED ANCHOR POINT

1 Select the object (or objects).

2 Click the Rotate tool.

3 Click an anchor point on the selected object to establish the rotation point.

4 Click and drag a different anchor point to rotate the object around the selected point, as shown in Figure 5-2.

> NOTE When you rotate with the Rotate tool, you can define the rotation point outside the selected objects(s). When you do this, you define a fulcrum outside the object. Then you can rotate the object around this fulcrum, something like moving an object at the end of a lever.

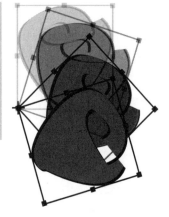

FIGURE 5-2
Using the Rotate tool provides more flexibility than simply rotating with the Free Transform tool; you can rotate around a selected point.

TRIPPING WITH MORE TRANSFORMING TOOLS

The Reflect, Twist, Shear, and Reshape tools provide even more options for warping, stretching, and basically mangling any selected object(s). These tools work in a similar way as the Rotate tool, but they produce different effects.

In all the dialog boxes for these tools, when they are available, the Preview check box shows your changes before you click OK or press ENTER. Objects and Patterns check boxes, when available, determine whether objects and/or pattern fills are transformed. I asked a friend to pose and demonstrate all four of these tools in this illustration.

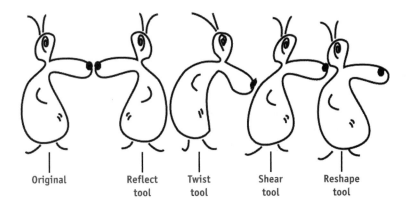

| Original | Reflect tool | Twist tool | Shear tool | Reshape tool |

The Reflect tool (in the Rotate tool pop-out) allows you to mirror selected objects precisely by using a dialog box. You can flip an object upside down by choosing the Horizontal radio button. Choosing the Vertical radio button mirrors an object without changing the top/bottom relationship. Or, you can rotate both horizontally and vertically by choosing the Value radio button and entering an angle in the Angle box.

The Twist tool (in the Rotate tool pop-out) distorts an object as it rotates it. If you hold down OPTION-ALT as you click and drag, a dialog box appears allowing you to define a twist angle. However, you can't open a dialog box by double-clicking the tool; you interactively use the Twist tool by clicking and dragging the selected object. If you first click once on the path, you can define a fixed point that will not move as you twist the object.

The Shear tool (in the Scale tool pop-out) skews selected objects. The shearing (skewing) takes place around the center point of the object unless you first click to set an anchor point. In that case, the anchor point is fixed while the rest of the object shears. You can also define shearing for a selected object by double-clicking the Shear tool to open a dialog box similar to the Rotate dialog box.

The Reshape tool (in the Scale tool pop-out) interactively works on selected objects to stretch and distort them. Click first to set a fixed anchor point, and then drag on another point to distort the object. The Reshape tool is not associated with a dialog box.

SUMMARY

You can transform a simple drawing in an infinite number of ways by using Illustrator's escalating set of transforming tools. You can apply these tools to single objects, sets of selected objects, or grouped objects.

You can elect to display bounding boxes on your artboard, which provide convenient anchor points around selected objects for sizing, mirroring, or rotation. For basic resizing or rotating, the Free Transform tool usually does the trick.

For more precise sizing or rotation, the Scale and Rotate tools allow you to assign exact size changes or rotation angles. Further, they allow you to select anchor points that stay in one place as you interactively resize or rotate an object.

The more esoteric Reflect, Twist, Shear, and Reshape tools provide more options for distorting selected objects.

 ON THE VIRTUAL CLASSROOM CD In Lesson 3, "Scaling and Distorting," I'll show you the quick-and-dirty way to rescale and reshape objects, as well as introduce tools for more precise scaling and transforming objects.

Pens and Paths

The unique power of vector drawing programs like
Illustrator lies in their ability to generate perfect curves. It's
amazing how much freedom you have to create illustrations by
combining straight lines and curves. And the ultimate curve tool
in Illustrator's arsenal is the Pen tool.

Other tools, like the shape tools I discussed in Chapter 4, or the drawing tools I explained in Chapter 3, are OK for creating already defined shapes. But to really unleash your creativity, you'll want to pick up the Pen tool. It gives you infinite control over the curvature of line segments and how they connect with each other.

THE MATH OF PATHS

Some Illustrator lovers like to fixate a bit on the underlying logic of curves generated by the Pen tool. Fair enough. Without this underlying math magic, you'd be without the freedom to create beautiful, precisely defined curves. So I'll explain how this logic works.

Virtually *all* the basic objects created in Illustrator—all vector objects—are in essence *curves*. Illustrator's vector objects are a combination of anchor points and a line segment in between (along with defined fills). Illustrator saves programming code (called PostScript, a page-description language) that defines the nature of each curve.

This vector-based method of saving graphic files is rooted in mathematical formulas for defining curves, pioneered by a French engineer named Pierre Bézier. Bézier's curves revolutionized the way graphic files were saved. As I explained briefly in Chapter 1, vector images are often smaller in file size, and they are always more easily resizable than bitmap images.

Vector graphics are, indeed, an efficient way to save illustrations. But they are also a dynamic and unique way to *create* drawings. Illustrator compensates for our humanly imperfect drawing skills. Even the most accomplished artist can't duplicate the precision and control that Illustrator provides over curves. If you don't count yourself among the drawing elite, you can still create perfect curves.

The most powerful and versatile tool for generating and altering curves is the Pen tool. The Pen tool creates anchor points, and line segments between them. The nature of the segments (curved or straight) is defined by the anchor points at either end of the segment.

Figure 6-1 shows an illustration created using the Pen tool, with a combination of curved and straight line segments and associated curved and corner anchor points.

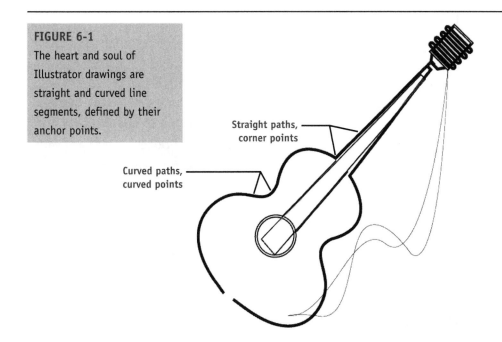

FIGURE 6-1
The heart and soul of Illustrator drawings are straight and curved line segments, defined by their anchor points.

Straight paths, corner points

Curved paths, curved points

As you explore and experiment with the Pen tool, you'll gain wizard-like ability to draw with it. And with some practice, it will become an extension of not just your hand, but your imagination.

CREATING AND EDITING STRAIGHT SEGMENTS

The easiest and most basic type of line segments you create with the Pen tool are *straight segments*: line segments with two straight corner points. To draw a straight line with the Pen tool, click once, and then click again at another location on the artboard. Complete the straight corner point by clicking a third time, as shown here.

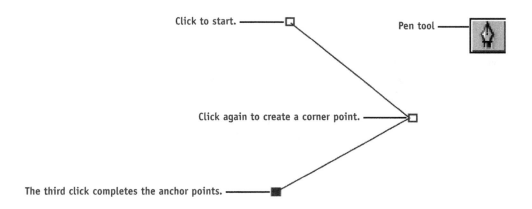

Click to start.

Pen tool

Click again to create a corner point.

The third click completes the anchor points.

When you have completed the set of line segments, hold down COMMAND/CTRL and click. Or you can select another tool to deselect the Pen tool. Another quick, easy way to do this is to use a keystroke shortcut (like the letter O) to quickly deselect the Pen tool. You can press P or select the Pen tool from the toolbox to begin a new set of line segments.

> **NOTE** Resist the natural impulse to click and drag to create line segments. Clicking and dragging with the Pen tool produces very counterintuitive results. In the remaining sections of this chapter, I'll illustrate how clicking and dragging with the Pen tool defines curved segments.

Alternatively, you can end a series of straight line segments by *closing* the path. Just move the Pen cursor over the original anchor point and click. As you move the cursor over the starting anchor point, the cursor displays as a circle. I'll discuss closed paths in more detail in the section "Penning Closed Paths," later in this chapter.

As you click to create straight corner points, you can constrain the line segments you draw to 45 degree increments by holding down the SHIFT key as you click to create new anchor points. If you turn on Smart Guides, 45 and 90 degree angle points are illustrated. (Choose the View menu, and make sure Smart Guides is selected.)

CREATING AND EDITING SMOOTH CORNER POINTS

Curved line segments are defined by the length and location of *direction lines* that you create and define as you generate a curve with the Pen tool.

To Create A SMOOTH CORNER POINT

1 Select the Pen tool, and click the artboard to create the first anchor point.

2 Move your cursor (without clicking and dragging) to the location of a second anchor point, and click. *Don't release the mouse button.*

3 Click and drag from the new anchor point to create a direction handle and generate a curved anchor point as shown in the illustration that follows.

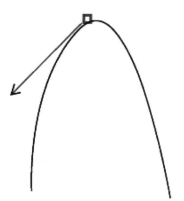

4 Click on a third point on the artboard.

5 Press COMMAND/CTRL and click to finish the path.

MAKING WAVES

Waves are a widespread phenomenon in nature, and therefore in art as well. One of my favorite uses of the Pen tool is to generate smooth, flowing, and easily altered waves.

The exercise of drawing a wave is also a good way to get a feel for how curves are defined by drawing direction lines.

To Draw A SET OF WAVES WITH THE PEN TOOL

1 To help draw evenly spaced waves, select View | Show Grid, and then select View | Snap To Grid.

2 Select the Pen tool, and click and drag vertically to create a vertical direction line.

3 Draw a second vertical direction line the same length. Use the (nonprinting) grid to space the second anchor point.

> **NOTE** Remember, you're not drawing a line now, you're drawing a direction handle to define a curved anchor point. You'll create the actual line when you define the next anchor point.

4 Draw a couple more direction lines—all the same length and evenly spaced—as shown here.

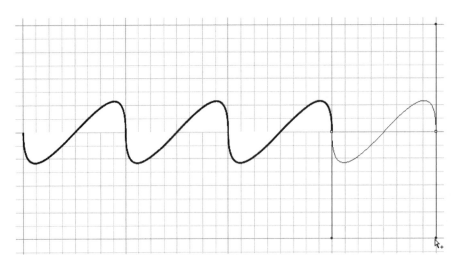

5 Press COMMAND/CTRL and click to end the path.

Once you generate a wave or set of waves, you can use all the transformation tools covered in Chapter 5 to resize, rotate, and otherwise distort your waves for effect.

MANIPULATING DIRECTION HANDLES

Once you have generated a curved anchor point, you can manipulate the curve of the attached line segment(s) by moving the anchor points. You can make a curve higher by extending the direction handles and shallower by shortening the direction handles, as shown here.

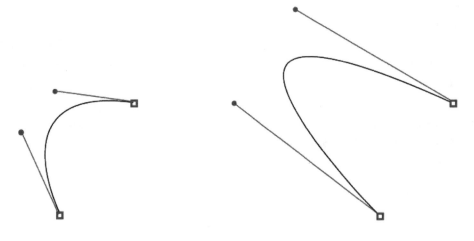

In addition, you can alter the angle of the intersection of curved line segments by rotating the direction handle.

To change the direction or length of a direction line, use the Direct Selection tool to select the anchor point. As you do, the direction line(s) become visible. Click and drag on the endpoint of a direction line to lengthen or shorten it, or to rotate it.

MIXING AND MATCHING STRAIGHT AND CURVED SEGMENTS

Complex drawings mix and match both straight corner and curved corner anchor points. To create a complex path of both curved and straight segments, use the Pen tool to generate your curve by clicking to create anchor points. For those anchor points you want to act as curved anchors, click and drag to generate a direction handle for the point. For straight corner points, simply click.

The following path combines *one* curved anchor point and a whole bunch of straight corner anchor points. Try it yourself—clicking and dragging to generate the one curved anchor point.

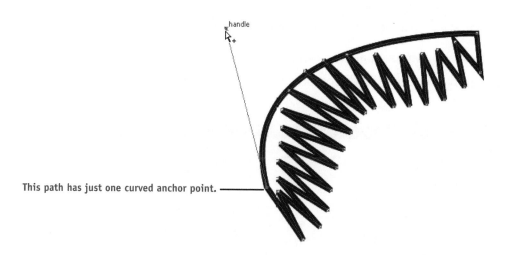

This path has just one curved anchor point.

Remember, you can always change the height and direction of a curved segment by *later* manipulating the direction handle. So first rough out your path, and then fine-tune the curve by clicking and dragging on the direction handle.

You can also *move* an anchor point by selecting the anchor with the Direct Selection tool, and then clicking and dragging that point to a new location.

ADDING AND DELETING ANCHOR POINTS

After you generate a path with the Pen tool, you can easily add or remove anchor points with the Add Anchor Point or Delete Anchor Point tool—both found on the Pen tool pop-out.

> **NOTE** Holding down COMMAND/CTRL as you use the Pen tool temporarily converts the Pen tool into the last used selection tool—either the Selection, Direct Selection, or Group Selection tool. A very handy trick for drawing and editing!

With the Add Anchor Point tool selected, click anywhere on a path to create a new anchor. The new anchor point is created with the attributes (curved or straight) of the existing segment. So, for instance, if you click a straight line segment with the Add Anchor Point tool, you'll create a new straight corner point.

You can also add anchor points automatically between *every* anchor point in a selected path. Perform this task by first selecting the path, and then choosing Object | Path | Add Anchor Points. You'll instantly double the number of anchor points, providing more flexibility in manipulating the path.

Similarly, you can use the Delete Anchor Point tool to remove unwanted anchor points. Point and click an existing anchor point, and it's gone.

To reduce the number of anchor points (and thus smooth out a curve), select Object | Path | Simplify. The Simplify dialog box appears (shown next).

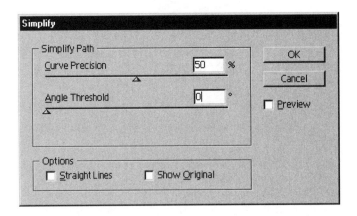

Use the Curve Precision slider to define just how much you want to simplify the selected path. Higher values simplify the curve less drastically, while lower values keep less of the original shape of the path.

You can use the Angle Threshold slider to protect some corner points from being simplified. If you define an angle threshold of 45 degrees, for example, then only corners with angles of 45 degrees or higher would be smoothed out when you applied the changes.

The Straight Lines check box changes paths to straight lines, and the Show Original check box displays both the original curve and the changed curve if you select the Preview check box. Use the Preview check box to display how your changes will appear before you click OK in the Simplify dialog box.

CHANGING POINT TYPES

You can transform points from straight corner to curved, or vice versa. The easiest way to perform this task is to use the Convert Anchor Point tool (in the Pen tool pop-out).

When you point and click on an anchor point with the Convert Anchor Point tool, curved points are instantly converted to straight corner points. In the following illustration, the guitar body taking shape as a curved anchor point is converted to a corner point.

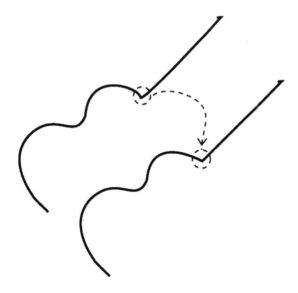

If you convert a straight point to a curved point, you can immediately click and drag to define and manipulate direction lines to edit the line segments that connect to that point.

MORE PEN TOOL TIPS

You'll almost always want to modify curves that you create with the Pen tool. And often, you'll want to quickly switch back and forth between touching up your curves and creating new ones. Illustrator provides many tricks for doing this.

Depending on when and how you use it and which keyboard keys you hold down, the Pen tool converts to several related tools.

In addition, Illustrator provides features for automatically smoothing or touching up your Pen-drawn curves, including the ability to line up anchor points, delete stray anchor points, or simplify a curve. I'll explain how to do all this in the next section.

THE MANY FACES OF THE PEN TOOL

Because the Pen tool is the most powerful and useful tool in Illustrator, you'll have it selected most of the time you create a drawing. By moving the cursor to different parts of a path, or by pressing COMMAND/CTRL or OPTION/ALT, you can temporarily change the functioning of the tool.

> **TIP** Like all drawing tools, the Pen tool cursor can be displayed as cross hairs for more accuracy. To display the Pen tool cursor as cross hairs, press CAPS LOCK on your keyboard. Pressing CAPS LOCK again reverts to the normal cursor display.

You can use the Pen tool to add segments to an existing path and to add or delete anchor points to a path. And the Pen tool can even be converted to temporarily function like the Convert Anchor Point tool.

ADDING SEGMENTS TO A PATH

To add segments to an existing path, move the Pen tool over an endpoint in the path. As you do, the cursor displays as a slash (/).

With the Pen tool cursor displaying as a slash, click the current endpoint in the path. Then, click again to define a contiguous segment. If you click and drag instead of just clicking, you'll define a new curved anchor point.

ADDING, DELETING, AND ADJUSTING ANCHOR POINTS WITH THE PEN TOOL

When you point to an anchor point, the cursor becomes a minus (–) sign, and the Pen tool takes on the persona of the Delete Anchor Point tool. Move the Pen tool over an existing anchor point, look for the minus sign cursor, and click. The selected anchor point disappears.

When you point to a path (but not an anchor point on the path), the Pen tool temporarily assumes the identity of the Add Anchor Point tool. Click to create new anchor points. The new anchor point assumes the characteristics of the line segment to which it is added. So a new anchor point on a curved line segment will be a curved anchor point.

When you hold down COMMAND/CTRL, the Pen tool changes to the most recently chosen selection tool. One frequent scenario is that you will add an anchor point by pointing and clicking on a path. After you've jumped to the Direct Selection tool once, the next time you need to toggle from the Pen tool to the Direct Selection tool, just press COMMAND/CTRL to convert the Pen tool on the fly to the Direct Selection tool. Now you're ready to adjust the direction handle on the new curved anchor point.

> **NOTE** A further possible conversion is to hold down OPTION/ALT with the Pen tool selected. This action temporarily converts the Pen tool to the Convert Anchor Point tool.

MORE PATHBREAKING TRICKS

You can use menu options to close a path and to "average" a path to align points. You can also use menu options to find and clean up those stray anchor points that are created when you click with the Pen tool but don't generate a path. Somehow, those darn things always seem to litter a complex illustration.

PENNING CLOSED PATHS

Closed paths are the ones whose last anchor point is connected to the first point. Closed paths provide more flexibility in adding pattern fills—as you'll see in Chapter 10.

You can create a closed path as you generate a curve by pointing to the original anchor point to finish the path. The Pen tool cursor becomes a circle as you connect the first and last anchor points in the curve. To convert an existing open path into a closed path, select the path and choose Object | Path | Join.

ALIGNING POINTS BY AVERAGING PATHS

In Chapter 4, I showed you how to align (as well as space) objects along a horizontal or vertical path. That method works for entire paths. But Illustrator also allows you to align *specific* anchor points within a path.

This trick can be handy when you need to create symmetrical or aligned objects. Generally, when you average paths, you'll want to apply the averaging only to selected points. Otherwise, averaging tends to mush your path into an unrecognizable mess.

> NOTE If you select two anchor points that are already in the exact same place and choose Object | Path | Join, you convert them into a single anchor point. If one of the merged anchor points is smooth and the other is a corner anchor point, you can use the Join dialog box to choose whether to convert the newly merged point to a smooth or corner point.

To Average POINTS IN A PATH

1 Use the Direct Selection tool to select two (or more) anchor points in a path.

2 With two or more points selected, choose Object | Path | Average. The Average dialog box appears.

3 Select Horizontal to align the selected points on a horizontal plane; select Vertical to line the points up vertically. If you select both, the selected points will move to the same location (and merge into one point).

4 Click OK to apply the changes to the path. The following illustration shows the effect of horizontal and vertical averaging on two points in a path.

> NOTE The easiest way to select just two anchor points is to select one, and then hold down SHIFT and select a second point. Because anchor points are tiny, it's sometimes hard to tell if they are selected. Selected anchor points display as filled squares instead of hollow squares, and they are easier to identify in Outline view. (Choose View | Outline to toggle from Preview to Outline view.)

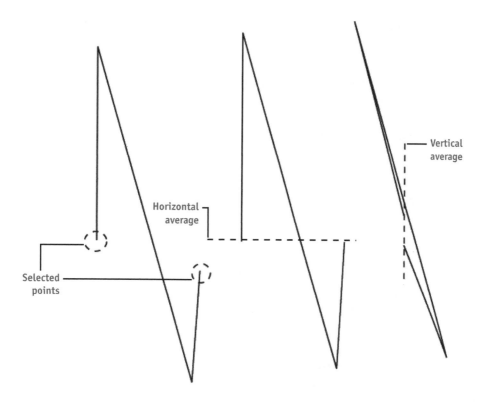

Vertical
average

Horizontal
average

Selected
points

CLEANING UP LOST ANCHOR POINTS

A click here, a click there, and suddenly, your artboard is littered with a bunch of invisible (unless selected) anchor points. Although they don't print, they mess up your project by adding space and size to exported files. And they cause confusion by appearing when you select objects and find you've also grabbed a few stray anchor points.

TIP Another way to clean up stray points is to select Object | Path | Clean Up. This strategy opens the Clean Up dialog box, with check boxes that allow you to get rid of stray points, unpainted objects, and/or empty text paths. You'll learn about text paths in Chapter 8.

You can see stray anchor points in Outline view, and you can delete them manually. Thankfully, Illustrator identifies and deletes these stray anchor points automatically. Just choose Select | Objects | Stray Points, and press DELETE to clean them up.

A Fun Pen Project

The only way to get comfortable with using the Pen tool to create and manipulate paths is to try it out! In the following exercise, you'll use the Pen tool attributes covered in this chapter, plus just a little bit of shapes and fills (from Chapter 4).

Don't feel you have to exactly duplicate the illustration here—freelance, simplify (or amplify), and definitely don't get frustrated if the drawing doesn't shape up easily. Using the Pen tool requires a whole new way of thinking and drawing. So use this practice as a way to get some experience. The final project will look something like the drawing here.

To Draw BY CREATING AND MANIPULATING PATHS AND ANCHORS

1 Draw the top half of the guitar body using the Pen tool, with both curved and corner anchor points, to create a path like the one in the following illustration. Remember, you can hold down COMMAND/CTRL to convert the Pen tool into the Convert Anchor Point tool and use that to transform curved anchors into corners, or vice versa.

> NOTE In this illustration, eight anchor points are used to define the path. If yours has too many to create a smooth path, try deleting some points.

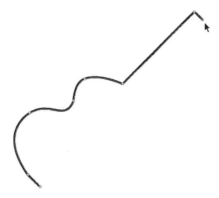

2 Use the Reflect and Rotate tools (see Chapter 5) to duplicate the half-guitar body you drew, and align it with the top of the guitar to make the body.

3 Create a closed path with the Pen tool to serve as the decoration on the top of the guitar, and use rectangles to create the tuning keys, as shown here.

4 Use circles (see Chapter 4) to create the hole in the guitar.

5 Use a closed path to draw a trapezoidal path to outline the strings on the guitar. Use lines to create additional strings.

6 Draw the guitar strap with two intersecting paths. The circles, straight line segments, and curved/straight paths are shown here.

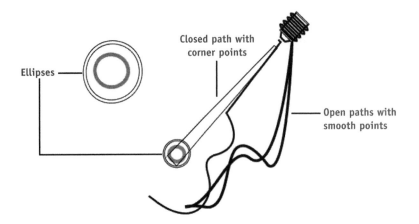

Ellipses

Closed path with corner points

Open paths with smooth points

7 If necessary, use the Direct Selection tool, the Convert Anchor Point tool, and perhaps the Add Anchor Point and/or Delete Anchor Point tools to touch up your paths.

8 Use the Paint Bucket tool to apply a fill color to selected areas of the guitar.

SUMMARY

You use the Pen tool to create paths. These paths are composed of line segments, bounded by smooth or curved anchor points. You create drawings in Illustrator with the Pen tool by defining and tinkering with these anchor points.

Once you create a path with the Pen tool, you can (endlessly) add, delete, and manipulate the generated anchor points. Illustrator has tools to convert corners to curves, and vice versa, to line up anchor points horizontally or vertically, and to infinitely fine-tune the size and direction of curves.

 ON THE VIRTUAL CLASSROOM CD In Lesson 4, "The Pen Tool," I'll demystify the unintuitive Pen tool and show you my tricks for generating smooth, precise curves.

7

Blending Away

Blends are used to generate transitional paths

in between two selected paths. Blending takes advantage of

the fact that vector images in Illustrator are defined mathe-

matically, and Illustrator performs some serious math cal-

culations on your computer's processor to generate these

"in-between" images.

Aesthetically, you can use blends to create a series of distinct transitional drawings, or to attach what appear to be effects like shading or gradient blending to images. Figure 7-1 shows blending used for both purposes.

You can generate blends between any two (or more) selected paths. That doesn't mean they will look good between any two paths. But in the sections that follow, I'll show you some nice techniques that you can use by applying blends.

> **TIP** You can't apply blending to bitmaps that you place in an Illustrator drawing. You also can't assign them to type. If you need to assign blending to text, you'll need to convert that text to outlines. (Select the type block and select Type | Create Outlines.) For more on working with type, see Chapter 8.

SETTING BLEND OPTIONS

Before you apply a blend, you'll need to use the Blend Options dialog box to define the kind of blend you want to apply. The main decision to make is what kind of spacing you want between the generated objects.

FIGURE 7-1
The blend on top uses hundreds of finely spaced iterations to create the illusion of a 3-D shadow, while the blend on the bottom uses a few steps to create animation-like transitions.

A very small spacing creates a smooth, gradient-like result, and it is often used for color gradation in effects like shadows or 3-D illusion. Larger spacing creates a series of distinct images, with distinct steps visible. The following illustration shows both smooth and step applications.

You define blend options (either in advance, or to a selected blend) by double-clicking the Blend tool. The Blend Options dialog box opens, as shown here.

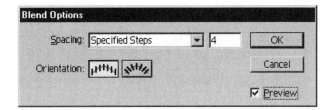

I'll explain the options in this dialog box in the following sections. Then, I'll show you how to apply a blend. But keep in mind that if you select an already applied blend with the Selection tool and then double-click the Blend tool, you will edit the blend. If you do that, the Preview check box in the Blend Options dialog box is handy—you can see how blend parameters will look before you press ENTER or click OK.

BLEND SPACING

There are two basic options for blend spacing: smooth or steps. But Illustrator offers further fine-tuning options for how to apply a blend.

If you choose Smooth Color Spacing from the Spacing drop-down list in the Blend Options dialog box, Illustrator calculates the optimum number of steps to create a smooth, gradient-looking blend.

If you elect to define a limited number of steps, you can either choose the number of generated intermediate shapes, or you can define spacing in intervals. To define a set number of steps, choose Specified Steps from the Spacing drop-down list, and enter a value next to the Spacing box.

If you want to define a set distance between steps, choose Specified Distance from the Spacing drop-down list, and enter a value and an increment. (You can type 12 pixels, or 12 px—short for pixels—.5 inches, .5 in, and so on.)

> **NOTE** The value you enter will define the number of *generated* shapes, not the *total* number of shapes. The total number of shapes is the number of generated shapes plus the original shapes.

> **NOTE** Illustrator converts the value and unit of measurement you enter into the Preferences dialog box for general units. To change your default unit of measurement, select Edit | Preferences | Units | Undo.

BLEND ORIENTATION

If you define a specified blend (either specified steps or specified distance), you can also define how objects rotate along a curve. This task is worth performing only if you create a curved path to define your blend. I'll show you how to do that very soon in this section. But just so this discussion makes some sense, the next illustration shows both kinds of orientation: aligned to a page, and aligned to a path.

Orientation along an aligned path means that the intermediate objects in a blend will rotate in conformity with the path along which they are generated. Orientation to the page means objects that start vertical, for example, stay vertical throughout the blend.

To define how orientation will be applied (and again, this concept is relevant only if you will be blending along a path), click either the Align To Page button or the Align To Path button in the Blend Options dialog box.

After you define blend options, close the dialog box by pressing ENTER or clicking OK. The options you defined will apply to each blend you create.

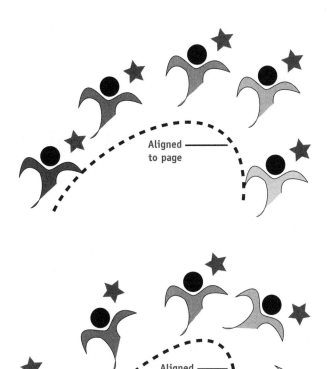

Aligned —
to page

Aligned —
to path

BASIC BLENDS

Blending can get rather complex—and fun! But before you explore the widest reaches of what you can do, you should get comfortable working with the two basic types of blends: smooth colors, and steps.

To get some experience blending, I'll walk you through a couple different exercises. First, you'll turn a square into a circle. Then, you'll use a blend to produce a smooth color blend that lends a bit of a shadow effect to a star.

EXERCISE: A STEP BLEND

Who says you can't pound a round peg into a square hole? In this exercise, I'll show you how to transform a circle into a square. You'll generate a five-step blend that creates intermediate shapes that transition from one shape into another.

To Blend A SQUARE INTO A CIRCLE

1 On a nice, clean artboard, draw a square on the left side. Apply a yellow fill and no outline.

2 On the right side of the artboard, draw a circle, about the same size as the square, with a red fill and no outline.

> **TIP** Refer to Chapter 4 for the steps to create squares and circles.

3 Double-click the Blend tool to open the Blend Options dialog box. Select Specified Steps from the Spacing drop-down list, and enter 5 next to the Spacing box.

> **NOTE** Because you're not yet blending along a path, it doesn't matter which orientation button is selected.

4 Click OK in the Blend Options dialog box. The Blend tool is still selected.

5 Click once in the middle of the square. Move the Blend tool over the circle. As you do, the cursor displays with a tiny plus (+) sign. Click in the middle of the circle to generate a blend. Your blend should look something like the one here.

EXERCISE: A SMOOTH COLOR BLEND

Now I'll show you how to use a smooth blend to create a star that uses blending to create a shadow. This blend will use the Smooth Color blend option and transition from a light color to a dark color to create a 3-D background shadow using two identical shapes.

To Apply A COLOR BLEND TO TWO STARS

1 You won't need an entire artboard for this exercise, just a little space. Draw a five-pointed star. (See Chapter 4 for instructions on drawing shapes, including stars, and for assigning fill and outline colors.)

2 Assign a light-colored fill to the star, and no outline.

3 With the star selected, hold down OPTION/ALT, and drag the star slightly up and to the left to create a duplicate that is mostly in front of the original star, as shown next.

4 Select the star behind the front star, and apply a black fill, no outline. The star in the background should look like a black shadow, something like the one shown here.

5 Double-click the Blend tool on the toolbar to open the Blend Options dialog box.

6 In the Spacing drop-down list, choose Smooth Color. Click OK in the dialog box.

7 With the Blend tool still selected, click once on the star in front and once on the star in back. The colors will blend, creating a 3-D like shadow, something like the one here.

Smooth color blends can also be effective in generating gradient-like transitions between an object on top of another object. In the following illustration, I placed a shape on top of another shape. The smooth color blend between the dark shape and the light shape creates the illusion of a cave entry with receding light.

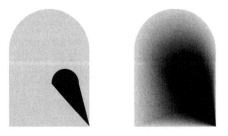

REVERSE A BLEND

Sometimes, you will want to modify a blend so that the object on the bottom of the blend moves to the top. This revises the whole blend and reverses the stacking order that was originally generated. Reversing the stacking order is useful (and relevant) only if your intermediate objects overlap each other.

To reverse the stacking order in a blend, select the entire blend using the Selection (not the Direct Selection) tool. Then select Object | Blend | Reverse Front To Back.

MAKE BLENDS GO AWAY

Finally, before I lead you into more complex blending, let me tell you how to undo a blend.

To remove a blend, first select it. You can select blends just like other objects. They aren't grouped—for purposes of the Selection tool, they are like a single path. So, before you start unblending, use the Selection tool to select the whole blend.

> **TIP** You can use the Direct Selection tool to select individual objects within a blend. Stay away from that tool for now because the goal is to select the entire blend.

With the blend selected, choose Object | Blend | Release. Now the blend is gone.

CHANGING BLENDS INTERACTIVELY

Once you generate a blend between two or more paths, you can modify the blend interactively on the artboard by moving one of the paths used to create the blend.

Start by selecting just one of the blended objects. You'll find this task much easier if you use the Direct Selection tool. Just click and drag with the Direct Selection tool, and watch the blend redraw itself as you move one object.

You can also select individual anchor points and anchor them on a blended object. The trick is, it's pretty hard to select an individual anchor in a blended object. This task is easier to perform with the Direct Selection tool in Outline view. (Select View | Outline.) That way, it's easier to see which anchor point is selected and to manipulate direction lines. The downside is that you can't really tell how the blend will look until you switch back to Preview view. (Select View | Preview.) When I need to do that, I resort to first selecting the anchor in Outline view with the Direct Selection tool, and then switching back to Preview view to actually edit the path.

BLENDING BETWEEN DEFINED ANCHORS

In the examples I've discussed so far in this chapter, I've shown you how to blend between two objects. You can fine-tune blends and create some interesting deviations on those blends by basing a blend on selected anchor points in the blended objects.

About the best way I can describe the result of blending from anchor points instead of objects is that the effect is interesting.

You can use anchor blends with either step or smooth blends. I find the most interesting and useful anchor point–based blends use smooth color transitions to tweak shading and 3-D effects. I'll walk you through that process in the following steps.

To Create A BLEND BETWEEN ANCHOR POINTS ON TWO DIFFERENT PATHS

1 Double-click the Blend tool to open the Blend Options dialog box.

2 Choose Smooth Color in the Spacing drop-down list, and click OK.

3 I find it easier (much easier!) to define anchor point blends if I can see the anchor points. Therefore, use the Selection tool to select both objects involved in the blend—making their anchor points visible.

4 Now that you can see the anchor points in both selected objects, choose the Blend tool. The anchor points remain visible.

5 Click an anchor point in one of the objects.

6 Move the Blend cursor over an anchor point in the second object. As you do, the anchor point and the Blend cursor display together as a black square. Click to generate the blend.

The main "rule" for creating anchor point blends is to experiment! After a while, you will almost be able to anticipate the effect you'll produce with various anchor point blends. Keep the Undo option on the Edit menu handy as you experiment.

The following illustration shows three different anchor blends applied to create smooth color blends between two objects, and the different resulting shading.

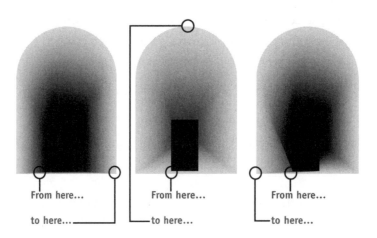

From here...   From here...   From here...
to here...   to here...   to here...

BENDING THE BLENDING PATH

You can further stretch the blending envelope by defining a custom path along which to generate the blend. This custom path is called a *spine,* and you can create it with any drawing tool (like the Pen or Pencil tool).

You can use blending along a spine to create a follow-the-path series of transitioning, blended objects. Or, you can use a smooth blend combined with a custom spine to create interesting shadow or 3-D effects like tubing, or a snakelike blend. The following illustration uses a smooth blend to create a snakelike curve.

This illustration uses a two-step blend to create a different effect—morphing a square into a star.

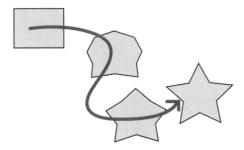

In the following steps, I'll walk you through the routine involved in creating a blend that uses a spine. I'll use an example of a blending spine to create a tubelike effect.

To Create A BLEND THAT USES A SPINE

1 Draw a small circle on the left side of the artboard. Assign a white fill and a black out-line to the circle. (Refer to Chapter 4 for help drawing shapes and assigning fill and stroke color.)

2 Create a second circle on the right side of the artboard. Make it about four times as large as the original circle. Assign a yellow fill and a black outline to the second circle.

3 Double-click the Blend tool, and set Spacing to Smooth and click on the Align To Path button in the Orientation area of the dialog box.

4 With the Blend tool, click on the edge of one circle, and then again on the edge of the second circle to generate a blend.

5 Underneath the generated blend, draw a wavelike curve, like the one shown here.

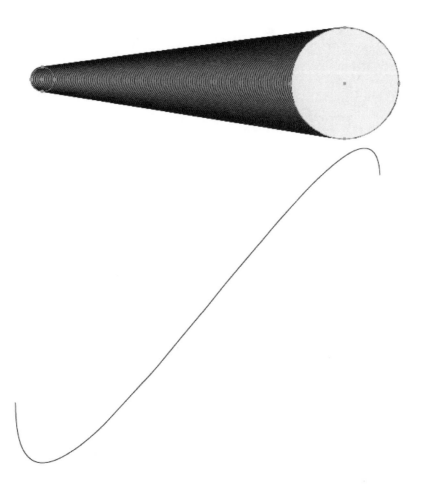

6 Select both the wavelike path and the blend.

7 Select Object | Blend | Replace Spine to align the blend along the path defined by the wavelike curve.

NOTE For instructions on drawing a wave with the Pen tool, see Chapter 6.

After you append the blend to the path, you can experiment with changing blend options. (Try both Align To Path and Align To Page). You can use the Direct Selection tool to select and move either the first circle, the second circle, or the spine path. And you can use editing tools like the Scale and Free Transform tools to alter either of the three elements of the blend.

You can reverse the direction of a blend along a spine by selecting Object | Blend | Reverse Spine. And you can select an entire blend—including a blend along a spine—and edit it with tools like the Free Transform and Scale tools.

BLENDING AND GROUPING

Ouch! Blending between two or more grouped objects can get weird. In general, blends work well between simple shapes, and they get ugly when you start to blend complex shapes.

This idea gets illustrated when you try to blend grouped objects. In general, the results are kind of a mushy mess. For example, in the following illustration, I blended the two grouped dancing figures, with not very pretty results.

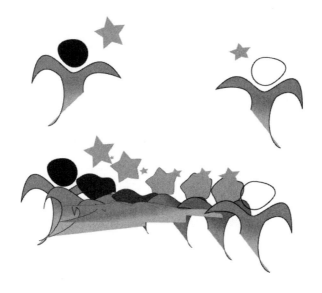

I got better results when I ungrouped my drawings and created separate blends between each object within the group. That way, in the next illustration, the heads, stars, and bodies all have separate blends, and the results are more distinct and useful blends.

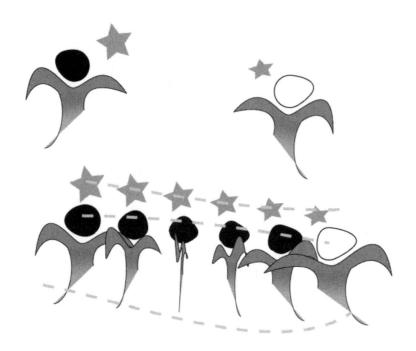

TWEAKING BLENDS

As you've seen, blending is a very versatile technique, which you can use for everything from seamlessly smooth color blends to animation-style sets of objects that transition from one shape to another.

Although you can do a lot to control blends—both in the Blend Options dialog box and by adhering a blend to a spine—sometimes you will want to *tweak* (adjust) the result of a blend.

For example, in the next illustration, I started with a blend, but I wanted to add some text and remove a couple of the generated transitional objects.

You can't do that kind of fine-tuning by using only a blend. The solution is to expand the blend. Expanding a blend converts each of the generated transitional shapes into a distinct, editable shape.

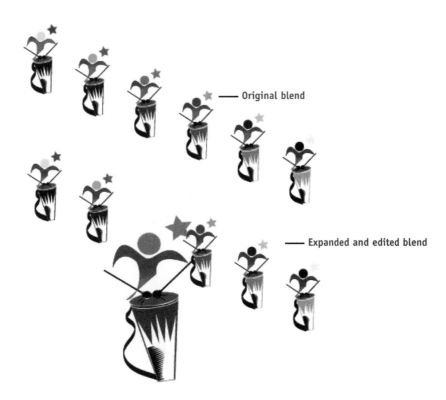

Original blend

Expanded and edited blend

To expand a blend, first select the blend. Then select Objects | Blend | Expand. The result will be a set of paths that you can edit. When you first expand a blend, the objects that made up the blend will be grouped, so ungroup them (Object | Ungroup) before you start editing individual objects.

Once you expand a blend, of course it loses all its blend properties. You can no longer adjust the blend options or work with a spine path.

BLENDS: A FINAL WARNING

As you spend time experimenting with blends, you'll see how exciting this feature is! And you'll be tempted to go out to lunch with it. The problem is that those beautiful color blends and entertaining step blends you launch with the click of a mouse are hard to handle in both print and web output.

The limitation with print output is that smooth color blends in particular can place undue demands on your print agency's ability to mix and merge colors.

I'll discuss this subject in more detail in Chapter 14, when I explain how to prepare Illustrator images for printed output.

The problem gets worse with web output. Because web design is generally constrained to 216 colors and a grainy 72 dots per inch (dpi) resolution, intricate smooth color blends will be reduced to banded (striped) bars of colors. I'll discuss the challenge of incorporating blends in web-bound art, including some available solutions, in Chapter 15.

Does all this bad news mean there is no place for blends? No—blends can be used in both digital and print output, but smooth blends especially pose a real challenge in both environments.

SUMMARY

Blends are one of the most powerful, versatile, and fun tools in Illustrator. You can use them to create transitional images. Or you can create smooth color transitions to use for shadows, for tubelike results, or for other interesting effects.

Blends take full advantage of Illustrator's underlying math-based curve logic. Unfortunately, they do tend to put some stress on your computer's processor because they involve a lot of calculation to generate. And some blends do not transition well to web output: an issue I'll return to in Chapter 15.

 ON THE VIRTUAL CLASSROOM CD In Lesson 5, "Blends," I'll show you how to create a smooth color blend, as well as how to use step blends to create transitional objects between two pieces of artwork.

8

Goin' Wild with Paths

Illustrator allows you to intersect objects to create many different effects. You can use the tools in the Pathfinder palette to cut up intersecting images. Or you can apply transparency and allow overlaying objects to function like a piece of tinted glass, revealing the underlying drawing but with the colors tinted, shaded, or distorted.

Another cool way that overlapping objects can react on each other is through masking. Mask objects reveal only a part of an underlying image. Think of a bright spotlight shining on a dark stage—revealing only those elements of the stage that are lit up.

And, before this chapter is done, I'll show you how to combine masking and transparency to create some really tripping effects.

TAKING ADVANTAGE OF PATHFINDER TOOLS

The ten tools in the Pathfinder palette basically allow you to combine and divide two or more intersecting paths. These tools provide a quick way to apply some complex anchor point and path changes that would be tedious if you did them with tools like the Pen tool or the Direct Selection tool.

When the tools in the Pathfinder palette combine two objects, the object on the bottom usually assumes the fill and stroke attributes of the object on top.

So, before you apply a Pathfinder effect, select Object | Arrange, and move the object in front of or behind another object to define how fill and stroke attributes will be handled.

> **NOTE** There are a couple exceptions to this rule—where the top shape assumes the properties of the bottom shape. Those odd tools are the Subtract From Shape Area and the Crop tools.

Pathfinders work with vector objects, including gradient fills. However, they don't work with bitmaps: for that, you can use a clipping mask, which I'll discuss later in the section "Clipping with Masks."

To access the tools in the Pathfinder palette, choose Window | Pathfinder. The following illustration identifies each of the tools.

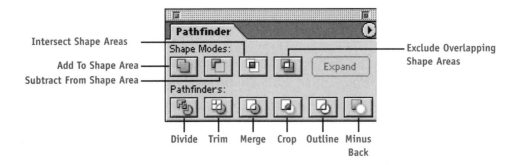

To access Pathfinder palette options, click the menu pop-out in the Pathfinder palette, and choose Pathfinder Options. The Pathfinder Options dialog box appears, as shown in the next illustration. The options define how intersecting objects will be combined. The Precision value determines how accurately intersecting objects will be combined or divided, and the default setting works fine. The

Remove Redundant Points and the Divide And Outline Will Remove Unpainted Artwork check boxes are useful. Each of them removes elements of a combined (or divided) object that aren't functional, simplifying the resulting paths. I advise activating these options before you start using the tools.

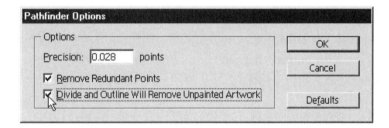

If you experiment with the Pathfinder tools, you'll discover some fun results that you can incorporate in drawings. The tools are divided into two rows: the Shape Modes, and the Pathfinders. I'll demonstrate how each of these tools works.

USING THE SHAPE MODES TOOLS

Illustrator 10 dubs the top row of the Pathfinder tools the Shape Modes set of tools. They basically generate new shapes from intersecting shapes. The following tools comprise the Shape Modes set:

▶ **Add To Shape Area** Combines selected objects into a single shape (previously referred to as the Unite button)

▶ **Subtract From Shape Area** Deletes the top shape from the bottom shape

▶ **Intersect Shape Areas** Removes everything but overlapping areas of selected shapes

▶ **Exclude Overlapping Shape Areas** Deletes shared areas of two overlapping selected objects

These short explanations give you a basic sense of how these tools work when applied to two overlapping objects. The following illustration demonstrates these tools.

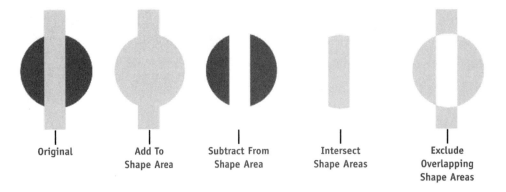

After you apply a Shape Modes tool, the resulting path is a compound shape. Compound shapes are kind of like grouped shapes, but the combination is more permanent: you can't "uncompound" a path and restore individual outlines, shapes, or fills.

NOTE You can undo a compound shape by selecting Release Compound Shape from the Pathfinder menu.

If you want to break apart a compound shape created with a Shape Modes tool, you can click the Expand button in the Pathfinder palette. Expanding a compound shape frees each of the newly generated paths for individual editing. This illustration shows the differences in paths once a generated shape has been expanded. Note the missing anchors and curves in the expanded objects.

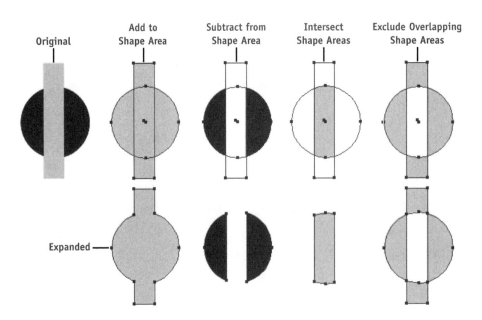

USING PATHFINDERS

The Pathfinders—the second row of tools in the Pathfinder palette—perform more complex transformations to overlapping objects than the Shape Modes tools. In earlier versions of Illustrator, they were called *divide* tools, which gives a little hint of what they are used for.

One basic function of Pathfinders is to combine overlapping objects, and then break them into a variety of *new* objects that can be ungrouped and moved, deleted, or edited individually. These tools comprise the Pathfinders set:

▶ **Divide** Splits the new combined object into individual shapes created by intersecting paths.

▶ **Trim** Deletes the covered portion of the bottom shape.

▶ **Merge** Works like the Trim tool, but merges contiguous shapes with the same color fill.

▶ **Crop** Uses the top object like a cookie cutter to cut away parts of the bottom object that do not fit within it.

▶ **Outline** Converts fills to outlines; the color of the fill becomes the color of the outline stroke.

▶ **Minus Back** Uses the bottom object as a cookie cutter to strip away intersecting areas from the front object.

After you apply one of the Pathfinders, the result is a grouped object. You can split that group and edit the newly generated shapes. In the following illustration, I've ungrouped and split up the shapes that resulted from applying a Pathfinders tool.

> **NOTE** As is often the case, the results of Merge and Trim are the same here. The only time the results are different is if there is a contiguous, divided area with the same color fill.

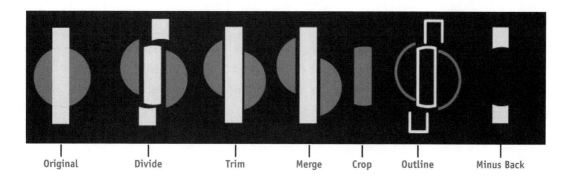

Original   Divide   Trim   Merge   Crop   Outline   Minus Back

HARD AND SOFT MIXES

You use the Hard and Soft mix options to combine colors in overlapping shapes. In previous versions of Illustrator, they were available in the Pathfinder palette.

In Illustrator 10, Hard and Soft mixes live on the Pathfinder menu. You can access these effects, and the rest of the Pathfinder tools, from the menu by choosing Effect | Pathfinder, and then selecting a Pathfinder effect.

Since the arrival of transparency back in Illustrator 9, you now have a more reliable way to combine colors in overlapping objects. Transparency produces color mixes that stand up better when sent to hardcopy or web output. Hard and Soft mixes remain on the toolbar, but they are no longer an important part of the Illustrator arsenal.

That said, if you want to try them, group objects before applying a Hard or Soft mix. Hard mixes add the values of overlapping colors—simulating overprinting hardcopy colors. Soft mixes are similar to transparency.

CLIPPING WITH MASKS

The "mask" metaphor in clipping with masks is a little weird, and requires some explaining. When you put on a mask, the only parts of your face that are visible are where the mask has holes in it, like for your eyes, nose and mouth. Think of clipping masks not as the *mask* in this scenario, but more like the *holes* in the mask. Rather than covering up part of an image, the object you use as a mask actually reveals part of an underlying image, and the rest of that underlying image is covered up.

In the next illustration, the star is the mask, and the bottle label is the masked object. As you can see, the only part of the label that is visible after masking is where the star is placed.

Clipping masks work something like the Shape Modes tools. However, there are a couple differences: you have much more control over cropping with a clipping mask, and, unlike the Shape Modes tools, you can use clipping masks on bitmap (raster) images.

MASK AWAY

There are two basic steps in clipping (trimming) an object with a mask. The first is to create the mask object, which can be any vector image (not a bitmap). But your mask object can be text. After I walk you through this process, I'll explain how to use a masking object to trim another object—the second step in clipping an object with a mask.

It doesn't matter which fill or outline you apply to an object that will be used as a masking object. The outline will disappear when the object is used as a mask. And the fill will become the section of the masked object that lies underneath the masking object.

Try the following steps to use a star shape as a mask over a larger drawing.

To Create A MASK OBJECT AND USE IT TO CLIP AN UNDERLYING OBJECT

▌ Start with any illustration using vector art.

2 To make it easier to work with your illustration, group it. (Select all objects and choose Object | Group).

3 Draw a star using the Star tool in the Rectangle tool pop-out.

4 Select a dark fill and no stroke (outline) for the star.

5 Move the star shape on top of the illustration. If the star ends up behind the illustration, choose Object | Arrange and move objects forward or backward until the clipping object (the star) is on top.

6 Select both the star and the illustration.

7 Choose Object | Clipping Mask | Make.

8 Click outside the object to see the effect of the clipping mask.

The clipping object (the mask) and the underlying masked object are linked. But only the masked section of the underlying object is visible.

Editing a Mask

Once you create a masked object, you can edit the shape and location of the mask. This works pretty much like editing any other object, except that your illustration is complex, and it's tricky to select your mask object.

Use the Direct Selection tool to edit the path of a masking object. Be careful to select the masking object, and not the (hidden) underlying object. Click and drag with the Direct Selection tool on mask object handles to change the area that is revealed, as shown next.

You can also move a masking object to different locations over the masked object. Do this by choosing the Group Selection tool, and dragging the masking object to a different location. Here again, be careful not to select elements of your underlying illustration with the Group Selection tool.

TYPE WORKS FOR MASKING

When you use type as a mask, you can adhere to your text the pattern of the underlying masked object. As I'll explain in Chapter 9, fill options for type are not as versatile as fill options for other paths. For instance, you can't assign a gradient fill to type.

You can get around that limitation, though, by using type as a mask over patterns of illustrations—including a gradient fill.

To Use A MASK TO APPLY A GRADIENT FILL TO TYPE

1 Create some text. This topic is covered in Chapter 9, but you can quickly whip up some text to experiment with by clicking the Type tool and typing a word.

2 Create a rectangle about the size of your text, and apply a gradient fill. (See Chapter 4 for the how-to on gradient fills.)

3 Move the type on top of the filled rectangle.

4 Select both the type and the rectangle.

5 Choose Object | Clipping Mask | Make.

6 Click outside your type to see the effect. This illustration is an example of type with a gradient fill.

PRODUCT OF FRANCE

RELEASING A MASK

When you use an object as a mask, you permanently wipe out any fill and/or outline you applied to that object before you applied it as a mask. You can unlink the masking object and the masked object, and the masked object will resume its original appearance. But the masking object will become a path with no outline or fill.

If you want to remove a mask from an object, select the (combined) masked object. Choose Object | Clipping Mask | Release. After you detach the masking object from the (previously) masked object, you can create a new fill and outline for (what was) the masking object.

CROPPING BITMAPS WITH MASKS

Bitmap images—either placed from other sources (like Photoshop) or created in Illustrator—can be cropped with masks. Photos or any bitmap illustration can be cropped using a vector object as a mask.

> **NOTE** For more on working with bitmaps, see Chapter 12.

The basic routine for creating a bitmap mask is to first place a bitmap on your artboard, and then place a vector image on top of the bitmap. With both the masking vector object and the underlying bitmap selected, choose Object | Clipping Mask | Make to generate a mask.

Because part of my business is promoting web sites I've designed, I've developed a little routine for putting together illustrations using bitmap masks to simulate an enlargement of sections of a site. I'll show you how I do that in the following fun project.

To Use A BITMAP MASK AS AN ENLARGEMENT

1 Set up your artboard for this little project by placing a bitmap image. (Select File | Place, and then navigate to and select a bitmap image.)

2 Duplicate the bitmap. (Copy and paste it.)

3 Use the Free Transform tool to enlarge the duplicate of the bitmap.

4 Create two circles, no stroke, white fill. Make one a bit larger than the other.

5 Use the Rectangle tool to draw a handle on the larger circle, so it looks like a magnifying glass. Move the smaller circle on top of the larger bitmap. The next illustration shows my project at this stage.

> **NOTE** Enlarging bitmaps distorts them. I know, sorry about that! That's one of the big limitations of bitmaps. I'm having you enlarge the bitmap for this exercise, but in real life, I have two different versions of the bitmap—one larger—so I don't have to distort the original.

> **TIP** Choose Object | Arrange, and then Bring To Front or Send To Back to change the stacking order of objects.

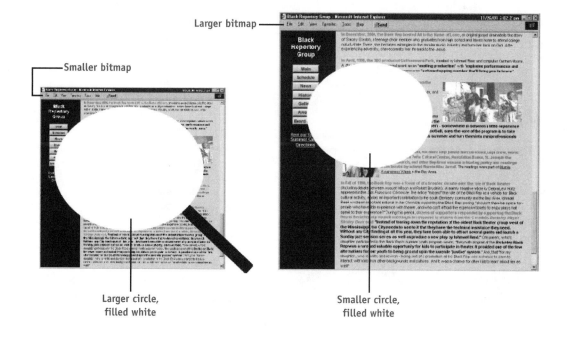

Larger bitmap

Smaller bitmap

Larger circle, filled white

Smaller circle, filled white

6 Now it's time to transform the smaller circle into a bitmap mask. To do this, select both the circle and the bitmap under it. The circle must be on top of the bitmap.

7 With both the bitmap and the circle selected, choose Object | Clipping Mask | Make. The result will be a masked section of the underlying bitmap image.

8 Drag the masked image on top of the larger white circle (the magnifying glass lens) to create the illusion of an enlarged section of the image, as shown here.

NOTE If you want to simulate my project, find a web page to use and view it in your browser. Mac users press COMMAND-SHIFT-3. The image will be saved as Picture 1 in the root directory of your hard disk. Windows users press PRINT SCREEN to capture the image to the clipboard. Then, paste or place the captured bitmap into Illustrator. Pasting a bitmap from the clipboard embeds that image in your Illustrator drawing.

APPLYING TRANSPARENCY

Transparency allows an object to be made partially see-through. An object stacked beneath a transparent object will be partially visible.

Of course, a fully transparent object, like the invisible man, would not be visible at all. So transparency is applied in degrees, ranging from 1 percent (almost completely opaque) to 99 percent (almost completely invisible). A 0 percent transparent object is opaque, and a 100 percent transparent object is invisible.

> **YOU NEED TO KNOW** that *transparency* has two meanings in digital graphic design to prevent confusion. Web graphics that have one color "knocked out" so that the web page background shows through are called transparent images. This feature can be applied to GIF or PNG format bitmap images. I'll explain how this works in Chapter 15. The transparency I'm discussing in this chapter is *partial opacity*, where an underlying image is partially visible. And, as a matter of fact, you can use this kind of transparency with printed output, but it is very difficult to transfer to images destined for the Web. Therefore, you should avoid it if you are designing web graphics.

MAKING AN OBJECT TRANSPARENT

To apply transparency to a selected object, activate the Transparency palette (choose Window | Transparency). The Transparency palette, shown next, becomes visible.

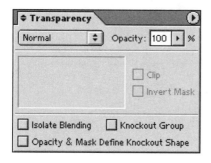

> **NOTE** Transparency is applied to both the fill and stroke of a selected object. In Chapter 13, I'll explain how to apply transparency selectively to strokes or fills using layers.

Use the Opacity area in the palette to define how much transparency you want for the selected object. Figure 8-1 shows transparency applied to different elements of an illustration.

FIGURE 8-1

Transparency lowers the opacity of objects, allowing the underlying objects to be partially visible. Here, lower percentages of opacity create more transparency.

Before transparency

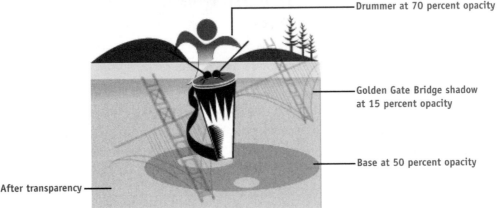

Drummer at 70 percent opacity

Golden Gate Bridge shadow at 15 percent opacity

Base at 50 percent opacity

After transparency

USING BLENDING MODES

In addition to plain, plastic wrap transparency, Illustrator's Transparency palette allows you to define blending modes that transform colors in the underlying layer. These blending modes work something like sunglasses or a colored piece of glass—tinting, distorting, or enhancing the effect of a transparent overlay layer.

The following blending effects are available from the Blending Mode list menu in the Transparency palette. The illustration shows the Blending Mode list.

▶ **Normal** Provides just transparency, no distortion of color.

▶ **Multiply** Darkens the resulting color.

▶ **Screen** Lightens the resulting color.

▶ **Overlay** Sharpens the contrast of a color (or pattern) filter by intensifying contrast.

▶ **Soft Light** Lightens the underlying object if the filtering object color is lighter than 50 percent gray. Otherwise, the underlying object is made darker.

▶ **Hard Light** Simulates shining a bright light on the underlying object.

▶ **Color Dodge** Brightens the underlying object.

▶ **Color Burn** Darkens the underlying object.

▶ **Darken** Changes underlying colors lighter than the overlay color to the overlay color.

▶ **Lighten** Lightens underlying colors that are darker than the overlay.

▶ **Difference** Calculates a new color based on the difference between the brightness values of the overlapping colors.

▶ **Exclusion** Changes color using the same kind of calculation as the Difference effect, but the contrast between the original and changed color is muted and less dramatic than the Difference effect.

▶ **Hue** Retains the color of the top filtering object(s) while assuming the saturation (intensity) and brightness of the bottom object(s).

▶ **Saturation** Retains the saturation (intensity) of the top filtering object(s) while assuming the brightness and color of the bottom object(s).

▶ **Color** Retains the hue and saturation of the top filtering object(s) while assuming the brightness of the bottom object(s).

▶ **Luminosity** Retains the brightness quantity of the top filtering object(s) while assuming the saturation (intensity) of the bottom object(s).

> NOTE **If your output is destined for hardcopy using spot color printing, avoid the Difference, Exclusion, Hue, Saturation, Color, and Luminosity blending modes. They're not supported by spot colors. For more on spot color printing, see Chapter 14.**

Many of the blending modes are determined by calculations based on hue, saturation, or brightness values. This tends to produce somewhat unintuitive results. You can look up color hue, saturation, or brightness values by choosing the HSB palette from the Color palette menu pop-out. As you experiment with different blending modes, you'll develop your ability to anticipate the effect they will have when used as filters.

CLIPPING WITH OPACITY MASKS

In this chapter, I showed you how to crop illustrations with masks and how to apply transparency to an object. Finally, I'm going to show you how to combine these tools by creating opacity masks.

Opacity masks reveal part (and only part) of an underlying object. But, while they reveal a section of an underlying object, they do it through an *opacity lens*; that is, they distort the brightness of the section of an underlying image that they mask.

Opacity masks are a little confusing because they combine two concepts (transparency and masking) that are both kind of confusing themselves. But you can create some of my favorite effects by using them, so I'll show you how it's done in the following exercise.

You can get a better handle on the impact of the effect of opacity masks if you use a gradient fill in your mask object. Unlike regular masking, fills matter when you apply an opacity mask. The lighter the fill, the more the masked illustration shows through the opacity mask. The darker the fill of the opacity mask, the less the underlying illustration shows through.

To Apply A GRADIENT FILL AS AN OPACITY MASK

1 Create or open an illustration that you will use as a masked object. It will be easier to keep track of your masked object and your masking object if you group the underlying masked object.

2 Create a circle to use as an opacity mask, and fill it with a black-to-white gradient fill, like the one shown at the top of the next page.

3 Move the masking object (the circle with the gradient fill) over the illustration.

4 Open the Transparency palette.

5 Select both the mask object (the circle) and the underlying illustration.

6 From the menu pop-out in the Transparency palette, choose Make Opacity Mask, as shown here.

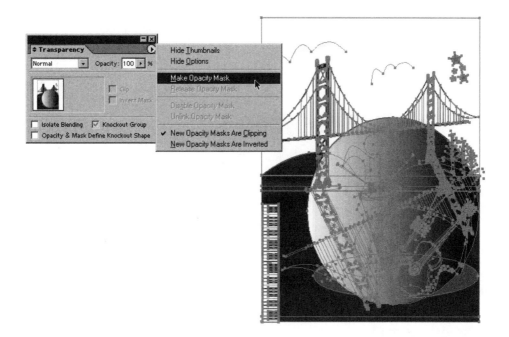

7 Click outside the masked set to reveal the results of the opacity mask. You can see my results here.

A few notes on editing opacity masks: If you deselect (the default) Clip check box in the Transparency palette after you apply an opacity mask, the mask functions like a regular transparency, not a mask. If you select the Invert Mask check box, you reverse the effect that dark and light colors have on the underlying image. If you reduce the opacity of the masking object, the resulting mask is more transparent.

You can click on the Link icon in the Transparency palette (visible when an opacity mask is selected) to unlink the opacity mask from the underlying image, as shown here.

When you unlink the opacity mask from the underlying image, you can move either the underlying (masked) image or the opacity mask to change the area that is revealed through the mask.

SUMMARY

In this chapter, you explored different approaches to cutting up images. Both Pathfinder tools, located in the Pathfinder palette, and masking, allow you to apply a cookie cutter to an existing image.

You also learned to apply transparency to objects. Because transparency allows some of an underlying image to show through an overlying object, you can use it to create all kinds of interesting effects.

Finally, you learned to combine transparency and masking to generate opacity masks. These masks reveal part of an object, but through a transparency lens that distorts the brightness of the underlying image.

 ON THE VIRTUAL CLASSROOM CD In Lesson 6, "Masking," I'll show you how to combine a masking object and a masked object to cut out a section of an illustration. I'll also show you how to create interesting masking effects by using transparent objects for masking.

Using Type

Illustrator offers two sets of tools for integrating

text into your artwork. The most dynamic and exciting type

tools allow you to shape text along a path, stuff it inside an

object, make it run up and down instead of right to left, and

generally mold text like putty to your illustration.

Other Illustrator tools function as a scaled-down word processing utility, allowing you to perform basic editing, formatting, and even spell checking on your text. In this chapter, you'll learn to use all these text features.

EDITING TEXT

You can incorporate paragraphs of text in your illustrations with Illustrator's type tools. I wouldn't throw out your word processor, but Illustrator edits, formats, and even spell checks text. But the real fun starts when you associate text with drawn objects—using text almost like a fill pattern.

Illustrator doesn't just do text: it bends it, shapes it, and allows you to use text as a fill for illustrations. The two main ways you do this in Illustrator are by using text to fill a curve, or by aligning text along a curve. Figure 9-1 illustrates both techniques.

NOTE I find Illustrator's ability to integrate text and curves impressive. But if you were hoping for a hybrid illustration program/semidesktop publishing package, you'll need to add Adobe PageMaker to your arsenal. Illustrator creates any kind of artistic text effect, but I think you'll find it a stretch to use Illustrator as a text manager, even for projects like a trifold brochure or a text-heavy full-page presentation.

Another easy-to-implement type trick is aligning text horizontally, or vertically, or even upside down. You'll learn how to achieve all these effects in this chapter.

FIGURE 9-1
The illustration on the left shows a drawing filled with text. On the right, text is bent to follow a path (the non-printing curve under the text).

CREATING TEXT

To start creating text in Illustrator, select the Type tool in the toolbox, and type. As you do, the cursor displays as an I-beam text cursor. A vertical line that is larger (depending on text size) indicates where the insertion point is set, as shown here.

Here comes the sun...

If you want to constrain your text box to a set width and height as you type, select the Type tool and draw a text box first. Then, click inside the text box (still with the Type tool selected) and type. Lines of text will wrap at the edge of the defined Type text box, as shown in the following illustration.

NOTE If you first define a text box and then type, all your text may not fit in the text box. I'll show you how to resolve this problem by *linking* text boxes in the section "Linking Text Boxes," shortly in this chapter. Other options include resizing the text box. You'll learn to do that in the section "Resizing and Reshaping Text Boxes" later in this chapter as well.

By first defining the height and width of a text box, you constrain the text to the width of that text box. Text automatically wraps at the edge of the text box - like it does in a word processor...

As you type, you can change the location of the insertion point by pointing and clicking with your mouse, or by using keyboard cursor movement keys. Some standard word processing rules apply in Illustrator:

▶ END Moves to the end of the block of text

▶ HOME Moves to the beginning of the block

▶ COMMAND/CTRL-UP OR -DOWN Moves up or down a paragraph

If you are copying text from a word processor or other source outside of Illustrator, you have several options. If you click and drag with the Type tool to create a text box, and *then* select Edit | Paste, the text will be constrained within the defined text box. If you choose the Type tool and select Edit | Paste, the text will be pasted with paragraph breaks preserved, but without the formatting of the original text. To paste text while preserving text formatting, don't select the Type tool first. Just choose the Selection tool, and then select Edit | Paste. When you copy text in this way, font, text size, attributes like boldface, and text-box width will be preserved from the original text.

To edit text in an existing text box, you can double-click the text with the Selection tool. The Type tool automatically becomes selected, along with the block of text.

You can select text by clicking and dragging, or by holding down SHIFT as you use navigation keys on your keyboard. You can use the Edit menu to select Cut, Copy, Paste, or Clear (the same as Cut, but the text is not saved to the clipboard).

To view nonprinting symbols like paragraph marks, blank spaces, or forced line breaks (use SHIFT-ENTER to create these), select Type | Show Hidden Characters.

PROOFING TOOLS

Illustrator offers enough basic word processing tools to keep bad spellers like me from making a fool of myself. You can also convert the case of selected text, and automatically generate quotation marks for the beginning and end of quotes.

To check spelling, it's not necessary (or worthwhile) to select a text box first. The spelling checker will check *all* the text in your document. Just select Type | Check Spelling. The Check Spelling dialog box will prompt you to correct spellings not found in Illustrator's dictionary. If you click the Language button in the Check Spelling dialog box, you can navigate to files with dictionaries for alternate languages.

To use Illustrator's smart punctuation tools, you can first select text within a text box by clicking and dragging with the Type tool. If you do, you'll have the option of applying smart punctuation changes to just the selected text, or to your entire document. Choose Type | Smart Punctuation to open the Smart Punctuation dialog box, as shown next.

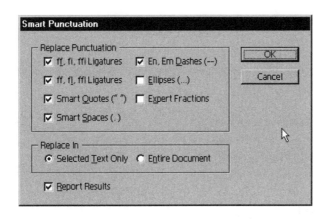

Use the available check boxes to make the optional conversions, for instance, from two hyphens (--) to an em dash (—), or from standard quotes (") to smart open (") or close (") quotes. After you click OK in the dialog box, you'll see a Report dialog box summarizing which changes were made to your text. As always in Illustrator, you can select Edit | Undo if the results are undesirable.

You can apply the Change Case feature only to selected text. First, select text by clicking and dragging with the Type tool, and then select Type | Change Text to open the Change Text dialog box. You can convert selected text to uppercase, lowercase, or what Illustrator calls *mixed text,* which is text with the first letter of each word capitalized.

> **NOTE** Some of the smart conversions are *too* smart for normal fonts, and require special OpenType fonts that are available only for Macintoshes.

The Find/Change option in Illustrator works only on an entire open document. Select Type | Find/Change to open a standard Find And Replace dialog box, and either find text or replace text throughout a document.

Linking Text Boxes

If you type more text than will fit in a defined text box, an almost impossibly tiny plus (+) sign appears in the lower-right corner of the text box, explained in the following procedure.

Overflow text can be continued in *linked* text boxes. The basic routine is that you select both the (overflowing) text box and another shape (any shape), and link the two objects. You can then flow text from one shape into another. The following steps demonstrate that process.

To Link TWO TEXT BOXES

1 Start by drawing a text box with the Type tool, about 1 inch square. After you draw the box, type enough text to fill the square.

2 Keep typing. As you enter more text than the text box can hold, you won't see the text, but Illustrator will store it and it will be available for a linked text box.

> **TIP** Bored of typing? Click and drag to select some text. Choose Edit | Copy and then Edit | Paste to quickly fill your text box.

3 After you've typed more text than your text box will hold, you'll notice the tiny plus sign on the right side of the text box.

4 Use the Rectangle tool to create a rectangle.

5 Use the Selection tool to select both the original text box and the new rectangle.

6 Select Type | Blocks | Link. Text will flow from the text box into the new rectangle.

You can unlink text boxes by selected them and choosing Type | Blocks | Unlink. Or, you can string together multiple text links by selecting more than one object and choosing Type | Blocks | Link.

When you link text in multiple objects, the text flows from the earliest created object into later created objects. Or, if you change the stacking order of objects that are linked text boxes (by selecting Object | Arrange and choosing a stacking option), then text flows from the top object into lower objects within the stacking order.

SHAPING TEXT

As is most often the case in Illustrator, there are many options and *alternate paths* (sorry, a new-age Illustrator pun) to shaping text.

Once you create a text box, you can resize it using the sizing and shaping techniques covered in Chapter 5. Or you can reshape the text box and the text within it using the path-editing tools that are explored in Chapter 6.

Another approach is to start with a shape, and then either align the text to a curve, or place the text within the path. I'll show you how to use these different techniques for shaping text in the next section.

RESIZING AND RESHAPING TEXT BOXES

You can reshape any text box using path-editing tools, like the Pen, Pencil, or Selection tool. As you do, text flows to fill the changed path. If you reshape or resize a text box so that text no longer fits inside it, the oh-so-tiny overflow icon (the plus sign) appears on the left edge of the text box.

> **NOTE** You'll need the Pen and Path tools covered in Chapter 6 to follow these steps.

The following steps illustrate just one technique for converting a standard rectangular text box into a shaped text box.

To Reshape A TEXT BOX

1 Select an existing rectangular text box, or create one.

2 Use the Add Anchor Point tool (in the Pen tool pop-out in the toolbox) to add a few new anchor points to the text box.

3 Use the Convert Anchor Point tool to change anchor points into smooth points.

4 Manipulate the anchor direction lines to change the contours of the text box. In Figure 9-2, I'm conforming the outline of the text box to match the shape of the guitar so the text will flow around the guitar.

By tweaking the location and curve attributes of the anchors in your text box, you can create text that smoothly flows around an adjacent shape. In the illustration below, I've deselected the text and shape to show how the text will look in a finished illustration.

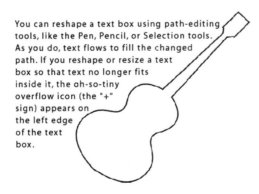

You can reshape a text box using path-editing tools, like the Pen, Pencil, or Selection tools. As you do, text flows to fill the changed path. If you reshape or resize a text box so that text no longer fits inside it, the oh-so-tiny overflow icon (the "+" sign) appears on the left edge of the text box.

FIGURE 9-2

By editing the location and direction handles on anchor points, I'm creating a text box that will flow along the side of the guitar.

Getting By
How do I get by,
When all there is to life
Is repetition, redundancy?
Each day the same as the one before
Each day worse cuz they are all the same
Not falling deeper, not getting higher
Consistency can kill, but slowly.
How do I get by,
When all there is to life
Is people pretending to think?
Faking emotions they can't remember how to feel
When falsity has gone from cheating deep to bone level
And the plastic people mimic hurt and joy
Reality set aside for the depressed.
How do I get by,
When all there is to life
Is struggling for the future?
Everything today focused on
tomorrow
The point of tomorrow
being the day after
No thoughts or cares for
here, now anymore
Maybe there never were
any.
How do I get by,
When all there is to life
Is competition and struggle?
Striving to do better solely for
the credit
Leaping to act only for glory
Never

RESHAPING TEXT BOXES...AND RESHAPING TEXT

In the previous example I just illustrated, I showed you how to change the shape and size of a text box without changing the size and shape of the text itself. That is, the text didn't get higher or wider as the text box was resized and reshaped. I often like to interactively resize text as I resize the text box. For example, sometimes I want to see how much room is left in an illustration for text, and then resize the text box and text size simultaneously to fill the available space.

To resize text as you resize a text box, you can use either the Scale tool or the Free Transform tool. Sometimes, the Free Transform tool is more effective, because it's easier to control sizing interactively, and it can also be used to rotate or even mirror text (for special effects).

As you resize a text box with the Scale tool or Free Transform tool, you'll see the text get wider and/or higher depending on how you resize the text box. Text spacing (both line spacing and word and letter spacing) adjusts proportionally as you resize the text box. In Figure 9-3, I'm resizing text and the text box to make them both higher and narrower.

USING THE SHAPE TYPE TOOL

Rather than starting with a text box and reshaping it, you can start with an existing drawing and simply fill it with text.

FIGURE 9-3
You can use the Scale and Free Transform tools to change the size of both a text box and the text itself simultaneously.

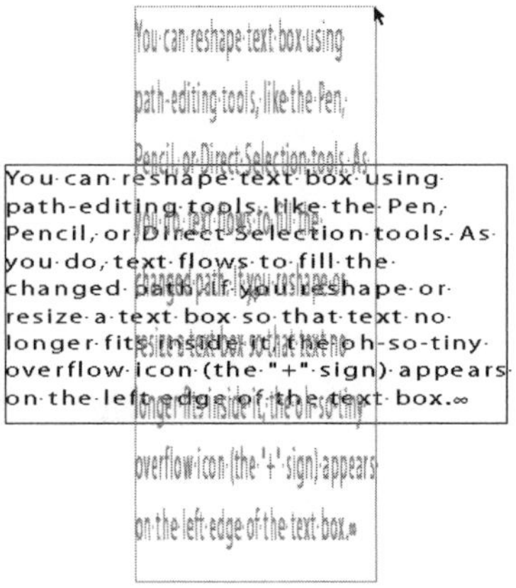

You can reshape text box using path-editing tools, like the Pen, Pencil, or Direct Selection tools. As you do, text flows to fill the changed path. If you reshape or resize a text box so that text no longer fits inside it, the oh-so-tiny overflow icon (the "+" sign) appears on the left edge of the text box.∞

To fill an existing path with text, you use the Area Type tool in the Type tool pop-out. The following steps walk you through the whole process.

To Fill A PATH WITH TEXT

1 Create a path with any drawing tool. It doesn't have to be a closed path.

2 Choose the Area Type tool from the Type tool pop-out in the toolbox.

3 Click the outline of the path you drew.

4 Start typing. The text will appear in the path, as shown here.

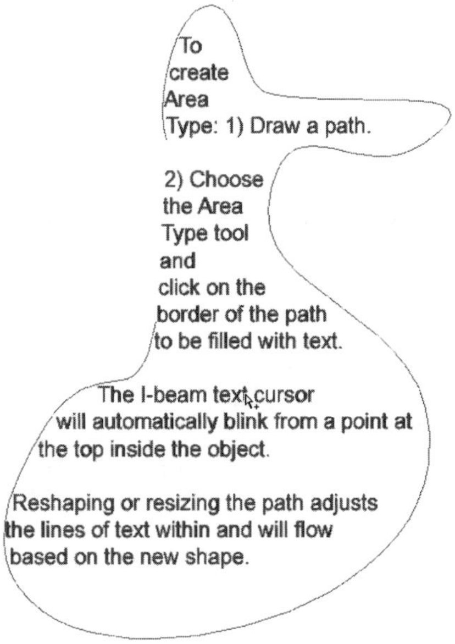

To create Area Type: 1) Draw a path.

2) Choose the Area Type tool and click on the border of the path to be filled with text.

The I-beam text cursor will automatically blink from a point at the top inside the object.

Reshaping or resizing the path adjusts the lines of text within and will flow based on the new shape.

TYPE SELECTION TRICKS Select a text box with its text using the Selection tool. With a text box selected, you can move it (or delete or copy it). You can select text within a text box by double-clicking the box with the Selection tool. This process automatically activates the Type tool. To select text within a text box, click and drag (or hold down SHIFT while using keyboard cursor keys). Triple-click with the Type tool to select an entire paragraph of text. With the Type tool and a text box selected, press COMMAND-CTRL-A to select all text in a text box. To select either a text box or only the text, use the Direct Selection tool. This tool is useful for resizing a text box without changing the size of the type, but it's tricky to do because most text box outlines are not stroked (invisible). Use Outline view to more easily select the text box outline with the Direct Selection tool.

ALIGNING TEXT TO A CURVE

Aligning type along the outside of a path is similar to aligning it along the inside of a path. You just use a different tool: the Path Type tool.

To attach type to a path, first create the path or use an existing path. Then select the Path Type tool from the Type tool pop-out, and click the path to which you want to align the text. In the following illustration, I'm typing along one of the curves in the bridge.

When you attach type to a path, the path stroke changes to no stroke. Illustrator assumes you created the curve only to use as a guide for the text, and you don't want it to be visible. If you want to see the curve to which the text has been attached, you can select that curve again and assign a stroke color and other stroke attributes.

> **TIP** Finding and selecting paths with no stroke or fill is like looking for a needle in a haystack—at night! Instead, you can resort to Outline view (select View | Outline) to select invisible paths, and then revert to Preview view (View | Preview) to resume editing.

To adjust the location of the text along the curve, select the I-beam text cursor with the Direct Selection tool, and drag along the path to reposition the text.

USING VERTICAL TYPE

The Vertical Type, Vertical Area Type, and Vertical Path Type tools work like their horizontal type cousins, except that text is presented vertically, usually from top to bottom.

For example, if you want to create vertical text, click the Vertical Type tool, click to create an insertion point on the artboard, and start typing. Text flows down, vertically, as shown here.

V
I
S
I
T

U
S

After you adjust to the oddity of a horizontal text I-beam insertion point, you can enter, paste, and edit text just as if it were presented horizontally.

FORMATTING TYPE

You can define text type (font) and size from the Type menu, but the Character, Paragraph, and Tab Ruler palettes provide even more control over character and paragraph formatting. Illustrator also allows you to set up column layout.

In addition, many graphical tools are applicable to text, like stroke and fill attributes. And, if you really want total control over text, you can convert type to outlines and format it like any other vector object in Illustrator. I'll show you how to do all of that now.

FORMATTING CHARACTERS

You can assign font face and size to type from the menu, either before or after creating the text. To define the font before you type, select Type | Font, and select a font from the menu. Where supported, font faces can have additional attributes like italic or boldface. To define type size, select Type | Size, and select a font size in points.

You can assign font size and face to existing type by first selecting the text, and then using the menu to define font style and size.

The Character palette provides additional options for formatting text. Select Window | Type | Character to display the palette, and choose Show Options from the palette menu to display all the formatting options. The expanded palette is shown here.

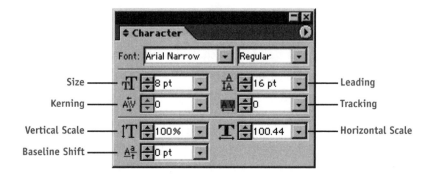

The following options in the Character palette provide microcontrol over how characters are spaced horizontally and vertically:

▶ **Size** Measures font size in points. You can enter size with other units of measurement (like .25 inches) and it will be converted, by default, to points.

▶ **Kerning** Microdefines spacing between two selected characters. Zero is the default value. The unit of measurement, "em,"—about the size of the letter *m*— and values are defined in units of 1/1000th of an em. Positive kerning values add spacing. More frequently, negative kerning is used to move a lowercase letter partially beneath a larger uppercase letter, as shown in Figure 9-4.

▶ **Leading** Increases line spacing. Leading is so named for the olden days when printers used extra shims of lead to separate lines of text. Combining 12-point text with 24-point leading produces the equivalent of double-spacing, while combining 18-point leading with 12-point text produces one and one-half line spacing.

FIGURE 9-4
Negative kerning between the *W* and the *e* moves the *e* underneath part of the *W*.

We!
We!

▶ **Tracking** Controls horizontal spacing between characters and words. Measured in ems, like kerning, positive tracking values increase space while negative values crunch type together.

▶ **Vertical Scale** Creates taller, thinner text when a positive value is used; creates shorter, thicker text when a negative value is used.

▶ **Horizontal Scale** Creates shorter, thicker text when a higher value is used. Basically the opposite of Vertical Scale.

▶ **Baseline Shift** Raises any selected character(s) when the baseline shift is positive, while negative values move selected characters below the text baseline. Usually reserved for individual superscript or subscript characters.

> **NOTE** You set default values for many type attributes in the Preferences dialog box. To adjust them, select Edit | Preferences | Type | Auto Tracing.

STROKING AND FILLING TYPE

By default, type has a fill color, but no stroke color. If you add a visible stroke, type becomes thick, and sometimes a bit ugly. But you can experiment with different stroke and fill colors and attributes to create some interesting text effects.

> **TIP** In the illustration showing the assignment of a stroke, but no fill, to the text, I used a very thick font (Impact), and made it even wider with a positive horizontal scale value (of 200) so that the outlining is effective.

If you assign a stroke to text, but no fill, the text appears outlined, as shown here.

You can assign stroke and fill attributes to type just like you would any path, using the Eyedropper or Paint Bucket tools.

A WORD ON MULTIPLE MASTER (MM) FONTS

Multiple Master (MM) fonts were promoted by Adobe in the late 90s as a kind of flexible, adjust-on-the-fly approach to modifying fonts. Faced with a public that already had too many typeface standards, Adobe has abandoned MM development, but Illustrator still provides a palette for modifying MM fonts.

If you have a Multiple Master type font installed on your system, you can modify that font using the MM Design palette.

To Use THE MM DESIGN PALETTE

1 Create text, and assign an MM font to that text.

2 Select the text, and select Window | Type | MM Design to display the MM Design palette.

3 Use the Height and Width sliders in the MM Design palette to adjust the thickness of the font and the width of the characters, as shown here.

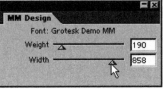

4 When you finish adjusting the look of the font, click outside the selected text.

Newer Illustrator type control tools, including options in the Character palette, perform much the same function as the MM Design palette, and do not require special MM fonts.

If you must experiment with MM fonts, you can purchase them at Adobe's web site (www.adobe.com). Or you can search for free ones on the Web. Free MM font sites seem to be on the way to extinction, but if you find one left or purchase an MM font set from Adobe, download the MM fonts into the Font folder for your operating system, and they will appear in your Type | Font menu in Illustrator.

WARNING MM fonts are not supported by all printers and print shops, so I advise against using them.

EMBEDDING FONTS

The fonts available for assignment in Illustrator depend on the fonts installed on your system. And those fonts can be viewed only if the person looking at your Illustrator file has those same fonts installed on his or her system. That presents a problem when sharing Illustrator files or when sending illustrations to a printer.

If the person viewing your file does not have the fonts you used in your illustration, his or her system will substitute a different font, or worse yet, have trouble opening your file. If you've ever opened an Illustrator file from a collaborator and been prompted to OK a replacement font, you've seen this process in action from the receiving end.

You can include (embed) required font types when you save a file, making them available to the person who opens that file. Most type-face license agreements allow this. If they don't, the type face is not good for much because only you can see the fonts you assign. But you should check on what rights you have to embed fonts if you have purchased custom fonts.

To embed fonts when you save your file, click the Embed All Fonts check box or radio button that appears in the Save dialog box for your selected format. The various Save dialog boxes (they differ depending on which format you are saving to) also provide options for you to restrict file size by saving only those characters (or font-type subsets) used in your illustration.

CONVERTING TEXT TO OUTLINES

The safest way to preserve the look of your formatted text is to convert it to outlines. And with text converted to outlines, you can apply all effects and path-editing techniques available for any other outline.

The downside of converting text to outlines—and it's a biggie—is that the text is no longer editable, and you cannot use any of the Type tools with it. Therefore, you might want to save your text first as type, and then create a copy that you convert to an outline.

To convert text to an outline, select the text box, and choose Type | Create Outlines. The resulting object will consist of a group of paths. To move or edit individual letters, ungroup the characters.

Converting text to outlines is especially useful for text destined for the Web. Because the "text" is actually a graphic image, all formatting characteristics are preserved, regardless of which fonts are supported by a viewer's system.

DEFINING PARAGRAPHS

The Paragraph palette is where you find tools to align type (Align Left, Align Center, Align Right, Justify Full Lines, and Justify All Lines), or define tabs. These features work like those in your word processor, and you'll pick them up with little advice from me.

Illustrator also has a useful and fairly powerful tool for laying out text in columns and rows. If you want to flow text from column to column, you'll want to use that feature.

ALIGNING TYPE

The Paragraph palette (select Window | Type | Paragraph to view it) provides tools for aligning and indenting text in a selected paragraph. The Paragraph palette is shown next.

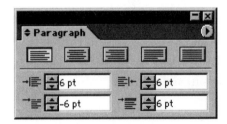

To align or indent text, first select a specific paragraph within a text box. You can perform this task easily by double-clicking with the Selection tool, and then clicking once within a paragraph with the Type tool.

With a paragraph selected, use the self-evident alignment buttons in the Paragraph palette to left-, center-, or right-align text. Use the Justify Full Lines button to justify all long lines in a paragraph with the right and left edges of the text box, and use the Justify All Lines button to stretch all lines to the left and right borders of the text box, regardless of how long they are. This last option will create very large spacing in short lines of text.

The following spinners define horizontal indentation (in pixels), except for the last one:

▶ The Left Indent spinner defines how far to indent the entire selected paragraph from the left edge of the text box.

▶ The First Line Left Indent spinner defines how far to indent (or outdent) the first line of the paragraph in relation to the rest of the paragraph. A positive value indents the first line of the paragraph. A negative value outdents the first line of the paragraph, and is useful, for example, for numbered lists where a number extends out to the left of the text.

▶ The Indent Right spinner defines space between the right edge of the text and the right edge of the text box.

▶ The Space Before Paragraph spinner defines line spacing ahead of the selected paragraph(s).

SETTING TABS

You set tabs and indentation with the Tab Ruler palette, similar to how you do this task in word processors like Microsoft Word. The Tab Ruler palette (shown in the following illustration) has four buttons to select the type of tab you want to define: Left, Center, Right, or Decimal Aligned. After you select a type of tab (usually left aligned), click the ruler to define the tab. Here, I'm defining a left-aligned tab at a ½ inch.

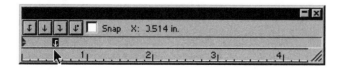

You can also use the movable markers on the left edge of the ruler to define first line (the top marker) or paragraph indentation. These options provide a graphical alternative to defining indentation in the Paragraph palette.

The unit of measurement for the Tab Ruler palette is determined by the selected unit in the Preferences dialog box. To change this unit, choose Edit | Preferences | Units | Undo. Choose a unit of measurement (like inches) in the General drop-down list to set the ruler increments for the Tab Ruler palette.

LAY OUT WITH COLUMNS

Illustrator allows you to lay out type in sequential rows or columns. The most useful application of this feature is to format text in columns.

To lay out type in a text box in columns, select the text box, and select Type | Rows And Columns. In the Rows & Columns dialog box, choose a number of columns. You must also choose a text flow option from the set of four buttons on the bottom of the dialog box. If you are flowing text from one column to the next, you will want to click the By Columns, Left To Right button, as shown here.

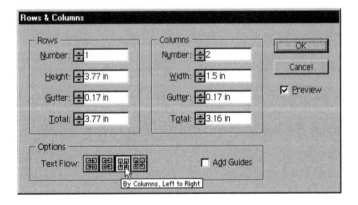

Select the Add Guides check box if you want to display nonprinting guideline dividers between columns and rows. These nonprinting guides are handy if you will be doing significant text layout.

SUMMARY

You can type text anywhere on the artboard using the Type tool. The Area Type tool allows you to constrain type within any selected object, while you use the

Path Type tool to apply type to the edge of any path. Each of these three tools has its vertical equivalent on the Type tool pop-out, so you can create text that goes from top to bottom instead of from left to right.

Illustrator's Type palettes provide control over character, paragraph, and tab attributes, whereas menu options provide word processing features like column layout and spell checking.

ON THE VIRTUAL CLASSROOM CD In Lesson 7, "Shaping Type," I'll show you how to place text inside a shape (filling the shape) or outside a shape (outlining the shape).

10

Applying Effects and Filters

Illustrator's Filter and Effect menus unleash an amazing array of path distortion and texture changes on your artwork. Effects and filters also include frequently used features like drop shadows or line arrows. Each effect and filter combines a whole array of changes to your artwork, saving you time and also making it easy to experiment with fun transformations in your artwork.

The main difference between filters and effects is in how they affect an object path. Effects do not change an object path, but simply alter the image based on the original path. Filters, on the other hand, do change the object path.

Effects have advantages over filters in that the underlying paths are not changed when they are applied. Therefore, after you apply an effect, you can still edit the original path. I'll start this chapter by showing you how to apply effects. But sometimes filters are more appropriate—for one thing, they can reduce file size. So I'll also show you how and when to use filters as well.

APPLYING EFFECTS

In a way, applying one or more effects allows you to transform an object, while keeping the original path intact. Think of looking at yourself in a fun-house mirror. You still have the same shape (fortunately!), but the image in the mirror is distorted. As you move, crouch down, or change your stance, the distorted image in the mirror transforms as well.

That's how effects work. You apply them, and they appear in any output (printed or digital). But the underlying outline is unchanged by the effect.

You can apply effects to selected paths. If you want to apply an effect to a group of paths, make sure to select all the paths to which you want to apply the transformation. Or, you can apply an effect to a grouped object.

> **NOTE** Options in the Styles and Appearances palettes provide other methods for altering how a path looks without altering the underlying path itself. The features in these palettes are relatively complex, advanced ways of assigning transformations to objects, but I'll introduce you to them later in this book: in Chapter 13, I'll discuss using the Appearances palette, and in Chapter 16, you'll learn to save time by applying sets of transformations using the Styles palette. Also, the Effect menu includes Pathfinder palette options, which I explained in Chapter 8.

With the object(s) selected, choose an effect from the Effect menu. Different effects display different dialog boxes with different options for defining the applied effect. For example, the Pucker & Bloat effect displays the dialog box shown here.

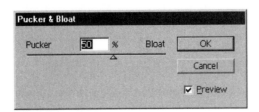

After you apply an effect, that effect and the settings you defined for it appear at the top of the Effect menu for easy reapplication to additional objects on the artboard. Illustrator remembers your last effect selection even after you close a document.

TWO TYPES OF EFFECTS

Two basic types of effects live on the Effect menu. The first group of effects distort vector fills and paths (and this applies to their cousins on the Filter menu). Other effects just alter fills.

When you open the Effect menu (or the Filter menu), the first set of effects—more or less—are those that transform both the path and fill, while the second group of effects transforms only fills. Both groups are shown in this illustration.

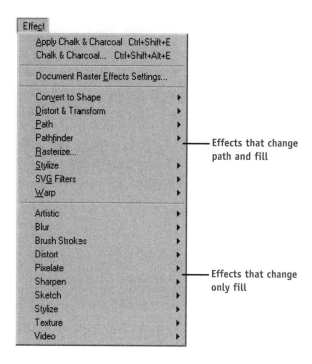

Figure 10-1 shows an example of both types of effects. The first effect is the Pucker & Bloat effect, which transforms the guitar into a spaced-out instrument. The second effect, from the set of fill-only effects, makes the guitar look like a woodcut.

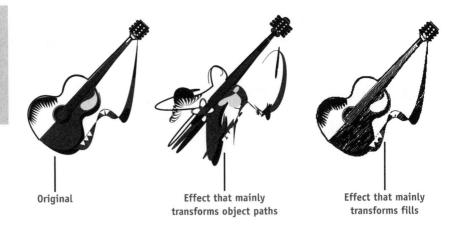

FIGURE 10-1

Effects fall into two basic categories—those that (mainly) transform the path of an object, and those that transform the fill.

Original

Effect that mainly transforms object paths

Effect that mainly transforms fills

There are some exceptions to the basic logic of how Illustrator divides up effects into these two groups, but I'll note those as I explain how each effect works.

PATH-BENDING EFFECTS

The first set of effects on the menu, the ones that distort the displayed outline of an object, all include a Preview check box in their dialog boxes. You'll appreciate that feature as you explore different effects because you can see each of these effects *before* you apply them.

Path-bending effects are organized into eight sets of effects: Convert To Shape, Distort & Transform, Path, Pathfinder, Rasterize, Stylize, SVG Filters, and Warp. I'll explain and illustrate each group of these effects next.

CONVERT TO SHAPE EFFECTS

The effects on the Convert To Shape menu convert a path to a rectangle, a rounded rectangle, or an ellipse. The only time I use this feature is when I want to create a rectangular or elliptical shape to use as a layout guide for old-fashioned pasteup.

DISTORT & TRANSFORM EFFECTS

The effects on the this menu offer a zany set of hypertransformations. I've illustrated the Distort & Transform effects next.

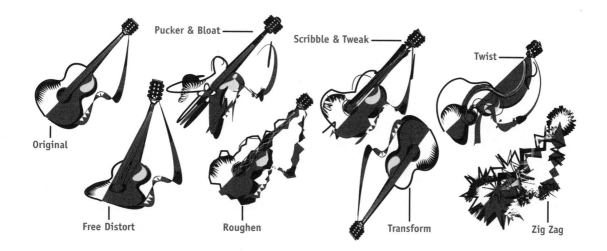

The Free Distort menu option opens an interactive dialog box for a selected image. You can click and drag on the corner handles in the dialog box to transform the selected object, as shown in Figure 10-2.

You use the Free Distort effect to alter the perspective on an object. The four corner handles function like vanishing points—dragging them creates the illusion of an object emerging or fading from front to back, or from left to right.

The popular Pucker & Bloat effect was known as the Punk & Bloat effect in earlier versions of Illustrator, and it creates pointy or puffy distortion of your original image. The slider in the dialog box allows you to assign relatively more pucker (pointiness) or bloat (puffiness).

FIGURE 10-2
The Free Distort dialog box allows you to interactively change the perspective of a selected object.

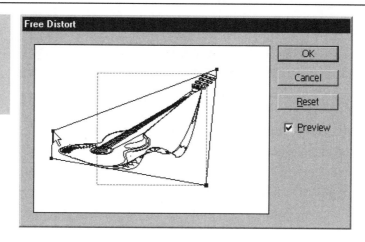

The Roughen effect is kind of the opposite of the Simplify Path menu command (Object | Path | Simplify). Instead of smoothing a path, this command roughens up a path by adding anchors. The Roughen dialog box allows you to choose either smooth or corner anchors. The Size slider defines how much the paths will be distorted either by percent (choose the Relative option) or in pixels or another unit of measurement (use the Absolute option). The Detail slider defines how many new anchors will be added. Lower settings produce less distortion.

The Scribble & Tweak effect is a little like throwing your object against a wall to see what happens! Lower Horizontal and Vertical slider settings produce less distortion. The Relative option assigns distortion levels relative to the object size, while the Absolute option defines the distortion in your selected unit of measurement. The Anchor Points, In Control Points, and Out Control Points check boxes in the Modify area of the dialog box allow

> **NOTE** In defining Scribble & Tweak, Illustrator uses the phrase *control point* to refer to anchor points and their direction lines. I explain how to use anchor point direction lines to alter curves in Chapter 6.

you to change anchor points, or alter only the control points (either In or Out control direction lines).

The relatively mundane Transform effect is similar to options provided by the Scale and Free Transform tools in the toolbox. The fairly self-explanatory options in the dialog box allow you to scale, move, or rotate a selected object. The Copies area of the dialog box allows you to generate additional copies of the object. And the Reflect X and Reflect Y check boxes allow you to flip the object horizontally and/or vertically. A grid allows you to define a pivot point for rotation.

The Twist effect is something like twirling an object and watching the shape and fill appear as if spinning around. You can increase the intensity of the effect by selecting a higher degree angle in the dialog box.

The Zig Zag effect literally applies zig zags or curvy distortion to paths in a selected object. The Size slider determines how large the zig zags or curves are. The Relative options define curves or zig zags relative to the size of the object. The Absolute option lets you use a unit of measurement like pixels to define zig or curve size. The Ridges Per Segment slider defines how many curves or zig zags to create. The Smooth option generates curves, and the Corner option generates zig zags.

PATH EFFECTS

When you select Effect | Path, you can choose from three effects that allow you to duplicate or transform an object outline: Offset Path, Outline Object, and Outline Stroke.

The Offset Path effect allows you to create a new path offset from the original. You can determine the offset distance by changing the value in the Offset area of the Offset Path dialog box. You can also change join types and miter values for those joins.

You use the Outline Object and Outline Stroke effects to convert complex objects—like those imported from a multilayer Photoshop file—into simpler paths. You use Outline Stroke to convert strokes, while you use Outline Object to simplify fills and strokes.

SEE ALSO For an explanation of the Stroke palette settings, see Chapter 4.

PATHFINDER EFFECTS

The Pathfinder effects (choose Effect | Pathfinder, and select an effect) are very similar to the tools available from the Pathfinder palette I discussed in Chapter 8. Like the tools in the Pathfinder palette, Pathfinder effects combine or divide intersecting paths, and the object on the bottom usually assumes the fill and stroke attributes of the object on top.

Before you apply any Pathfinder effect, you will want to arrange objects front to back (choose Object | Arrange).

Pathfinder effects don't work with bitmaps, but they do work with type and vector objects.

RASTERIZE EFFECTS

You can apply many of the transformations available from the Effect menu to raster (also referred to as bitmap) images only when they are exported to web graphics or printed. Illustrator provides a really unique option for applying these effects: you can create a raster *version* of your vector object, while preserving the underlying vector paths and anchors.

In short, you get the best of both worlds. You can still edit paths and anchors, and your objects are still easily rescalable. But you can also apply effects that work only on raster images. After you rasterize an image, it will appear as a bitmap on the artboard—jaggy lines, course resolution, and all those other attributes associated with bitmaps. If you want to see the paths and anchors, choose View | Outline to view your object without the bitmap attributes.

To rasterize a selected object, choose Effect | Rasterize. The Rasterize dialog box opens, as shown here.

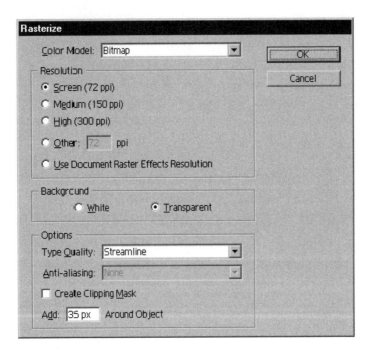

If your graphic is destined for a web site, choose 72 ppi from the set of Resolution options. If your graphic is going to be used with print output, select a higher resolution. The Color Model options are those available for digital or web graphics: RGB (best for web graphics), Bitmap, or Grayscale.

Choose the Transparent option for web graphics in the Background section of the dialog box when you want the web page background or background color to show through behind uncolored portions of the image.

The Type Quality options allow you to save type as type fonts (Streamline), or convert type to outlines (Outline). And Anti-Aliasing options allow you to smooth out some of the jaggies in type that is converted to bitmaps. If you select the Create Clipping Mask check box, you apply a clipping mask as you rasterize. (See Chapter 8 for a full discussion of clipping masks.)

After defining Raster conversion options, click OK in the Rasterize dialog box. Raster options are explored in more detail in Chapter 15.

STYLIZE EFFECTS

Somewhat buried in Illustrator's vast Effect and Filter menus are the very useful Stylize effects. They include such popular appearance changes as arrowheads on lines, drop shadows behind objects, and cool color tinting.

To add arrowheads to a path, first select the path, and then choose Effect | Stylize | Add Arrowheads. The intuitive Add Arrowheads dialog box appears, as shown here.

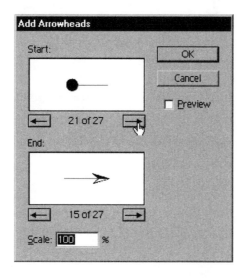

You can define an arrowhead for the start and/or for the end of a path. The Scale area allows you to adjust the size of the arrowhead relative to the size of the path stroke. Clicking on the arrows scrolls through a set of symbols to use as arrowheads. Use the Preview check box to watch changes interactively on the artboard.

The other Stylize effects alter path or fill effects. Experiment with different options in the dialog boxes with Preview checked to see changes on the artboard before you finalize effect settings. The Inner Glow and Outer Glow effects add subtle glowing tints to colors, moving either toward the center (Inner Glow) or beyond the edges (Outer Glow) of a selected object. Both effects are illustrated next.

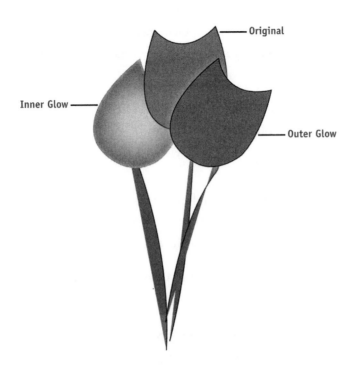

The Drop Shadow effect is great for quick shadows. Feather creates a transitional fade at the edges of an object, and Round Corners produces some interesting distortions of your original image. Figure 10-3 shows the Drop Shadow, Feather, and Round Corners effects.

SVG FILTER EFFECTS

Adobe is promoting Scalable Vector Graphics (SVG) format for web browsers. The SVG Filter set provides interesting vector-based mutations of the fill for a selected object. If you are saving your illustration to SVG format, you'll be able to preserve and display these effects in web graphics.

Unlike other vector-based effects, SVG Filter effects don't have dialog boxes, much less a preview option. You can try 'em, like 'em, or undo 'em.

For an explanation of SVG graphics, how to use them, when they work, and their limitations, see Chapter 15.

WARP EFFECTS

You can use Warp effects to create waving flags, surf on water, or create distortion-like bulges and arcs in selected objects.

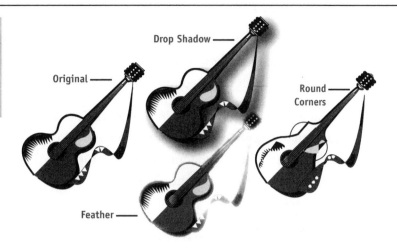

FIGURE 10-3
Stylize effects provide quick, easy ways to apply useful sets of changes to paths and fills.

Illustrator makes it easy to experiment with Warp effects because they are all available in the dialog box of any warp you select. To experiment with warps, select an object, choose Effect | Warp, and then select any Warp effect. The resulting dialog box allows you to choose from the entire array of warps. And by activating the Preview check box, you can try on any warp from the same dialog box, as shown here.

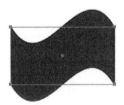

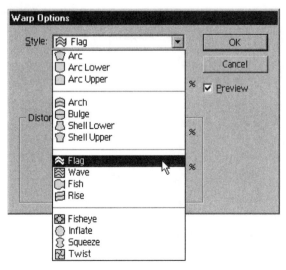

EXPLORING FILL EFFECTS

The second set of effects, those that affect only fills, are the kind of artistic alterations that are usually available only to raster images. You can apply them in Illustrator without losing the nice shape-editing properties inherent in vector images.

What's so cool about applying these effects in Illustrator is that you can apply effects that you can usually apply only to a bitmap image. However, when you assign these effects, you can still edit the underlying vector path. For example, you can reshape an object by moving anchor points, and the applied fill will expand to fill the new path.

There are dozens of fill effects available on the Effect menu. I won't illustrate each of them, but I'll give you some tips for experimenting with them.

After you select an object, choose a fill effect from the Effect menu. The resulting dialog box will have a preview area at the top, as shown in Figure 10-4. Different effects provide different option sliders, but you can always preview the changes in the small preview area right in the dialog box. Use the plus (+) and minus (−) signs to zoom in and out. Zooming out shows more of your image, while zooming in displays the details of the effect, as shown in this figure.

APPLYING FILTERS

The options available from the Filter menu are similar to those available from the Effect menu. However, as I mentioned at the beginning of this chapter, after you

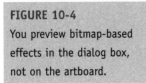

FIGURE 10-4
You preview bitmap-based effects in the dialog box, not on the artboard.

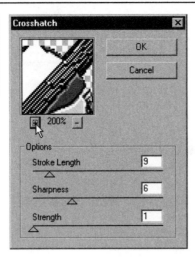

apply a filter, you can no longer edit the original underlying structure of the object's path. The positive side of this is that you can edit the new path that the filter generated.

In Figure 10-5, I've applied an effect Drop Shadow effect and a filter Drop Shadow effect (with similar option settings). As you can see, the effects are similar.

Now take a look at the underlying paths, as revealed in Outline view. As you can see in Figure 10-6, the paths and anchors of the filter-generated drop shadow are entirely changed, while the paths and anchors of the effect-generated drop shadow are unchanged.

Like the Effect menu, the Filter menu is divided into two sets of effects (OK, *filters!*). Those filters that apply to vector paths are listed in the top section of the menu. Those filters that apply to bitmap fills are organized on the bottom part of the menu. However, unlike the Effect menu, the bitmap fill effects on the bottom part of the Filter

> **TIP** Objects displayed as bitmaps by selecting Effect | Rasterize cannot be used with bitmap filters. They aren't really raster objects; they just display that way.

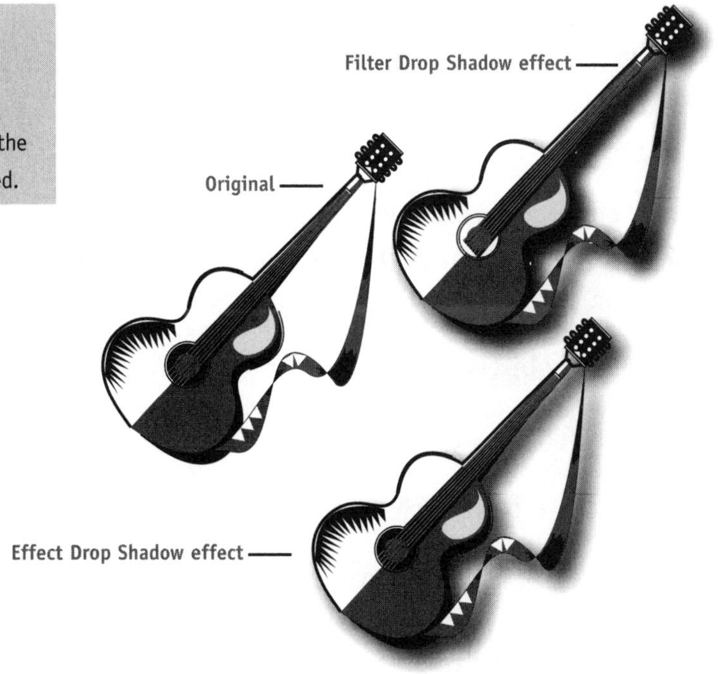

FIGURE 10-5
The filter and effect drop shadows look similar; the real difference is in how the underlying path is handled.

Filter Drop Shadow effect

Original

Effect Drop Shadow effect

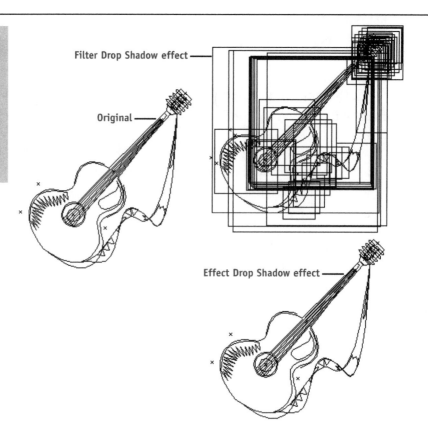

FIGURE 10-6
The filter Drop Shadow effect and the effect Drop Shadow effect produce the same results, but the effect Drop Shadow effect preserves the object's underlying paths and anchors for future editing.

Filter Drop Shadow effect

Original

Effect Drop Shadow effect

menu can be applied only to raster images. These raster objects can either be placed (using File | Place) or converted (using Object | Rasterize).

Those filters that act on vectors come with dialog boxes that include a Preview check box, just like their effect cousins. Experiment with settings in the dialog box with Preview checked, and watch the filter effect appear on the artboard. Then click OK to assign the filter.

Those filters that act on raster objects display with a preview box similar to those available for their effect cousins.

APPLYING A GRADIENT MESH

Gradient mesh effects are one of the more powerful and exciting Illustrator tools. They act something like gradient fills, except that they can be more finely controlled and applied. They're also a bit trickier, but worth the trouble of getting comfortable with.

Gradient meshes are based on intersecting paths within an object that are used only to define color blending. These special paths and anchors aren't visible, but you can edit them to control how colors blend from one part of an object to another.

To Apply A GRADIENT MESH

1 Create a simple shape to experiment with, or use an existing shape. A rectangle or ellipse will work fine to experiment with. I'll use a section of the guitar illustration I've used as a model for much of this chapter.

2 Assign a solid color fill to the object.

3 Select the Gradient tool in the toolbox (or just press u on the keyboard).

4 Use the Fill swatch in the toolbox to select a color to assign to the gradient mesh point you are about to create.

5 With a fill color selected (use a light color if your object color is dark, or vice versa), click somewhere near the middle of the fill for the object to which you are applying the gradient mesh. You'll generate a mesh point from which the color radiates, as shown in Figure 10-7.

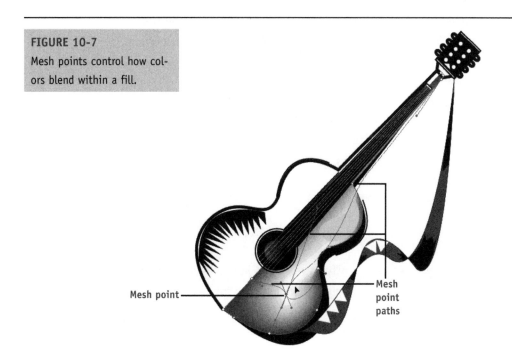

FIGURE 10-7
Mesh points control how colors blend within a fill.

Mesh point

Mesh point paths

6 Mesh points are generated as the intersection of special mesh point paths. The generated anchors have direction lines like regular paths. Edit the fill by using the Direct Selection tool to edit these paths and anchors, or adjust the direction lines.

7 Add more than one mesh point to a path.

8 Change the mesh point color by selecting a mesh point and clicking a color in the Color palette.

Gradient meshes have the same limitation as regular gradient fills: they tend to look "banded" (like strips of color instead of smooth gradation) when converted to bitmaps or used in web output.

SUMMARY

There's nothing that magical about effects and filters; they are simply sets of changes to an object path and fill. But by packaging groups of stroke and fill changes, Illustrator provides a handy set of one-stop shopping tools for altering your images.

Some effects and filters are pretty esoteric, but others—like drop shadows or line arrows—are on an illustrator's "most wanted" list. Other effects and filters are great for warping, distorting, stylizing, and generally having fun with shapes.

The difference between effects and filters is that effects do not change the underlying path of an object, while filters generate a whole new path. Use effects when you want to edit the underlying paths and anchors in a drawing. Use filters to save file size.

Finally, in this chapter I introduced you to gradient meshes. These work like gradient fills, merging one color into another. But they are infinitely more flexible because you can adjust them using the special anchors, paths, and direction lines generated by the Gradient tool.

 ON THE VIRTUAL CLASSROOM CD In Lesson 8, "Filters and Gradient Meshes," I'll illustrate how filters and effects work and how they differ from each other. I'll also show you how to apply a gradient mesh to create complex and powerful gradient fills.

Using Pattern Fills and Strokes

A *fill* pattern is a single, repeating, small

illustration that fills a path to which it is applied. If you

have designed or observed patterns that repeat to form the

background of a web page, you've observed this concept. The

process of repeating a single illustration to fill a path is called

tiling: a metaphor invoking the tiles laid end to end on a

kitchen floor.

A similar kind of repeating image can be used to generate a brush *stroke* pattern. Stroke patterns tend to get a little more complicated, because you often want the shape of a stroke pattern to "bend" as it goes around corners. Therefore, some stroke patterns are actually composed of more than one illustration.

You access stroke patterns from the Brushes palette, and you access fill patterns from the Swatches palette. Illustrator comes with a starter set of brush and swatch patterns, but the real fun is creating your own patterns and applying them to achieve unique effects in your artwork. I'll show you how to do just that in this chapter.

APPLYING PATTERN SWATCHES

You can whet your appetite for designing unique pattern swatches by checking out the prefab ones that come with Illustrator. Do that by choosing Window | Swatches to display the Swatches palette.

The first four icons at the bottom of the Swatches palette allow you to display all swatches, color swatches, gradient swatches, or pattern swatches. These icons are illustrated here.

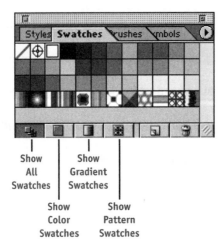

Show All Swatches

Show Color Swatches

Show Gradient Swatches

Show Pattern Swatches

The fifth icon in the Swatches palette—New Swatch—copies a selected pattern fill, and the final icon is Delete Swatch. You can drag existing swatches onto this icon to remove them from the palette.

Color and gradient swatches are just a convenient way to access colors or gradient fills that you use frequently. I explained how to select colors and define gradient fills in Chapter 4. And I'll dig more into managing color in Chapters 14 and 15, when I focus on sending your illustrations to hardcopy or web output.

In this chapter, I want to focus on the pattern swatches. When you select the Show Pattern Swatches icon, you'll see the preset patterns that come with Illustrator.

You can change the way these patterns are displayed by choosing Small Thumbnail View, Large Thumbnail View, or List View from the Swatches palette menu. In the following Illustration, I'm choosing to view the available fill swatch patterns as large thumbnails.

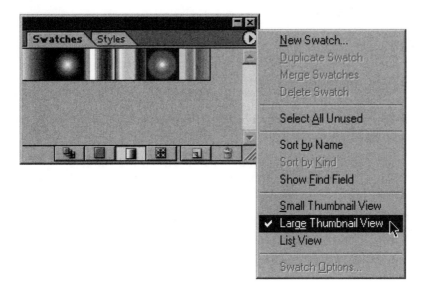

To experiment with the preset pattern fills, create a quick path or shape (or use an existing one). With the path or shape selected (with the Selection tool), click one of the pattern fills.

Try moving your pattern fill within the path by holding down the tilde (~) key as you click and drag within the object. The object itself doesn't move (as long as you hold down the tilde key), but if you look closely, you'll see that the pattern fill has scrolled to a different position behind the path.

You can switch pattern fills by simply clicking a different one in the Swatches palette. Or choose a color from the Color palette to replace your pattern fill with a solid fill color.

CREATING PATTERN SWATCHES

OK, now that you've seen how much fun pattern fills can be, you're ready to create your own custom fills.

Pattern fills are nothing but Illustrator objects—repeated over and over to fill a path. They can be composed of strokes, fills, text, and/or shapes. Unfortunately, you can't use gradients, blends, many filters and effects, or bitmap images in fill patterns. Nor can you include objects to which a mask has been applied in a fill pattern.

USING TEXT AS A PATTERN FILL

In Chapter 9, I showed you how to fill an object with type and how to bend type to conform to a defined curve. Here, I'll show you how to take a block of text and simply have it repeat to fill an object.

The first step is to create a block of text. You can review that process in Chapter 9, but the short version is to select the Type tool, click, and type some text. You can use the spacebar to add a space to create white space between the tiling text or not.

After you've created a block of text, you can drag that text into the Swatches palette. (Make sure that the Show Pattern Swatches tab is selected using the icon at the bottom of the palette.)

Once your fill pattern has been added to the Swatches palette, you can select any object and click the New Swatch icon to apply that fill to the selected object. In the next illustration, I've applied my text swatch to a star.

After you place your new fill, hold down the tilde key while you click and drag on the shape fill to adjust how the fill shows up in the shape.

CREATING SEAMLESS FILLS

Sometimes you want to create fills that don't look like they are tiled images. For example, you might use a fill to create a wavelike background that will look like waves, not like a repeating image. The trick is to create an image that can tile without appearing to tile.

One useful technique for accomplishing this task is to create symmetrical shapes. In the following exercise, I'll show you how to create a tiling zig-zag line for a heart-monitor-type effect.

To Create A TILING ZIG-ZAG LINE

1 To make it easier for your zig-zag lines to tile smoothly, select View | Show Grid | and View | Snap To Grid.

2 Using the Pen tool, draw a zig-zag line. You can create any kind of zig zag, but make sure the final point of the line is on the same horizontal grid line as the first point, as shown here.

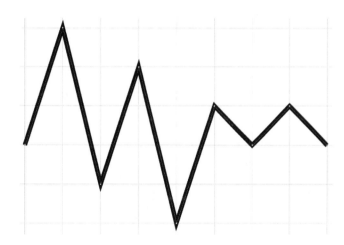

3 Make sure there is a stroke applied to the line, but no fill.

4 Drag the zig-zag path into the Swatches palette. (Make sure the Show Pattern Swatches icon is selected at the bottom of the Swatches palette.)

5 Now that you've defined your pattern swatch, draw a rounded rectangle, and use the new swatch as a fill.

6 Use the Selection tool with the tilde key pressed to adjust how the zig-zag line appears within the rounded rectangle until your drawing looks something like the one here.

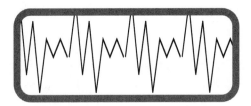

CREATING FILLS WITH BOUNDING BOXES

For more complex fills that involve many paths or shapes, you will often want to use a bounding box to define the positioning and spacing of the tiles that make up your fill. By *bounding box*, I'm not referring to the outline of a path that displays when you choose View | Show Bounding Box. Here, I'm using the term to refer to a shape (usually a square) that defines the outer limit of the tile you create for a pattern fill.

This concept is best explained with an example, so try these steps:

To Create A PATTERN USING A BOUNDING BOX

1 Draw several ellipses with both fills and strokes within a small area—about an inch square—as shown here.

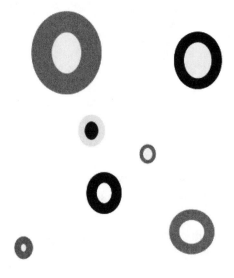

2 Draw a square over the shapes you've just drawn. Assign a bright or light color background to the square (like yellow), and no stroke.

3 With the square selected, choose Object | Arrange | Send To Back to move the square behind the shapes. Your illustration should look something like this.

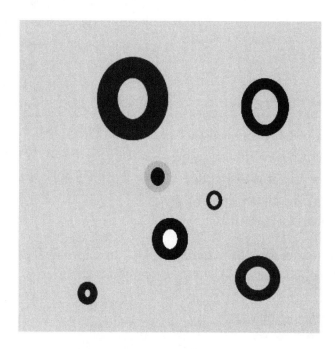

4 Use the Selection tool to select both the square and all the objects inside it. Drag the selected group of objects into the Swatches palette. (Make sure the Show Pattern Swatches icon is selected at the bottom of the Swatches palette.)

5 Draw a shape and apply your new fill to it. Select the fill with the Selection tool, hold down the tilde key, and adjust the display of the pattern fill.

Because you used a square as a "bounding box" for your tile, your fill can be more complex and irregular than if you simply dragged a shape into the Pattern Swatches palette.

Using Brush Patterns

Brush patterns are similar to fill patterns, with two major differences: brush patterns are applied to strokes instead of fills, and they are adaptive in that they change depending on the direction of the stroke path.

Illustrator comes with a nice set of Brush libraries from which you can choose stroke patterns. Or, you can mix up your own stroke pattern by adapting any vector image. I'll show you how to use the existing set of brushes and how to make your own brushes.

APPLYING A BRUSH PATTERN

You can get an idea of how brush patterns work by selecting one from the Brushes palette and using it as a stroke pattern. To view the Brushes palette, choose Window | SBrushes. You can use any of the symbols in the palette as a stroke pattern.

> **NOTE** You can apply a brush pattern to shape tools,\ like the Rectangle, Ellipse, or Star tools, the Paintbrush tool, or drawing tools in the Line Segment tool pop-out set of tools. You can't apply a brush pattern to text or to the Symbol Sprayer tool. (Choose a pattern from the Symbol library for that tool.) The Paintbrush tool works only with a selected brush pattern. I'll explain how that works in the section "Using Brush Pattern Libraries" later in this chapter.

You can get a better idea of how a brush pattern will look by choosing Thumbnail View from the Brushes palette, as shown here.

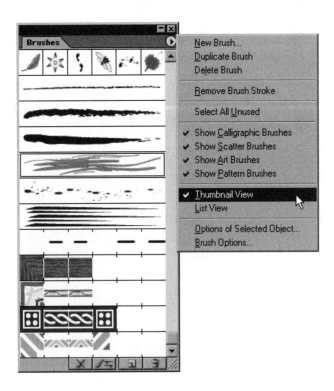

To Apply THE BRUSH PATTERN TO A STROKE

1 Click the brush pattern in the Brushes palette.

2 Select a drawing tool, like the Pencil or Pen tool.

3 Draw a path or shape. The selected brush pattern will be applied to the outline.

After you apply a brush pattern to an outline, you can change that stroke pattern by dragging a different brush pattern onto a selected path. Or you can remove a brush pattern from a selected path by choosing Remove Brush Stroke from the Brushes palette menu.

> **NOTE** You can apply a fill to paths independent of the stroke pattern.

USING BRUSH PATTERN LIBRARIES

Illustrator comes with many sets of Brush libraries. These brushes are illustrated in a nice Portable Document Format (PDF) brochure on the Illustrator CD. If you plan to do much with brush patterns, you should open and print this file. You'll find it in the Brush Libraries folder on the CD, which is in the Illustrator Extras folder. You'll see each set of brushes illustrated on a page, like the one here.

To make additional Brush libraries available in Illustrator, choose Window |
Brush Libraries | Other Library, navigate to the Illustrator Extras folder, and
then open the Brush Libraries folder. Double-click a library to display that
brush palette.

You can apply additional brush strokes from new libraries in the same way I
described for applying default brush strokes. Many of the additional brush strokes
work better if you widen the stroke to which they are applied using the Stroke
palette. In the following illustration, I've dragged a pattern from the Silhouettes
library (found in the Sports folder) onto a curve I drew with the Pen tool. By
widening the stroke to 8 points, I've fleshed out my basketball player.

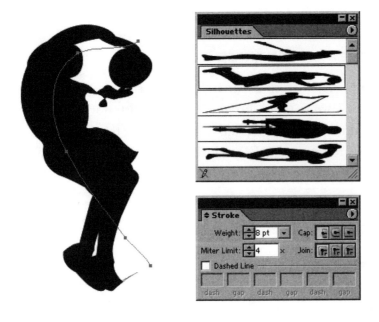

Brush strokes you use from additional libraries are added to the Brushes palette
associated with your file, and are available next time you open the file.

CREATING YOUR OWN BRUSH PATTERNS

There are four different types of brush patterns, and each type of pattern creates
different types of effects when applied to a path. Calligraphic brushes create
strokes that look like those drawn by a calligraphy pen. Scatter brushes "scatter"

pattern objects along a path. Art brushes stretch a single image—like the basketball player in the previous illustration—from one end of a path to the other. Pattern brushes can include up to five different tiles that are applied to the sides, corners, and endpoints of a stroke.

Each type of brush pattern has options for different kinds of adjustments. Art brushes, for instance, can be flipped so they run from the last anchor point in a path to the first anchor point.

Because brush patterns are fairly complex, and because Illustrator comes with a large selection of premade ones, the easiest way to create a custom brush pattern is to modify an existing brush and save it as a new brush. In the following sections, I'll explain how to do this for each type of brush stroke.

CREATING CALLIGRAPHIC BRUSH STROKES

Calligraphic brush strokes mimic real brushes. You can alter the size, angle, roundness, and *randomness* (variety) in the brush stroke width.

To Create A NEW CALLIGRAPHIC BRUSH STROKE THAT IS 7 POINTS WIDE

1 Select the 10 Point Oval brush stroke from the Brushes palette.

2 Choose Brush Options from the Brushes palette menu to open the Options dialog box for this brush.

3 In the Calligraphic Brush Options dialog box, change the name of the brush to 7 pt Oval, as shown here.

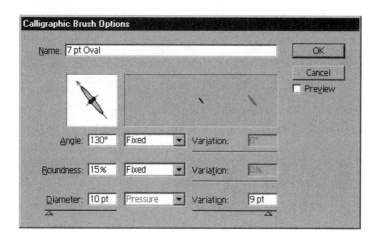

4 Enter 7 pt in the Diameter box to change the (new) brush stroke to 7 points.

5 Type 25% in the Roundness box, and choose Random from the Roundness list.

6 Type 10% in the Roundness Variation box.

7 Type 45° in the Angle box, and leave this setting as Fixed.

8 Click OK to save the new calligraphic brush pattern.

> **NOTE** If the original pattern has been applied to existing paths, you'll be prompted to either apply the new stroke to those paths or leave them alone.

Experiment with your new stroke pattern by using the Pencil tool with a stroke weight of 2 points. Try drawing letters using the Pencil tool, like these.

CREATING A SCATTER BRUSH

To experiment with creating a new scatter brush pattern, select the Ink Drop pattern in the Brushes palette, and choose Brush Options from the Brushes palette menu.

In the Scatter Brush Options dialog box that appears, enter a name for your new pattern. Use the sliders and lists in the dialog box to modify the pattern. Size controls the size of the pattern in relation to the original drawing. Spacing controls the space between pattern pieces. Scatter defines how far the pattern pieces will *scatter* (depart from) the selected path. And the Rotation setting defines how much objects will rotate when the pattern is applied to a curved path.

The Rotation setting can be applied relative to either the path or to the page. This setting is similar to the rotation options for blending, which I explained in Chapter 7. If you choose Random from the list associated with each setting, a second slider becomes active that controls how much variation occurs in the setting.

For example, if you choose Random for the pattern size, the second slider defines the percentage of size variation of the pattern object.

COLORIZING BRUSH PATTERNS The Colorization Method drop-down list in the Scatter Brush Options dialog box defines whether and what colors are added to the original stroke color. The various options are illustrated clearly if you click the Tips button in the dialog box. You'll see a handy colorization chart that details the effect of each colorization method.

CREATING AN ART BRUSH

Art brushes stretch a pattern tile to fill the entire path to which they are applied. Therefore, most of the work of defining an art brush takes place when you create the drawing right on the Illustrator artboard.

Start with a selected drawing, and choose New Brush from the Brushes palette menu. Click the New Art Brush radio button in the New Brush dialog box that appears, and click OK to open the Art Brush Options dialog box. The selected drawing will appear in the preview window of the dialog box, as shown here.

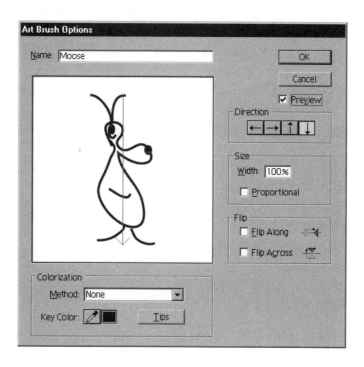

Use the Direction arrow buttons to define how the pattern object will be applied as you draw a path. Use the Stroke From Bottom To Top button to have the pattern appear right-side up as you draw a line from the bottom of the artboard to the top.

Use the Size box to define how big the symbol will display in the stroke path, and use the Proportional check box to keep the height and width ratio unchanged if you resize the object. The Flip check boxes allow you to reverse the symbol either horizontally or vertically.

After you define an art brush, you can modify it. As you change the settings, use the Preview check box to see how the modified stroke pattern will change on paths to which it has been applied.

THE FIVE SIDES OF A PATTERN BRUSH

Pattern brushes are the most complicated to modify or create because they involve as many as five different object panels. You can use a separate symbol for the start, the finish, the side (center), the inside corner, and the outside corner panels.

It's often not necessary to use all these panels. You can see how pattern brushes work by examining some of the samples in the oak pattern brush, for example, which uses just two different panels, as shown in Figure 11-1: one for sides and one for outside corners.

Pattern brushes can include any symbol saved to the current document's Swatches palette. So if you want to create a pattern brush from scratch, the first step is to create all the tiles you will use and save them to the Swatches palette.

To Create A PATTERN BRUSH WITH TWO DIFFERENT TILES

1 Start by viewing the Swatches palette (choose View | Swatches). You add drawings to the Swatches palette to use as pattern brush tiles.

2 Draw a slightly curved path, and assign an 8-point, dashed line stroke to the path, something like the one shown next.

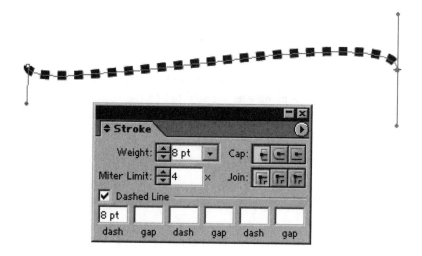

3 Draw two circles about the same diameter as the width of your line (about 8 points in diameter, but no need to be too exact). Assign a black 1-point stroke to both, and assign a black fill to one and a white fill to the other.

4 One by one, drag each of the three objects (the curved path and the two circles) into the Swatches palette, adding them to your list of swatches.

FIGURE 11-1
This pattern brush applies two different patterns to a selected stroke: one for straight paths or mild curves, and the second for corners.

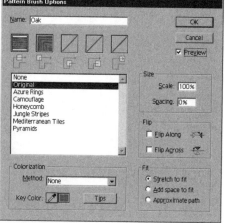

5 Double-click each of the new swatches, and enter a name for each swatch in the Swatch Name text box in the Swatch Options dialog box.

6 Now that you've added three swatches to the Swatches palette, you can use them in creating a pattern brush. Make sure no objects are selected on the artboard, and choose New Brush from the Brushes palette menu.

7 In the New Brush dialog box, choose the New Pattern Brush radio button and click OK.

8 In the Pattern Brush Options dialog box, enter Curve and Circles in the Name text box.

9 Click the Side Tile button in the Pattern Brush Options dialog box, and then click the curved line that you added to the list of swatches.

10 Click the Outer Corner Tile button in the dialog box, and click the black-filled circle that you added to the list of swatches. Assign the same black-filled circle to the Inner Corner Tile button as well.

11 Click the Start Tile button, and select the white-filled circle from the list of swatches. Add the white-filled circle to the End Tile button as well. Your dialog box should look something like the one here.

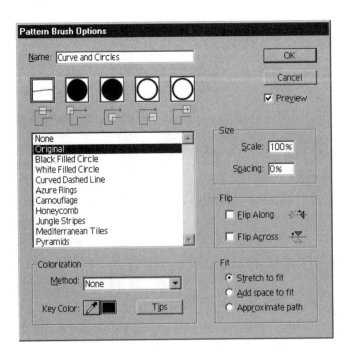

12 Leave the rest of the default settings as they are, and click OK to define the pattern brush.

Select the pattern brush from the Brushes palette, and then select a drawing tool. Try creating both curved paths and sharp angles. Experiment by assigning the new pattern brush to curves you create with the Pen, Pencil, Paintbrush, and different shape tools.

CREATING BRUSHES FROM SCRATCH

If you want to create a new brush from scratch, the process is similar to that of modifying an existing brush, except that you need to start with a drawing that will be used as the brush symbol.

With a path selected, choose New Brush from the Brushes palette menu. Depending on the nature of your selected path (not all paths work for all types of brushes), you'll be prompted to select a type of brush in the dialog box shown here.

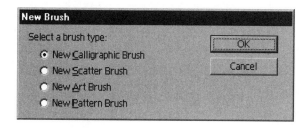

After you choose a brush type, click OK in the New Brush dialog box. A Brush Options dialog box will appear, and you can name and define your new brush based on the selected path.

SHARING CUSTOM FILLS AND BRUSHES

What if you want to access custom brush and fill swatches in a different file? It can be done. Illustrator lets you open the Swatch library of one file within a different file. One technique I find handy is to have a special Illustrator file that I use just to store fill and stroke swatches. That way, I can import that set of swatches into any open document and access my full library of custom fills.

To Open a Swatch or Brush library from a file into a different open file

1 With a document open, choose Window | Brush Libraries, or Window | Swatch Libraries, depending on whether you want to import brush stroke swatches or fill swatches from another file.

2 Select the Other Library submenu option.

3 Double-click the Illustrator (AI) file from which you want to import a swatch library. The new (additional) Swatches or Shapes palette appears in your open document.

4 You can access brush shapes or swatches directly from the imported Swatches or Shapes palette. However, if you want to incorporate one or more selected swatch or shape patterns into your open document, you can drag them from the imported palette into your document's own Swatches palette.

SUMMARY

You can have a lot of fun and unleash your creative juices by experimenting with Illustrator's sets of pattern fills and brush stroke fills. These fills are vector-based, so they have all the advantages of other vector graphics. They demand little memory, and you can easily rescale them without the graininess that results when you resize bitmap fills. Fill patterns also keep file size small because they consist of repeating illustrations that *tile* (repeat) to fill an object.

Fill patterns are found in the Swatches palette. Stroke patterns are assigned in the Brushes palette.

In addition to using Illustrator's built-in set of stroke and fill patterns, you can create and save your own patterns. These patterns are saved with your Illustrator document and can be accessed from other Illustrator documents as well.

 ON THE VIRTUAL CLASSROOM CD In Lesson 9, "Complex Custom Fills," I'll show you how to define brush patterns with bounding boxes to create repeating pattern tiles, and I'll show you how to use text for brush patterns.

A Little Bita'
Bitmaps

Just as I was writing this chapter, one of my students asked me, "When are they gonna combine Illustrator and Photoshop?" I'm ready. But Adobe isn't. If you need to do some serious color, contrast, and brightness tweaking of a photo, or a little airbrushing on your headshot, you'll need to cough up the extra money for either Photoshop or another graphics program that specializes in working with bitmap (or raster) files.

What Illustrator *will* do is apply to bitmaps many of the same effects and tools that you use to edit vector images. And Illustrator will embed bitmap images from other programs into your documents.

ANOTHER ANGLE ON BITMAP VS. VECTOR GRAPHICS

Throughout this book, I've touched on the differences between vector and bitmap images. In most cases, I've been emphasizing the attributes and features that make vector images so useful. In this chapter, I'll show you how to work with bitmap images in Illustrator. So I want to briefly explain how bitmap images work.

I prefer to use the term *bitmap* over *raster* because bitmap kind of explains what's going on behind the scenes with these types of image files. Whereas vector graphic files are saved by storing descriptions of paths and fills, bitmap images are saved by recording the character (color, brightness, transparency, and other attributes) and location of every single pixel in an illustration.

Although bitmaps are a less efficient way to save image files (compared to vectors), the bitmap file logic makes it easier to fine-tune attributes like color on a level not available with vectors. Therefore, photographs in particular are best suited for editing in bitmap programs.

Sometimes bitmaps are the only show in town. This is still mainly the case on the Web, where vector-based illustrations must rely on plug-ins like the Flash Player to be seen in browsers. I'll explain how to convert vector images to bitmaps for the Web in Chapter 15. What I'm going to focus on here is working with images that come to you as bitmaps.

BITMAP DO'S AND DON'TS

When you bring bitmap images into Illustrator, you can—as I already noted—use many of the powerful editing tools and effects available for vector objects. The following lists summarize and give examples of what you can and can't do with bitmaps in Illustrator.

What you *can* do with bitmaps in Illustrator:

▶ Apply transparency, and place transparent objects over bitmaps.

▶ Apply many filters and effects.

▶ Place bitmaps in layers.

▶ Group bitmaps, including in combination with vector objects.

▶ Cut, copy, and paste (and duplicate) bitmaps using the clipboard.

▶ Add bitmaps to your Symbol swatch.

▶ Apply crop marks for printing.

What you *cannot* do with bitmaps in Illustrator:

▶ Make bitmaps bigger without distorting them.

▶ Edit color.

▶ Wrap type around bitmaps.

▶ Edit paths and fills. (There aren't any in bitmap images.)

▶ Use bitmaps as patterns for brushes.

PREPARING BITMAPS FOR ILLUSTRATOR

Because two of the most important things you cannot do to bitmaps in Illustrator is resize or recolor them, you need to arrange to have photos or other bitmap artwork sized and colored before you bring it into Illustrator.

OK, you can resize images in Illustrator, but when you make them larger, they get grainy. For example, Figure 12-1 shows an enlarged bitmap image compared to an enlarged vector image. The bitmap is obviously distorted and displays with jagged edges.

NOTE Actually, it's only 90 percent correct to say that you can't assign colors to bitmap images in Illustrator. You can assign the color of *monochrome* (one color) bitmaps using the same Fill swatch in the toolbox that you use to assign fill colors to vector objects. But, again, this works only for monochrome bitmap images. You can also alter the coloration of an entire bitmap image by choosing Filter | Colors | Adjust Colors and then tweaking the color of the entire selected bitmap. However, these color changes are applied to all colors in the bitmap image. Tinting coloration with a filter is a useful effect, but it doesn't serve as a coloring editor for a photograph.

FIGURE 12-1

On top, the vector image did not distort, while the bitmap version (bottom) is trying to fill a larger space with the same number of defined dots.

Similarly, color tuning, tinting, and defining the outline of a bitmap image should be done in a bitmap editor (like Photoshop) before you import that graphic into Illustrator. Even the free image-editing software that comes with your scanner, your digital camera, or other accessories has more photo color tweaking features than Illustrator.

If the size and color of the image are set, then the bitmap is ready to import. Illustrator can handle over a dozen bitmap file formats, including the following:

▶ **.bmp** Bitmap, which is used with many Windows applications

▶ **.flm** Filmstrip, which is used for editing movie frames

▶ **.gif** Graphics Interchange Format, which is used for web images

▶ **.jpeg** Joint Photographic Experts Group, which is used for web photos

▶ **.pcx** PC Paintbrush, which is used with some Windows applications

▶ **.pdf** Portable Document Format, which supports both vector and bitmap objects

▶ **.pcd** Kodak Photo CD, which is supported by Kodak film developers

▶ **.psd** Photoshop files, which come into Illustrator with layers and other features intact

▶ **.pict** The Macintosh PICT format, which is used with many Macintosh programs

▶ **.png** Portable Network Graphics, which is similar to the .gif format for web-compatible graphics

▶ **.pxr** PIXAR, which is used for 3-D imaging

▶ **.tga** Targa, which supports enhanced gamma (intensity) settings, and is used with the Truevision video board

▶ **.tiff** Tagged Image File Format, which is used by many scanners as a default image format

This list of supported bitmap formats is extensive, but not complete. So you should make sure that any bitmaps you are bringing into Illustrator have been saved to or exported to one of these formats.

> **NOTE** In addition to these important bitmap formats, Illustrator also imports text from the following formats: Microsoft Word (as well as text in the .txt format), other vector graphic files like CorelDRAW, .emf and .wmf (Windows vector formats), and CAD (used with AutoCAD and other technical design programs).

MANAGING BITMAPS IN ILLUSTRATOR

There are two ways to manage imported bitmap images in Illustrator. You can embed them, in which case, they are saved in your Illustrator file as part of your illustration. Or you can link them, in which case, the imported bitmaps remain independent files. I explain the pros and cons of each method a bit later in this chapter, in the sections "Using Linked Bitmaps" and "Embedding Bitmaps."

Whether you link or embed a bitmap, you put it into an illustration by choosing File | Place. Navigate to the folder with your bitmap file. (It must be in one of the supported formats listed in the previous section.)

The Place dialog box has a check box option for Link, as shown here.

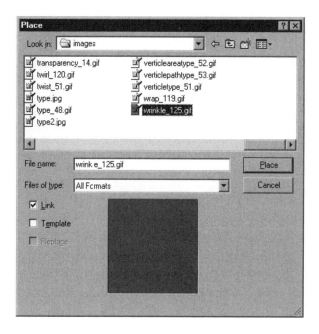

If you want to import your image as a linked file, select this check box.

A placed bitmap will look like any other vector object on your artboard. You can move it, and apply many effects and filters.

> **NOTE** The Template check box in the Place dialog box will import your image as a nonprinting, uneditable template layer.

ORGANIZING BITMAPS WITH THE LINKS PALETTE

The Links palette is actually somewhat misnamed—it displays both linked and embedded images. In any case, it allows you to view, find, and manage all the embedded and linked images in your open document.

To view the Links palette, choose Window | Links. All linked and embedded bitmaps will display in the Links palette, as shown at right.

The Links palette menu allows you to sort the display of linked and embedded images by name, type (file type), or status (linked or embedded). The menu also allows you to show all images (choose All from the Links palette menu) or just embedded images (choose Embedded from the Links palette menu).

Other options on the Links palette menu allow you to control how linked images are handled. I'll explain those options next.

In the Links palette, you can change the size at which linked and embedded images are displayed by choosing Palette Options from the Links palette menu, and choosing from the thumbnail-size options.

USING LINKED BITMAPS

Think of linked bitmaps as borrowed images. You borrow them from another application, you use them in your illustration, but ultimately, they belong to the other application.

When you place a bitmap as a linked object, you can assign all the effects and filters you wish in Illustrator. Those effects stay with the imported bitmap, even if the picture is edited in its original application. Let's say, for example, that you've imported a photo from Photoshop, and you applied several effects in Illustrator. Then, in this scenario, you later edit the photo back in Photoshop. When you update the link in Illustrator, the effects you applied will still be associated with the photo, but any changes made to the photo in Photoshop will also be applied to the photo in Illustrator.

To define how you want this updating to work, choose Edit | Preferences | Files & Clipboard. The Preferences dialog box offers three Update Links options, as shown here.

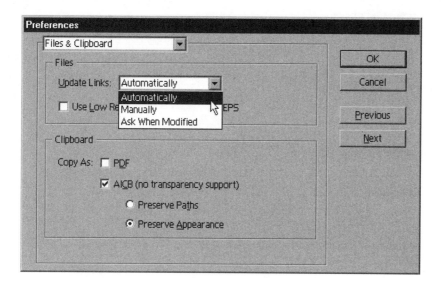

If you choose the Automatically option, Illustrator will modify the linked image whenever you change the file using another program. The Ask When Modified option prompts you to make changes. Ask When Modified is the way to go; that way, you'll have a chance to reject changes if you want to.

The Manually option requires you to click an object in the Links palette, and choose Update Link from the Links palette menu before a newer version of your image will be substituted.

You can conveniently edit a linked image in your system's default bitmap editor by choosing Edit Original from the Links palette menu. After you edit a linked image in your bitmap program, exit the program, and you'll be prompted to apply the changes to the version of the linked image in Illustrator.

You can not only edit a linked image in your bitmap editor and have it change in Illustrator, but you can also replace a linked image with a different linked image, and still retain all the effects you applied in Illustrator. Here's how.

To Replace A LINKED IMAGE IN ILLUSTRATOR

1 Place (File | Place) a picture in an Illustrator file, and be sure to select the Link check box in the Place dialog box as you import the image.

2 Move the image, rotate it, apply affects, or resize it.

3 View the Links palette (Window | Links), and select the image to be replaced in the Links palette.

> NOTE I know, I warned you earlier that resizing doesn't tend to work well with bitmaps in Illustrator. But you can get away with making bitmaps smaller, or sometimes even a little bit bigger, without too much distortion.

4 Choose Replace from the Links palette menu. The Place dialog box opens.

5 Navigate to the bitmap image file you wish to substitute for the selected image, and click the Place button in the Place dialog box. The new image will replace the old one, with the same size, location, and effects.

After you place the image, all the effects and other editing you applied to the original image are applied to the new bitmap.

When you open an Illustrator file that includes linked bitmaps (or other linked files), the linked files will automatically be opened in the document. However, if any of the linked images have been deleted or moved, you will be prompted with a dialog box like the one here asking if you want to replace the file with another one.

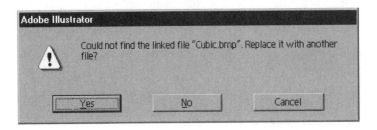

If you have moved the file or have another file you want to use, click Yes. The Replace dialog box will open. It's just like the Place dialog box: you can use it to navigate to and select a new image (or find a moved image). When you select a replacement image, click the Replace button in the Replace dialog box to substitute the new (or moved) file.

EMBEDDING BITMAPS

Embedding bitmap images is simpler and safer than linking them. It's safer because you don't have to worry about sending a bunch of linked images along with your Illustrator file to a client, or about whether you've broken links to images by changing your file folder structure in the process of transferring Illustrator files.

> **TIP** My general rule of thumb is that if someone is providing me with Illustrator files, I prefer to have placed bitmaps linked so I have more freedom to switch them or edit them in a bitmap editor.
> If I'm sending a file to a client, I generally embed images so they don't get lost, or the client doesn't accidentally break links by moving, renaming, or deleting linked images.

By not selecting the Link check box when you place an image in Illustrator, you embed the file. Images you copy and paste into Illustrator will be embedded, not linked. After all, if you copy and paste images into Illustrator, you haven't even identified a file to link them to.

You can convert linked objects to embedded images by selecting a linked file either on the artboard or in the Links palette, and then choosing Embed Image from the menu.

EFFECTS AND FILTERS THAT WORK WELL WITH BITMAPS

Illustrator's set of effects and filters includes a few that work especially well with bitmaps. The blur effects, Gauzian and Radial, are available from both the Filters and the Effects menus, and so is the Unsharpen Mask effect.

> **SEE ALSO** Filters and effects—and their differences—are explored in Chapter 10. In brief, filters make permanent changes to images, while effects make changes that can be removed.

To apply a blur effect to a selected bitmap, choose either Filter | Blur, or Effect | Blur. Then choose either Gauzian or Radial. The Gauzian blur does what it sounds like: creates a heavenly type gauzy blurriness on your photo or other bitmap. Use the Radius slider to increase the blurriness, and check out the effect in the preview area of the dialog box associated with this effect, as shown next.

The Radial blur creates funhouse-mirror-type distortion. If you select the Zoom radio button in the dialog box associated with this effect, the effect is as if your bitmap were created with wet paint and then spun, throwing paint to the outside of the image. If you choose the Spin radio button, as shown here, the image looks like it's being spun around so fast that it creates a blur.

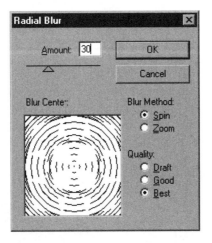

The Draft, Good, and Best radio buttons in the Radial Blur dialog box generate different resolution qualities, ranging from rough (Draft) to more crisp (Best). This dialog box doesn't have a true preview area, so you have to experiment and be ready to choose Edit | Undo to start over again if you don't like the results.

You can also define some bitmap attributes within an illustration using the oddly named Unsharp Mask effect. With a bitmap selected, choose Effect (or Filter) | Sharpen | Unsharp Mask. A dialog box displays with a preview area, as shown here.

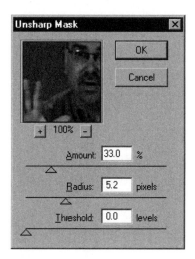

Actually, this effect either unsharpens (I guess the word *blur* was already taken) or sharpens an image. Sharpening is done by increasing contrast between different colors in the bitmap. The Amount slider in the Unsharp Mask dialog box defines how much sharpening you want to apply. (Higher values equal more sharpness.) The Radius slider defines the pixel size used to apply sharpening. Smaller values create more subtle color variation, whereas larger values create large splotches of color. The Unsharp Mask effect gives you a small taste of the kind of bitmap tweaking you can do with a full-featured bitmap editor like Photoshop.

Summary

Vector graphics have many advantages over bitmaps in scalability, file size, and range of available effects. However, bitmaps generally do a better job of handling the detailed color nuances of photographs, and therefore are going to be around for a while. Illustrator does not perform many of the basic photo-editing techniques required to touch up and work with photos, but it does let you import already formatted bitmap images into a document.

Imported bitmaps can be saved two ways. Embedded bitmaps are saved as part of the Illustrator file and become an integral part of the illustration just like the vector objects in your drawing. Linked bitmaps remain independent files that can be updated and edited in Photoshop or other bitmap editing programs.

13

Arranging Illustrations with Layers

Layers are a tool for both organizing complex

illustrations and for creating particularly complex effects.

The organizing part comes from the fact that you can separate

different elements of a drawing into different layers and edit

them without being distracted by the rest of your illustration.

Even more importantly, layers allow complex meshing of objects and effects to create really interesting artwork. Think of layers as transparent sheets of acetate that you can draw on. You can place any Illustrator object on a layer, including shapes and type. Because they are transparent, the content of different layers is visible even when you stack them one on top of each other. Objects on a top layer may cover up (or partially cover up) objects on lower layers. But you can achieve some really complex effects by controlling the opacity of each layer and of the separate objects on any given layer.

LOOKING AT LAYERS

If you've bumped your head up against the difficulty of selecting and editing sections of a complex drawing, you're ready to use layers to help solve your problem. Plus, you can use layers to apply effects and other editing tools *layerwide*—for example, all objects within a layer can have a set level of transparency applied to them.

You can create many layers in a single illustration. Once created, you can move the layers (i.e., change their order), lock them to prevent changes, group them together, and even apply styles to them.

Getting into the habit of creating objects on separate layers will end up saving you time as you create more complex illustrations.

EXPLORING THE LAYERS PALETTE

To view the Layers palette, choose Window | Layers or press F7. Note that both of these actions are toggles, meaning that if the palette is not visible, pressing F7 or choosing Window | Layers will show the palette, and pressing F7 or choosing Window | Layers again will hide the palette.

The Layers palette is normally grouped together with the Actions and Links palettes. To suit the way you work, though, you can choose to tear off the Layers palette and use it alone, or combine it with other palettes. To tear off the palette, simply click and drag the Layers palette tab away from the palette. To rejoin the palette, drag and drop it back

> **TIP** Hovering the mouse over the various parts of the Layers palette will bring up a small ToolTip that describes that part of the palette.

onto the grouping of the Actions and Links palettes. You can, of course, decide to group the Layers palette with any of the other palettes, using the same technique.

There are two columns of icons to the left of each layer. The first column toggles visibility, allowing you to display or hide the selected layer. The second column toggles locking, which either allows you to edit a layer (unlocked), or it prevents you from editing a layer (locked). Figure 13-1 illustrates the Layers palette.

> **NOTE** Layers and sublayers appear with a gray background on the palette, while paths and groups contained within a layer appear with a white background.

CHANGING LAYER OPTIONS

Sometimes you may want to work on a particular object, and you need to have a clear, uncluttered view of it. Having your objects occupy different layers can be a real lifesaver at that time because you can control the visibility of separate layers.

To toggle the visibility of any layer, simply click the Visibility icon (the small eye icon to the left of the layer's name in the Layers palette). Because this is a toggle, you can reverse the process by clicking the same area to make the layer visible again. (The eye won't be visible, of course, indicating that the layer is hidden.)

FIGURE 13-1
Each individual layer can be either visible or hidden, locked or editable.

Toggles visibility
Toggles lock

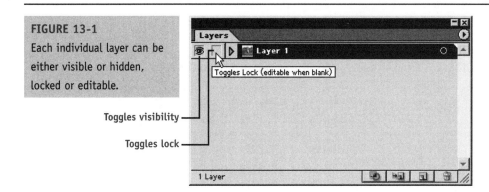

Locking a layer prevents you from being able to select its contents. Thus, you can select objects on overlapping layers without affecting the objects on the locked layer. With a layer locked, you can click and drag the Selection tool to select partly obscured objects while preventing other objects from being selected.

To toggle the lock on a layer, click the space to the right of the Visibility icon next to the layer that you want to lock. Again, because this is a toggle, you can unlock the layer by clicking the small lock icon that appears in the same space.

It's nice to be able to see at a glance what a layer contains. You can help the process along by using meaningful names for your layers. Naming a layer is quite easy. To name an existing layer, double-click the layer's entry in the Layers palette to open the Layer Options dialog box. In the space provided, enter a new name for the layer, as shown in this illustration.

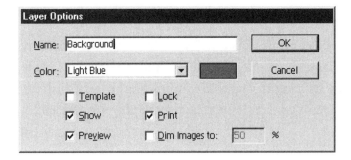

Every layer has an icon associated with it. The icon is a small thumbnail representation of that layer's contents. Depending on the size and resolution of your screen, this thumbnail may be rather difficult to see. Fortunately, you can change the size of the thumbnail view.

To Change THE SIZE OF THE THUMBNAIL

1 Open the Layers palette menu.

2 Choose Palette Options to open the Layers Palette Options dialog box.

3 In the Row Size area of the Layers Palette Options dialog box, choose Small, Medium, Large, or Other.

NOTE If you choose Other, enter a size (in pixels) for the thumbnail to be displayed.

Along with their names, layers have colors associated with them. You can leave the default setting, like with the name of a layer. However, you are also free to set the color of any given layer yourself.

To Set THE COLOR OF A LAYER

1 From the Layers palette menu, choose Options For *Layer Name*. (*Layer Name* will be the actual layer name.)

2 In the Layer Options dialog box, choose a color from the list or click the small color swatch to open the Color Picker dialog box.

3 After you select a color for your layer, click OK to close the Layer Options dialog box.

CREATING LAYERS

As you create more objects in an illustration, you should create them on their own separate layer, unless they are to be grouped together with objects on an existing layer.

To create a new layer, click the Create New Layer icon, located at the bottom of the Layers palette, as shown here.

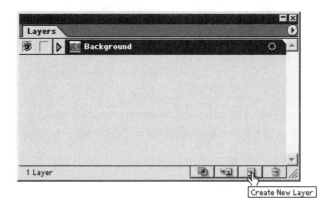

Sublayers, like layers, enable you to further organize your work. You can use sublayers to group like objects together under one layer and still have the same organizational control like with layers. To create a new sublayer, click the Create New Sublayer icon located at the bottom of the Layers palette.

You can create as many layers and sublayers as you need. Once you create a layer, you can expand it to display all sublayers and objects by clicking the triangle to the left of the layer or sublayer (so it points down). You can collapse layer display by clicking the triangle again (so it points right).

In the next section, I'll explain how to use layers to organize the objects in your illustration to make them easier to find and edit.

USING LAYERS TO ORGANIZE YOUR ILLUSTRATION

Sometimes you'll need to reorganize the layout of your illustrations. You may want to have certain objects appear below other objects rather than above them. With your work organized into layers and sublayers, this is an easy proposition. You can easily move layers around within the Layers palette.

To change a layer's order, just click and drag it within the Layers palette. You can drag a layer downward, effectively moving it below other layers, or drag it upward to move it above other layers.

To change the order of a sublayer, simply click and drag the sublayer within the Layers palette. You can drag a sublayer downward, effectively moving it below other sublayers, or drag it upward to move it above other sublayers.

> **NOTE** You cannot move a sublayer above other layers, i.e., a sublayer must remain a sublayer of the layer under which it was created.

DELETING LAYERS

Of course, not every object makes it into the final illustration. To that end, you will sometimes need to remove layers along with the objects they contain. There are several ways to remove unwanted layers.

You can remove a layer by selecting it in the Layers palette and then clicking the Delete Selection icon in the lower-right corner of the Layers palette, as shown next.

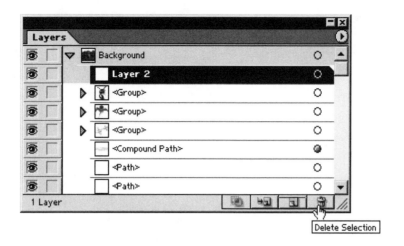

Another way to delete a layer is to click and drag the layer onto the Delete Selection icon. Mac users will find this intuitive because it reflects the Mac trash bin. Yet another way to delete a layer is to select it, open the Layers palette menu, and choose Delete Selection.

DUPLICATING LAYERS

Sometimes you will want to duplicate a layer. This approach can come in handy if you want to experiment with some of the artwork contained on a layer, but you want to be sure that the original artwork remains untouched. Another good reason to duplicate layers is when you're creating frames for an animation. Often, you'll need the same object duplicated and simply moved to create the animation. That's where duplicating a layer comes in.

You can copy a layer by dragging and dropping an existing layer in the Layers palette onto the Create New Layer icon at the bottom of the Layers palette. Or you can choose Duplicate *Layer* from the Layers palette menu, as shown next.

> **NOTE** The layer will be called *layername* copy, where *layername* is the name of the duplicated layer. To rename the copied layer, double-click it in the Layers palette and enter a new name in the Name box in the Layer Options dialog box.

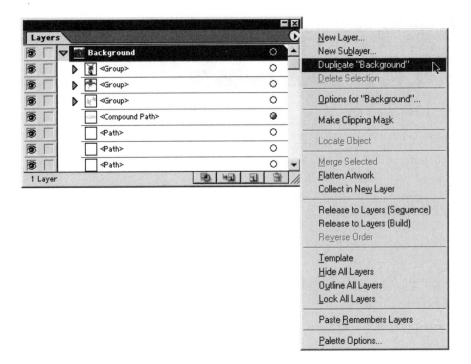

CONSOLIDATING LAYERS

Sometimes you might want to collect layers with similar objects in them onto sub-layers under one layer rather than keeping all of the objects on separate layers. Illustrator provides for such an occurrence. This strategy can be extremely helpful if you've created many objects on a single layer.

To collect existing layers onto one layer, select the layers you want to collect by clicking the first layer you want. You can then add to the selection by holding down SHIFT (to select contiguous layers) or COMMAND/CTRL (to select noncontiguous layers).

With the layers you want to collect selected, choose Collect In New Layer from the Layers palette menu, as shown next.

MOVING OBJECTS ONTO SEPARATE LAYERS

Often, you will begin work with a single layer or even several, but eventually, your project will outgrow the layer structure you originally set up.

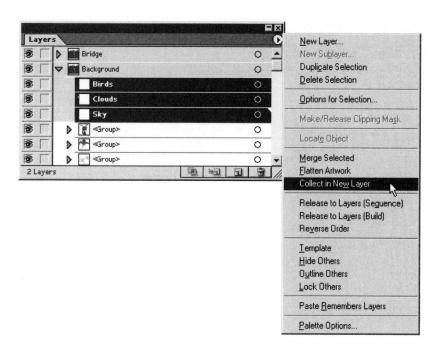

You can move objects from one layer (or sublayer) to another by dragging them in the Layers palette. If you use large row sizes, you can see useful icons that help identify each object on a layer.

In addition to organizing objects onto layers "by hand," Illustrator offers options for automating the process. You can automatically generate layers or sublayers for your illustration. To do this, you use sequencing or building features in the Layers palette menu. I'll explain how to do that next.

SEQUENCING OBJECTS TO NEW LAYERS

If you've created a number of objects on a layer and you'd like to have each of the objects on a separate layer, you can accomplish that task with relative ease. Rather than cutting and pasting each of the objects, you can release the objects to separate layers.

To release objects to separate layers (also referred to as *sequencing*), choose Release To Layers (Sequence) from the Layers palette menu, as shown next.

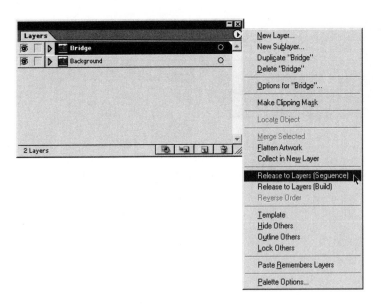

Sequencing creates a series of sublayers containing each of the objects from the original layer.

BUILDING LAYERS

You can also build a series of layers containing the objects cumulatively. This technique is handy for creating series of layers for animation purposes. Each successive layer will contain one less object than the previous layers. Say, for example, you have a layer with a rectangle, a triangle, and an ellipse. Choosing Build will create three layers; the first will have all three objects, the second will contain the rectangle and the triangle, and the last layer will contain only the rectangle.

To release objects to separate layers (build), choose Release To Layers (Build) from the Layers palette menu.

Releasing objects to separate layers creates a series of sublayers containing an accumulation of the objects from the original layer, as described previously.

MERGING LAYERS

Although it's nice to have layers to organize your work, illustrations with many layers take up more memory than those with fewer layers. Sometimes, you'll find that the objects on different layers could just as easily be collected together on one layer. You can accomplish this task by merging any two or more layers you wish.

To merge a series of layers, select the layers you want to merge by holding down COMMAND/CTRL and clicking to select the layers you want to merge.

With the layers you want merged selected, open the Layers palette menu and choose Merge Selected, as shown in this illustration.

> NOTE If the layers are contiguous, you can select a group of layers by clicking the first layer you want merged and then pressing SHIFT and clicking the last layer you want merged.

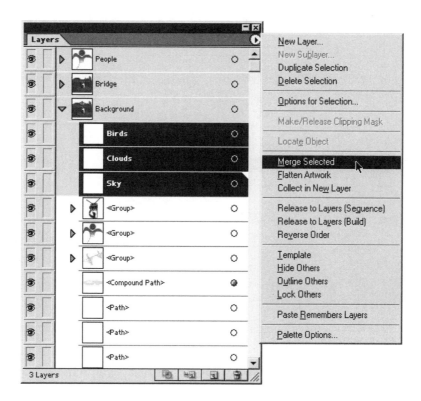

To save space in a file, especially after you're done doing all your tricky editing, you may actually want to flatten all of the layers in your illustration. Flattening the layers places all of your artwork onto one single layer.

To flatten the layers in your illustration, choose Flatten Artwork from the Layers palette menu.

CHANGING LAYER DISPLAY

You can also use the Layers palette to change the way artwork is displayed. You can choose from Preview view or Outline view. When computers were much slower, it was often better to have objects displayed in Outline view to prevent the slow redrawing times of objects displayed in Preview view. These days, that seems less important, but it's still often handy to see selected layers in Outline view when you want to be able to easily identify paths and aren't so interested in fills.

> **NOTE** Another way to toggle between Outline and Preview views is to press COMMAND/CTRL and click the eye icon in the Layers palette. The eye icon will appear hollow for layers with Outline view set.

To change the view of all objects on all layers, choose either Outline All Layers or Preview All Layers from the Layers palette menu.

To change the view for one layer, double-click the layer's name in the Layers palette. In the Layer Options dialog box, select or deselect the Preview check box, as shown here.

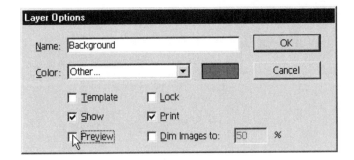

FINDING OBJECTS ON A LAYER

In a multilayered illustration with a large number of objects, it may seem like locating an object's corresponding layer or sublayer might be a tough task. However, when you select an object with the Selection tool, you can more easily locate the corresponding object in the Layers palette.

You can find selected artwork in the Layers palette by choosing Locate Object from the Layers palette menu. The selected artwork's layer or sublayer will appear in the Layers palette, as shown in Figure 13-2.

SETTING TRANSPARENCY WITH LAYERS

One of the most powerful ways to give depth and dimension to an illustration is to have objects appear through other objects, in effect, having the uppermost

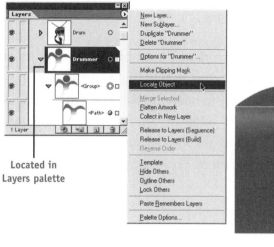

FIGURE 13-2
In complex illustrations, it can be difficult to locate objects in the Layers palette. The Locate Object menu option solves the problem.

Located in
Layers palette

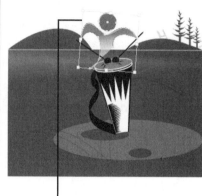

Selected object

objects be transparent to some degree. You can control the transparency of layers in Illustrator by using the Transparency palette.

To view the Transparency palette, choose Window | Transparency, or press SHIFT-F10. This action is a toggle: it will turn on the palette if it's not visible and turn it off if it is visible.

To change the transparency of a layer, select the layer by clicking its name in the Layers palette and then change the Opacity setting in the Transparency palette, as shown in Figure 13-3.

SEE ALSO For a full discussion of transparency and opacity, see Chapter 8.

FIGURE 13-3
Changing opacity for a layer changes the transparency of all the objects in the given layer.

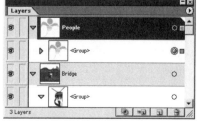

USING SCANNED ARTWORK AS A TEMPLATE LAYER

A popular method of creating artwork in Illustrator is to scan in existing hand-drawn artwork to use as a template for recreating the artwork using Illustrator's drawing tools. Many cartoonists, for example, will draw their creations in pencil or pen, scan the resulting artwork in Photoshop, and then use the scanned work as a template in Illustrator to draw the lines, shapes, and text. This artwork can then be saved and imported back into Photoshop, where final touchups and effects can be added.

Illustrator has the capability to display layers as templates to make this process much easier.

To Create A TEMPLATE LAYER

1 Create a layer you wish to use as a template, for example, by scanning a graphic and placing it on a layer.

2 Double-click the layer that you want to use as a template.

3 Select the Template check box in the Layer Options dialog box.

Objects in a template layer are *locked,* meaning that they cannot be selected, moved, or edited. Objects in a template layer will not be printed.

SELECTING LAYER OBJECTS

It's fairly easy to select all objects on any given layer. You can, of course, use the Selection tool to select any given object or number of objects. There are other ways to select all objects on a layer, though, by using the Layers palette itself, that you may find saves you time.

To select all of the objects contained on a layer, click the right edge of a layer in the Layers palette or press OPTION/ALT and click the layer name in the Layers palette.

A small square will appear to the right of the layer name, indicating that the objects on the layer are selected. The square will be filled with the color of the layer as set in the Layer Options dialog box, as shown here.

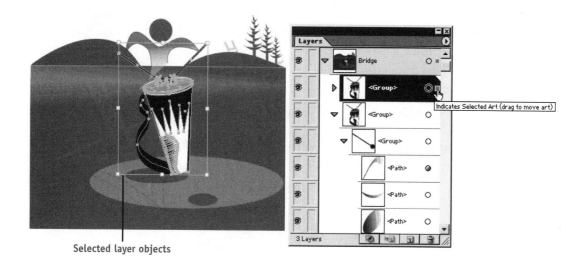

Selected layer objects

USING STYLES WITH LAYERS

Along with applying styles to objects, you can target layers and sublayers for styles. You can apply predetermined styles, such as drop shadows, buttons, and textures, to the objects residing on any given layer or sublayer. Applying these types of effects would normally require a great deal of work if you were to try to apply them without the use of Illustrator's styles. Styles and layers work together through the use of the Target icon in the Layers palette and the available styles in the Styles palette.

> SEE ALSO I'll return to using styles in Chapter 16.

The Target icon, which has four different appearances, is just to the right of a layer's name in the Layers palette. This rather tiny icon displays with subtle (hard to see!) differences depending on which styles are associated with a layer.

Normally, when all of the objects are not selected on a layer, the icon will appear as an empty circle, even if some of the objects are selected.

If all of the objects on a layer are selected, then the Target icon will have another circle drawn around it: that is, the icon will have two circles, one inside the other.

If the inner circle is empty, it means that the layer is targeted but has no style or appearance attributes associated with it.

NOTE Being targeted means that a layer will acquire appearance attributes or styles if a style is selected when the layer is targeted.

If the Target icon has a filled three-dimensional appearance, the selected layer has a style or appearance attributes associated with it, but it is not currently targeted. If the Target icon is filled, three-dimensional in appearance, and has an additional concentric circle outside of the inner circle, that means the layer has a style or appearance attribute associated with it, and it is currerntly targeted.

To target a layer, click the Target icon on the layer. To target a sublayer, click the Target icon on the sublayer. With a layer or a sublayer targeted, you can apply a style by clicking the style you wish to apply in the Styles palette.

USING CLIPPING MASKS WITH LAYERS

Clipping masks, which you already explored in Chapter 10, partially obscure the objects below them, allowing portions of the object to show through. You can create really cool effects by using clipping masks. Here, I'll briefly review how to create them in the course of explaining how to use clipping masks with layers.

Objects used for a clipping mask must be on the same layer as the objects being masked, because clipping masks do not affect objects on other layers.

To Create A CLIPPING MASK

1 Create at least two objects on a single layer. The uppermost object will become the mask, and the underlying object(s) will be masked.

2 With the objects selected, click the Create/Release Clipping Mask icon in the lower-left corner of the Layers palette, as shown next.

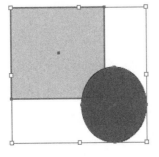
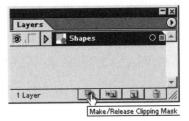

If you find that you no longer want the clipping mask to mask out an object, you can release the clipping mask. Just click the Create/Release Clipping Mask icon in the lower-left corner of the Layers palette. The masked object releases from the mask and becomes a regular object again.

> **NOTE** The masking object will lose all of its fill and stroke properties, and they will be reset to none.

USING NONPRINTING LAYERS

Sometimes, you'll want objects or layers that appear in your artwork not to print, even though they are visible. There are several ways of preventing parts of your artwork from printing.

To prevent artwork from being printed, you can do one of the following:

▶ If the artwork is on a specific layer, you can make that layer a template, as I explained earlier in this chapter in the section "Using Scanned Artwork as a Template Layer."

▶ You can toggle off the visibility of a layer by deselecting the eye icon next to the layer name.

▶ Finally, you can turn off printing in the Layer Options dialog box. To open the Layer Options dialog box, double-click the layer's name in the Layers palette. In the Layer Options dialog box, clear the Print check box to leave the layer visible but to cancel its ability to print, as shown here.

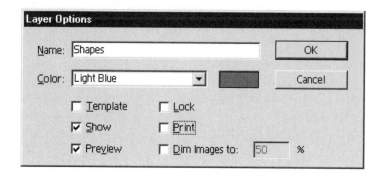

SUMMARY

You use layers to organize objects in complex illustrations and to control the properties of different objects grouped into layers.

You can organize objects onto layers and sublayers by dragging them around inside the Layers palette. Illustrator also has tools to automatically organize objects onto separate layers.

Layer properties can include the following: hidden or visible, printing or nonprinting, and locked or not locked. Hiding layers simply makes it easier to identify and work with selected objects in a crowded illustration. You can use nonprinting layers as templates—like a scanned photo or drawing, for instance—and build artwork around them. Locking layers prevents you from messing up artwork on a layer while you edit artwork on another layer.

Finally, you can assign attributes to layers that affect how all objects on the layer are displayed. In this chapter, I showed you how to apply transparency to every object on a selected layer.

 ON THE VIRTUAL CLASSROOM CD In Lesson 10, "Layers," I'll demonstrate how to use layers to organize work on a complex illustration, and how to apply effects like transparency to an entire layer.

14

Hardcopy Output

You've created a spectacular illustration, but you want to get it into print. The bad news is that what you see on your computer monitor is a long way from printed output. The process of displaying an image on your low-resolution but million-plus color monitor is very different than printing your illustration to paper, vinyl, fabric, or on the cover of a CD.

The good news is that Adobe Illustrator is the most widely supported graphic design tool, and print shops and preprint processing shops are all familiar with Illustrator and welcome Illustrator files. And printers and preproduction service bureaus are an invaluable source of assistance in achieving the results you want when you send your illustration to print.

AN OVERVIEW OF YOUR PRINT OPTIONS

There are essentially three ways your Illustrator artwork can end up in a printed form. You can print the artwork on your own desktop printer. Your artwork can be incorporated in a publication using a desktop publishing program. Or you can send your Illustrator file directly to a print shop for commercial printing.

Each of these options has its own rules and peculiarities. Artwork printed on your desktop printer will not necessarily accurately reflect how your artwork will appear when sent to a commercial printer because the color management process is different. And illustrations that are embedded in a publication usually have to conform to file format specifications defined by the publication. For example, the illustrations I'm preparing for this book are in color on my screen in Illustrator, but they appear in grayscale when printed in the book.

The point is that as you create your illustration, or before you submit your file to a printer, you need to know the constraints posed by the medium to which you are printing. And the best way to do that is to consult with the people who will handle your printed output.

If you are creating just a small number of copies of your illustration, it might be appropriate to use your desktop printer. Modern desktop printers do a reasonably good job of presenting colors you assign in Illustrator.

If your illustration is destined for a publication, it is important to find out which file format is best for that publication, and to properly save your file.

If your illustration is going to be printed by a commercial printer, you will need to work closely with the printer and the prepress service bureau that prepares the *plates* (film) that will be used on the printing press to apply layers of color to create printed copies.

Because desktop printing and embedded files in other publications are a little less complex a challenge, I'll explain them first. Then I'll walk you through the do's and don'ts of preparing an Illustrator file for commercial color printing.

PRINTING ON YOUR OWN PRINTER

With the proliferation of better and cheaper color printers, you have the option of testing your illustrations right on your desk. Better desktop color printers using high-quality glossy paper can create rather impressive hardcopy illustrations. Or, your desktop output can give you a fairly good idea of how your professionally printed illustrations will appear in their final form.

The printable section of your illustration is generally the section of the artboard within the page layout. To define the page layout for an open document, choose File | Document Setup. The Artboard area of the Document Setup dialog box opens. Use the Size and Units lists and the Width and Height areas to define the size of your printed page. The orientation buttons let you quickly toggle between portrait and landscape orientation.

The Tile Imageable Areas radio buttons in the Artboard area of the Document Setup dialog box *tile* large illustrations—printing several sheets of paper that can be taped together to create a full-size object. Tiling does not produce sufficiently neat results for professional display, but you can use it to create draft or test proofs of large print jobs.

> **TIP** If you're looking for more desktop publishing controls to print booklets, brochures, and so on, you'll have to look elsewhere. Unlike CorelDRAW, with its jack-of-all-trades approach, Illustrator leaves all desktop publishing tasks to its Adobe cousin, PageMaker.

Your desktop color printer almost certainly uses four different color ink holders (likely packaged in less than four cartridges) to create a broad spectrum of colors. The four primary colors for printing are cyan, magenta, yellow, and black. As I'll explain more in the section "Service Bureau Do's and Don'ts" later in this chapter, one of the major challenges you face when you prepare illustrations for printing is that the red-green-blue (RGB) color-generating system on your monitor is more versatile and flexible than the cyan-magenta-yellow-black (CMYK) color-mixing system used in hardcopy printing. Therefore, the colors you get from your printer often don't match those on the monitor.

In experimenting with the enhanced color printing features of Illustrator 10, I've been rather amazed by how reliably Adobe has managed to match screen and print colors, especially if your printer meets or comes close to the settings of those on the list of printers supported by Illustrator's color settings.

To Coordinate YOUR COLOR PRINTER WITH YOUR MONITOR COLORS

1 With your document open, choose View | Proof Setup | Custom.

2 In the Proof Setup dialog box, choose your printer, or one close to it in the Profile list, as shown here.

> **NOTE** Of course the match between monitor and printer colors is only approximate, given that they are created with completely different processes. This becomes a major issue in preparing commercial press output, where you will want to test and verify printed output colors before authorizing a print job.

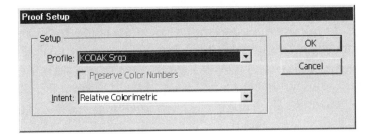

3 Click OK to close the Proof Setup dialog box.

4 Choose View | Proof Colors. The colors on your monitor will adjust to approximate those produced by your selected output printer.

> **NOTE** The four options in the Intent list provide different ways of handling colors and their relationships. The default, Relative Colorimetric, makes minimal adjustments in colors to conform to the constraints of four-color printing. Leave this option set at the default.

EXPORTING TO OTHER FILE FORMATS

If you are preparing illustrations for inclusion in a publication, your drawings will be embedded in a file using a desktop publishing program like Quark or PageMaker. The folks you work with in integrating your artwork into a publication will provide you with file types that they prefer to use.

While, in general, the production staff decides which graphic file types are used, you can also contribute your input as an Illustrator artist. Ask if the publication can support Encapsulated PostScript (EPS) file format graphics instead of raster (bitmap) images. Curves, effects, blends, and transparency are supported better by an EPS file than with popular bitmap formats like TIFF. And EPS files are generally smaller as well.

Once you have determined the best file format, you should make sure your illustration is saved correctly, and to the correct file format.

CLEAN UP BEFORE SAVING

Generally speaking, you should save illustrations that will be embedded in a publication without additional artwork in the illustration. In other words, unless you have made specific arrangements to provide cropping or trimming information, your file should contain only the artwork intended for publication.

One of the most frequent mistakes I see in files saved or exported for publications is stray anchor points that increase the area of the drawing board that is saved or exported to a file. Stray anchor points are easy to create: a touch with the Pen tool and zap, you've got an anchor point. And they're hard to find. So, before you save your file or export it, check for stray anchor points. To do this, choose Select | Object | Stray Points. A red line will appear on the artboard showing the entire area formed by your artwork, including any stray points. In the illustration shown next, a stray point in the upper-left corner of the page has expanded the area that will be saved or exported to a file.

After identifying stray points, delete them before saving or exporting your illustration to a file format.

EXPORTING TO VECTOR AND RASTER FILES

One of the great advantages of using Illustrator to prepare artwork is that it is *the* industry standard for vector graphics. Virtually all professional-level desktop publishing programs smoothly support Adobe Illustrator files.

ILLUSTRATOR'S VECTOR GRAPHIC FILE FORMATS

Illustrator has four native vector file formats to which you can save files:

▶ Illustrator (AI) files, which open fully editable in Illustrator. Among the options in the Illustrator Native Format Options dialog box is the Compatibility list, which allows you to create a version of the file that can be opened in older versions of Illustrator. In general, all the features you assign are preserved in the down-versioned file, but features like transparency will not be editable. Therefore, if you save to an older version of Illustrator, you should save a separate version of the file in Illustrator 10.

▶ Encapsulated PostScript (EPS) files, which also open fully editable in Illustrator.

▶ Portable Document Format (PDF) files, which preserve many effects assigned in Illustrator, but which are not editable.

▶ Scalable Vector Graphic (SVG) files (or compressed SVGZ files), which are used with XML and web publishing, and are not editable in Illustrator.

Illustrator, EPS, and PDF formats include options to generate *thumbnails* (small preview versions of the illustration), and to embed fonts with the file so that it can be opened even if the recipient's system does not have all the fonts in the document.

> **NOTE** If you save a file without embedding fonts, and the recipient does not have those fonts on his or her system, the recipient will be prompted to substitute a different font when opening the file.

In many cases, you simply need to know which version of Illustrator a file should be saved to, and whether to save the file in Illustrator or EPS format. All of the aforementioned file formats preserve the scalability and file-size economy of vector graphics.

EXPORTING TO RASTER FORMATS

If you are preparing images for integration into a web site, you will want to save them to GIF (Graphics Interchange Format) or JPEG (Joint Photographic Experts Group) formats, or alternatively as SWF (Macromedia Flash file format) files for display in the Flash Viewer or SVG format. I'll discuss these file format options in Chapter 15.

Sometimes publication specs require files be submitted as a raster file like TIFF (Tagged Image File Format) or PICT formats. To save a file to a bitmap format, choose File | Export, and choose a file format from the Type drop-down list in the Export dialog box. Click Save.

Depending on the selected export file format, a new dialog box will open with specific options for your raster file format. These options include color model, resolution, anti-aliasing options, and a choice between PC or Macintosh processing. Resolution for images destined for monitor display need not be higher than normal monitor resolution (72 or 96 dots per inch). Generally, bitmap images destined for printed output should conform to instructions provided by the print production people to whom you are submitting your illustrations.

Because raster images are not scalable, they get grainy when enlarged. And even unenlarged raster images tend to get *jaggies*: corners or points that look like they are composed of small squares instead of smooth corners. Anti-aliasing reduces the jaggies in bitmaps, and it is a check box option for exported raster image formats.

OTHER EXPORT OPTIONS

Along with supporting popular generic raster file formats, Illustrator also allows you to export to various proprietary formats, including Adobe's own Photoshop format. However, you can open Illustrator files right in Photoshop, so in most cases, that's a simpler and more effective option.

Other supported file formats include the CAD format used in technical design programs like AutoCAD, the TGA (Targa) format used in video production, and the Windows Metafile (WMF) format that incorporates vector images into Windows documents.

PREPARING FILES FOR COMMERCIAL COLOR PRINTING

While your computer monitor creates colors by mixing together tiny red, green, and blue pixels, printing color is created by mixing and overlaying different ink colors.

There are two basic approaches to color printing. *Spot* color usually involves two or possibly three colors. Examples of spot color are brochures, signs, banners, and T-shirts that use black plus one additional color in designs. While spot color usually involves just one color (in addition to black), you can use different gradations of spot colors to produce complex color effects. For example, if you use red as a spot color, you can overprint black with a 50 percent transparency over a red spot color object design, or you can use 50 percent transparency red to create pink.

PRINTING TRICKS AND TIPS

When you prepare your artwork for commercial printing, you'll need to understand a few terms and concepts to communicate clearly with your printer, and to have your artwork appear like you want it to look.

Bleeding is not as violent as it sounds; it's a process for allowing ink to extend to the edge of a piece of paper or other material. *Trapping* is a way of handling four-color printing that minimizes the tacky look you sometimes see in color newspaper photos where the different colors aren't properly aligned. And *overprinting* is a way to manage how colors are laid down on top of one another.

BLEEDING

Many times you will want your final artwork to extend to the very edge of the material on which it is printed. Because no printing press prints all the way to the very edge of the paper, fabric, plastic, and so on, material is trimmed after printing so that the material conforms to the edge of the artwork. To a viewer, it will appear like your artwork printed to the very edge of the paper or other material, but in reality, this effect will be achieved by trimming the material.

You can define a bleed area in the Print dialog box, or you can ask your printer or preprint service bureau to bleed your artwork to the edge of the page. In either case, you will want to design an area of your artwork that extends beyond the area that will appear in the final output. In other words, you need to create a bit of artwork that will be cut off and thrown away during the final production process. A simple way to do this is to create a large filled rectangle behind your artwork that can be trimmed.

I'll explain how to set a bleed area when you print in the section "Preparing Process Color Separations," later in this chapter.

TRAPPING COLORS

Because colors are applied by using up to four color plates, the plates must match perfectly so that the final output doesn't have a blurry, mismatched look. The process of matching plates is called *registration*. However, in the real world, plates don't always match perfectly. Trapping is a technique for creating some overlap between colors to avoid registration errors. For example, if you are printing a black outline around a green object, you can extend both the width of the outline and the size of the green object so that even if the plates don't register exactly, no mismatch will be evident in the final output.

Color trapping is used only with the CMYK color set for process printing. And you always use the CMYK color set for process printing. So before you assign trapping, make sure you are using the CMYK color model. One quick way to do this is to choose File | Document Color Mode | CMYK Color.

To Assign TRAPPING FOR TWO OR MORE OVERLAPPING OBJECTS

1 Select the overlapping objects to which you will apply trapping.

2 View the Pathfinder palette by selecting Window | Pathfinder.

3 Select Trap from the Pathfinder palette menu, as shown here.

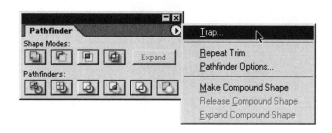

4 In the Thickness area, enter a stroke width of between 0.01 and 5000 points.

5 The Height/Width box allows you to change the relative size of the horizontal trap compared to the vertical trap. For now, leave this at the default setting of 100 percent.

> **NOTE** The amount of thickness determines how much overlap there will be between your images. Larger values create more overlap, which provides an additional guarantee that you won't see white space between misregistered plates.

6 The Tint Reduction box defines how much of the overlap area will have the color of the lighter color in the overlap. For now, leave this at the default of 40 percent, which creates a smooth merging between lighter and darker colors.

7 Select the Traps With Process Color check box to convert spot colors to process colors.

8 Generally, trapping is done by expanding the lighter color of the overlapping colors. In some rare cases where the overlapping colors are close in darkness, you might want to reverse the process and expand the darker color. Select the Reverse Traps check box to reverse trapping.

9 After you have defined your trap options for the selected objects, click OK.

OVERPRINTING

Overprinting is another way to guard against misregistration in process color printing.

Normally, when two differently colored objects overlap, the bottom object is cut away during printing. Figure 14-1 shows how overlapping objects are handled in process printing.

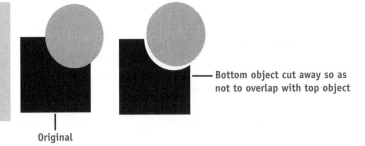

FIGURE 14-1
In process printing, the bottom object is cut away so that the ink from the top object does not print over the bottom object.

Original

Bottom object cut away so as not to overlap with top object

The normal process of cutting out the bottom object during process printing ensures that the color of the top object and the color of the bottom object will not mix or blend. This method of printing produces clean, uncorrupted colors just as you assign them in Illustrator. The downside is that if registration is slightly off, odd spacing or awkward overlapping will occur between the objects.

By assigning overprinting, you can add the color of a top object to that of a bottom object when objects overlap. The printed result is less vulnerable to misregistration. The following illustration shows overprinting applied to a fill and to a stroke.

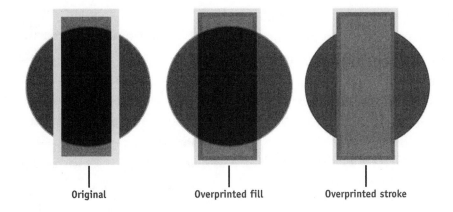

Original   Overprinted fill   Overprinted stroke

To Assign OVERPRINTING TO OVERLAPPING OBJECTS

1 Select both (or all) objects to be overprinted.

2 Choose Window | Attributes to display the Attributes palette.

3 Click the Overprint Fill check box to assign overprint to the fill of the top object(s).

4 Click the Overprint Stroke check box to assign overprint to the stroke of the top object(s). The illustration here shows both check boxes selected.

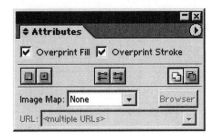

5   To see the effects of overprint options on your monitor, choose View | Overprint Preview.

PREPARING COLORS FOR PROCESS PRINTING

As you are aware by now, process color printing is called CMYK because it combines cyan, magenta, yellow, and black to create a full spectrum of colors. *Full spectrum*, however, is a relative concept. You won't have the same range of color options with CMYK printing that you will have on your monitor.

To prepare an illustration for process color printing, it's necessary to separate the illustration into four color plates. These plates are made from film prepared by a preprint service bureau. And your service bureau will use Illustrator to generate separate film for cyan, magenta, yellow, and black.

The most important element in preparing an illustration for process color is to work exclusively with colors from the CMYK color palette. There are different ways to do this, but two of the easiest are the following:

> NOTE Some print shops now use six plates instead of four to provide an increased color spectrum. The same basic process described here is used to prepare six-color printing, but additional color plates are created. Consult your service bureau and printer for advice if you are using six-color printing, but the general rules described here for adhering to the CMYK color set applies when preparing illustrations for six-color printing.

▶ Choose File | Document Color Mode | CMYK Color.

▶ Choose CMYK from the Color palette menu, as shown next.

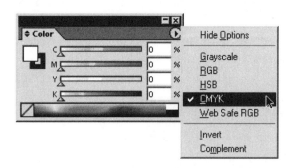

DEFINING PROCESS COLORS FOR YOUR DOCUMENT

Once you define CMYK as your document color model, all colors will be defined as relative mixes of cyan, magenta, yellow, and black.

Cyan is a color close to turquoise. Magenta is close to a bright plum color. With CMYK selected as the color model for your document, you can literally "mix" combinations of each color using the four color sliders in the Color palette. In the illustration here, I'm using the color sliders to define a color mix that is 100 percent cyan and 0 percent other colors.

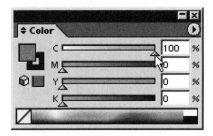

If your document has colors already assigned using the RGB model, those colors might not convert perfectly to CMYK colors. The solution is to set your document colors to CMYK when preparing output for printing.

PREPARING PROCESS COLOR SEPARATIONS

You can get a general sense of your final color output from your monitor by choosing View | Proof Colors. And you can see an approximation of your final print colors using your desktop color printer. However, onscreen color proofing and printing to your desktop color printer are not accurate enough to verify how your print job will look after it comes off a commercial color printing press. For an accurate color proof, you must have your commercial printer prepare test proofs.

The test pages you print on your desktop printer will help your commercial printer verify and apply process color. Some print shops and service bureaus also want you to provide color separations yourself so they can verify their own separations. You can print color separations if you have a PostScript printer installed. Alternatively, if your service bureau insists on you printing color separation pages and you don't have a PostScript printer, you can install one (like the Apple LaserWriter), and then print to a file.

To Print COLOR SEPARATIONS

1 Choose File | Print, and select a PostScript printer from the list of available printers. Depending on your operating system and the printer you select, the dialog box that opens will vary, but the basic options will be similar.

2 In the Print dialog box, click the Separation Setup button.

3 The Separations dialog box will show a list of the four process colors, as shown here. If you applied colors using a different color setup than CMYK, those colors will be listed as well, and you should click the Convert To Process check box to convert them to one of the four process colors.

> **NOTE** If your Separation Setup button is grayed out, your printer is not a PostScript printer and does not support color separation. Your option is to install the drivers for a PostScript printer (like Apple LaserWriter), and use the Print To File checkbox in the Print dialog box when you "print" a file in order to send that print file to disk instead of to your printer.

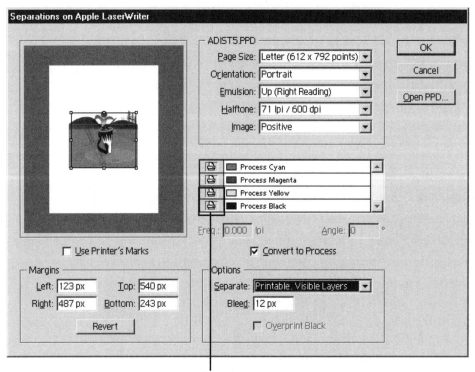

Separation colors

4 From the Separate list in the Options area of the Separations dialog box, choose Printable, Visible Layers to print only layers that are not marked nonprinting.

5 In the Bleed box, enter a value that will define how much of your illustration will be trimmed in the final production process. The bleed value will be displayed in the preview area on the left side of the Separations dialog box.

6 Click the Use Printer's Marks check box to print guides for your printer to use in trimming the final output and calculating registration between plates.

7 After you define printing options, click OK to print separate pages for each color. You can provide these pages to your service bureau and printer to help them check and create the real separation plates that will be used for your print job.

> **NOTE** The Overprint Black check box automatically overprints black objects in your illustration. Because black covers over other colors, this is a helpful way to prevent mismatched layers in your final output. For more explanation of overprinting, see the "Overprinting" section earlier in this chapter.

SPOT COLOR PRINTING

Spot colors are defined by a wide range of commercial color sets. The most widely used is the PANTONE matching system, but there are many others as well. If you are preparing a job for two-color printing, spot printing is more economical because instead of mixing cyan, magenta, yellow, and black in four press runs to produce your color, the selected ink color is simply applied in one press run.

Because there are so many sets of available process colors, they are difficult to simulate on a monitor. You really need to rely on the process color pattern sheet provided by your printer to know which color to expect in your final output.

Because spot colors are applied by running your paper, fabric, or material through a printing press more than once, the basic procedure for preparing illustrations for spot color is very similar to that for preparing illustrations for process color. The main differences are that with spot coloring, you usually use only one color (plus black), and that color does not have to be a product of mixing cyan, magenta, yellow, and black, but can be any color paint or ink provided by your printer.

SELECTING AND PREVIEWING SPOT COLORS

Even though matching process color and monitor color is tricky, Illustrator does what it can to simulate spot output colors onscreen. You can select from a list of process color sets, and choose a process color from a list provided by Illustrator. Illustrator then simulates a close approximation to that color on your monitor.

To Choose A SPOT COLOR TO DISPLAY

1 Choose Window | Swatch Libraries, and select a color set from the list, as shown here.

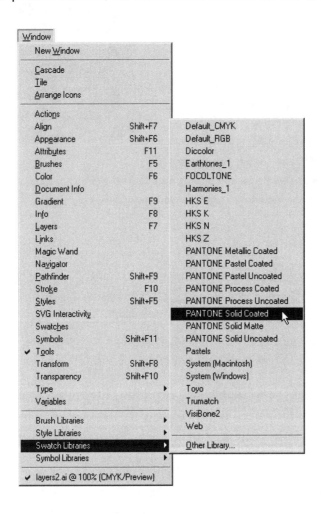

2 After you define a color swatch set, that set of colors will appear in a palette on the artboard. Choose to view spot colors in List view by choosing List from the Swatch palette menu, as shown next.

3 If you have one color from a spot color set that you will be using in your illustration, drag that color from the spot color swatch to the Swatch palette for easy access.

NOTE If your color set is not listed, you can choose Other Library, and navigate in your Illustrator program files folder to the Swatches folder for additional color set options. Or, if a color set is provided on disk by the ink manufacturer or print shop, you can load a swatch set from their file.

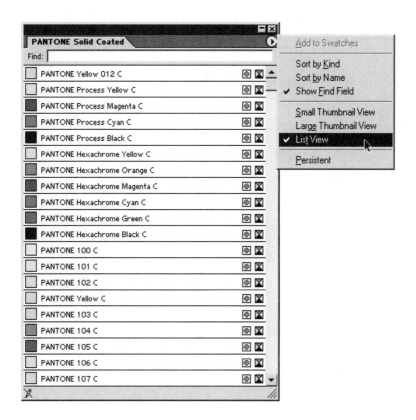

PREVIEWING SPOT COLOR PLATE SEPARATION

You can create your own separations for spot color printing pretty much the same way as I explained how to prepare process color separations in the section "Preparing Process Color Separations." The difference is that in the Separations dialog box, your printer will display process colors (cyan, magenta, yellow, and black) plus any spot color(s) you applied in your illustration.

If you are using two (or three) color spot printing, the only colors assigned to objects in your illustration should be those you will be using for spot coloring. If you have objects with other colors assigned, you need to recolor those objects because you won't have access to the process color set using spot color printing.

In the Separations dialog box, click to display the printer icon in the Print column to print process black, and the one (or two) spot colors you have applied. Figure 14-2 shows the Separations dialog box defined to print pages for black, and one selected spot color.

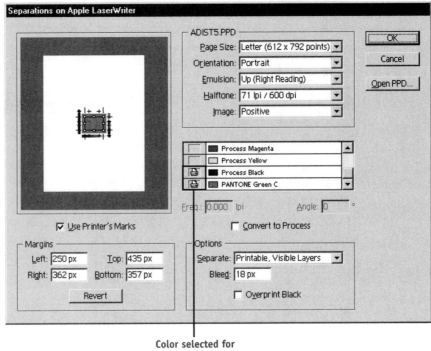

FIGURE 14-2
In this illustration, I'm using PANTONE Green C for spot color with process black and printing two plates.

Color selected for
separation printing

PROVIDING CROP MARKS

Sometimes you will submit illustrations to either a production manager or a printer that require cropping. Crop marks must be defined by a nonrotated rectangle.

To Create CROP MARKS

1 Draw a rectangle around the area that you wish to define with crop marks.

2 With the designated rectangle selected, assign no fill and no stroke to the rectangle.

3 Select Object | Crop Marks | Make.

You can convert the crop marks back to a regular rectangle by selecting Object | Crop Marks | Release.

Because you use only one set of crop marks in a document, you can replace the assigned crop marks by creating and selecting a new rectangle and assigning crop-mark properties to that shape. The old crop marks will revert to being a regular shape.

When you print color separations for spot or process printing, the crop marks you set on the artboard define the printed area for separations.

Service Bureau Do's and Don'ts

Your Illustrator file can end up as a book cover, a brochure, a calendar, a CD cover, a sign, a banner, a label, or almost any printed output. It can end up on a billboard, a business card, or be any size in between. The folks who make this happen are print shops and service bureaus.

Print shops produce printed output by running your material—paper, plastic, fabric, etc.—through a printing press. Additional colors are applied by running your material through the presses as many as six times, with colors overlaid to create additional colors.

Service bureaus produce film that is used to cut printing plates, and because color printing requires multiple passes through a printing press, up to six such films are required for commercial color print jobs.

Printers and print service bureaus are experts at converting your Illustrator files into the desired final output. As early as possible in the development process, you will want to establish a relationship with a printer and a service bureau, explain to them exactly what kind of final output you want, and carefully note and comply with the advice they give you for preparing your artwork in Illustrator.

The following checklist will help you prepare your illustration for commercial printing:

▶ Which version of Illustrator or EPS files will they accept?

▶ How do they want fonts handled? Do they want you to embed fonts? Do they have a set of fonts that you are allowed to use? Or do they want you to convert fonts to outlines? (If so, select all of the type in your document, and choose Type | Create Outlines before submitting the file to the printer.)

▶ If you are doing two-color printing, which set of spot colors do they use, and what advice do they have about how they come out?

▶ How should you handle sizing and scaling? Remember the movie *This Is Spinal Tap*? The band wanted a 10-foot high Stonehenge but got a 10-inch Stonehenge. Many printers or service bureaus will rescale artwork for you, especially artwork intended for billboards, banners, posters, and other large-scale venues. But make sure everyone is clear about what the final size should be.

SUMMARY

A quick trip to the Yellow Pages will provide you with a list of printers that can transfer your Illustrator artwork onto a billboard, a business card, a T-shirt, or a glossy brochure. As soon as you know the destination of your artwork, establish a close working relationship with your printer and seek advice on how best to prepare your artwork for final production.

In some situations, your artwork will be incorporated into a larger publication, usually managed with a desktop publishing program like Quark or PageMaker. In that case, you will likely need to export your artwork into a file format accessible to the team managing the publication. The Illustrator EPS file is widely recognized, and maintains the scalability and small file size inherent to Illustrator vector graphics.

Process and spot color printing are processes where colors are created by printing sequential plates on top of previously printed pages. If you are preparing artwork for process or spot color printing, you will need to restrict your colors to those supported in the CMYK palette, or to spot colors provided by your printer.

15

Illustrating for the Web

There is an interesting challenge to presenting

your Illustrator artwork on the Web. The Web is a raster (bitmap)

environment, while Illustrator excels at creating vector graphics.

Nevertheless, there are many good reasons to prepare Illustrator artwork for the Web, and some recent developments in the Web itself make it a more friendly environment for Illustrator graphics.

VECTOR ART IN A RASTER WORLD

Unfortunately, web browsers still support mainly two image file formats: GIF (the G is pronounced either as in "get" or as in "gee") and JPEG ("jay-peg"). A third widely interpreted web graphic file format, the PNG ("ping") format, is similar to GIF. All three are raster (bitmap) file formats, and they do not support the scalability features of Illustrator-created vector art.

OK, that's the bad news. But there's good news on two fronts: Illustrator has powerful tools for converting artwork to JPEG and GIF, and also, the Web is becoming a more vector-friendly environment.

THE CHALLENGES OF WEB GRAPHICS

For many reasons, you need to start preparing images for the Web when you first design your illustration. Web images are constrained to low-resolution monitors—usually 72 dots per inch (dpi). Further, different operating systems support different sets of reliable colors. And conventional web-design wisdom dictates that you restrict your color palette for graphics used on the Web to the 216 *browser-safe,* or *web-safe,* colors, which are colors that are supported by all systems.

And, unlike printed output, you don't know exactly which relative size your drawing will be in a web browser. An image that is 640 pixels wide will fill the entire width of a small, low-resolution monitor, but it will fill only half the width of a higher-resolution and larger monitor.

Finally, you have to factor in the download time required for graphics intended for the Web. A large image with many colors might look beautiful in printed output, but it could take an unacceptably long time to download into a visitor's browser window.

To solve these problems, follow these two guidelines:

▶ Plan ahead! As you create web graphics, anticipate what will and what won't work on the Web. (I'll share some advice on these issues in the next section of this chapter).

▶ Use Illustrator's powerful Save For Web dialog box to experiment with web graphic settings and preview the end result.

I'll devote most of this chapter to helping you through the process of converting Illustrator images to GIF or JPEG files.

NEW FRONTIERS IN WEB GRAPHICS

Over the past three or four years, the Web has become a much more vector-friendly place. To give credit where credit is due, this is mainly because of the widespread adoption of Macromedia's Flash Player (formerly the Shockwave Player) plug-in.

The Flash Player allows web surfers to view SWF format vector graphics by using the Flash Player plug-in. The Flash Player integrates with browser software to create a vector-supportive display environment on the Web. Before the widespread acceptance of the Flash Player, vector graphics could be used on the Web only if a designer knew which (if any) vector graphic program was installed on a viewer's computer.

Now, web designers generally assume the availability of the Flash Player, and therefore, the ability for web visitors to see vector graphics. While the Flash Player program itself is best known for its ability to create animation and interactive programs, its viewer supports static vector graphics as well.

An even newer, and as yet mostly unproven, venue for supporting vector graphics on the Web is Scalable Vector Graphics (SVG). Like the SWF format, it supports all the good aspects of vector graphics—scalability, economy of file size—and does a better job of supporting the array of effects and filters available in Illustrator.

SVG takes advantage of XML, a more advanced and powerful page description language than traditional HTML. As of this writing, SVG is still in its infancy, and it remains to be seen whether it will achieve the broad acceptance of SWF. The SVG option is available when you know that the people viewing your web pages will be using XML-enabled browsers.

PLANNING AHEAD: WEB GRAPHICS DO'S AND DON'TS

In spite of the emerging options for vector images on the Web, most illustrations for the Web must still be converted to GIF or JPEG format. Planning ahead will help you avoid disappointing results when you convert Illustrator files to GIF or JPEG.

One of the best points about converting Illustrator files to web images is that the red-green-blue (RGB) color system used on the Web supports more colors than cyan-magenta-yellow-black (CMYK) color mixing for hardcopy output. On the other hand, different operating systems and browsers present the same RGB color mix differently, so you will want to work with web-safe colors when you design artwork for the Web.

Another problem to prepare for is that web graphics must download to a visitor's computer, and bigger graphics take longer to download. In general, web graphic file size is a product of the size of the image and the number of colors used. So web graphics should be small, and they should use the minimum number of colors necessary for the effect you are striving for.

Finally, keep in mind that web graphics are low resolution. Unlike printed output, which composes your illustration using hundreds or thousands of dots per inch, monitor resolution presents graphics with less than 100 dpi. So avoid intricate detail and very small type fonts.

ADDING WEB ATTRIBUTES TO ILLUSTRATIONS

Before we dive into the process of exporting Illustrator graphics to web-friendly formats, I want to introduce you to some features in Illustrator that add web-useful features to images.

You can define link targets for images in Illustrator so that when the object is placed in a web site, it serves as a link. You can also create *image maps*: graphics that contain several links in a single image. For instance, you can create a map with different clickable areas that lead to different link targets.

Web site locations are referred to as URLs (Uniform Resource Locators). They're the *www* addresses assigned to web sites.

Generally, I recommend that you assign links and link targets in your web design program, such as Dreamweaver. It's usually easier to define links in web design software, and also it's more likely that you will be in a position to know which links to assign to an image.

Sometimes, however, it's appropriate to assign link properties in Illustrator. For instance, if you are creating a logo, ad, or banner that will appear on many sites, and you want to link that banner to a defined web site, you will want to embed that link information right in the image.

ASSIGNING LINKS IN ILLUSTRATOR

You assign links to objects by using the Attributes palette. You first select the object to which you want to assign a link, and then use the Attributes palette to define the link itself.

Links in Illustrator can be assigned either to a rectangular area or to a polygon. Rectangular links generate a rectangular-shaped clickable area around the selected image that will include space that is not part of the image itself. Figure 15-1 shows the clickable area for a logo generated by both a rectangular and polygonal link.

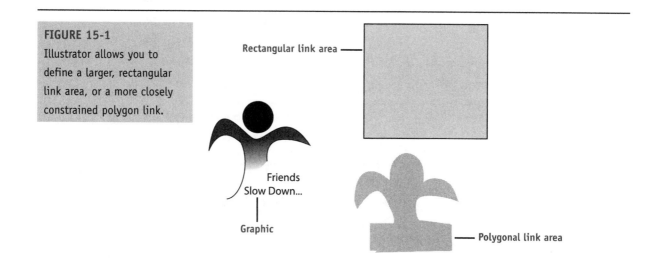

FIGURE 15-1
Illustrator allows you to define a larger, rectangular link area, or a more closely constrained polygon link.

Rectangular link area

Friends
Slow Down...

Graphic

Polygonal link area

To Create A LINK

1 Select an object or objects.

2 Choose Window | Attributes to display the Attributes palette.

3 From the Image Map drop-down list in the Attributes palette, choose either Rectangle or Polygon.

4 In the URL text box in the Attributes palette, enter a URL, as shown here.

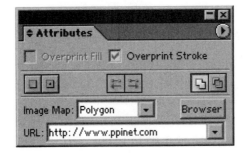

5 When you save your file, the URL you selected will be embedded in the graphic.

> **NOTE** You can easily launch your system's default web browser by clicking the Browser button in the Attributes palette.

CREATING IMAGE MAPS

You define image maps by creating more than one clickable area in an illustration. You create image maps pretty much the same way as you assign a URL to a single object.

In the next illustration, I'm assigning each symbol on my map its own link. When the illustration is saved as a single graphic file, it will contain multiple links. Depending on where a visitor clicks on the image, he or she will go to a different link target.

> **NOTE** As you assign links within a drawing, Illustrator keeps a list of those links available. You don't need to retype a link if you use it twice; just use the URL drop-down menu in the Attributes palette to access a list of saved URLs.

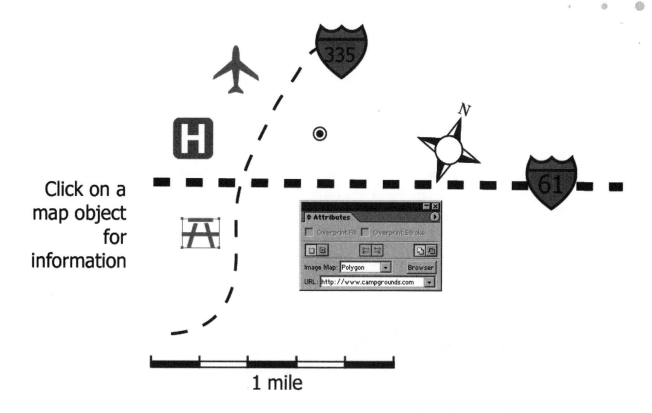

Click on a map object for information

1 mile

CONFIGURING ILLUSTRATOR FOR WEB GRAPHICS

If you are preparing your illustration for the Web, you'll want to define the Illustrator environment so web-friendly features are assigned and accessible.

You can confine yourself to colors that are supported by web browsers. You can view illustrations as they will appear when exported to raster format. And you can define your artboard so it simulates a web page instead of a printed page.

USING WEB-SAFE COLORS

As I mentioned earlier, images destined for the Web must use RGB color settings. The RGB color system defines how colors are presented on monitors, and it provides a different set of colors than those available for hardcopy output using the CMYK color-mixing system.

While the RGB color system is capable of creating millions of colors, not all monitors will display all these colors. And, in general, different operating systems and different browsers present the same RGB color mix differently. So, for example, the deep purple and bright orange you see on your monitor might look like pale blue and dark yellow on another system. To minimize the variation in color display for web graphics, be sure to use web-safe colors.

Competing browsers and operating systems generally support a very limited set of common colors—216, to be exact. If you want to ensure that the color you see on your system will look the same to a web visitor, you should choose colors from this set of 216.

To set your color palette for web-safe colors, choose Web Safe RGB from the Color palette menu, as shown here.

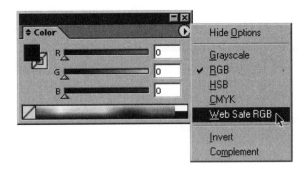

If you look closely at the Color palette after you assign Web Safe RGB, you'll notice that the continuous flow of the normal RGB palette has been converted to a more granular, choppy color palette. The almost infinite number of colors in the RGB palette has been pared down to the 216 colors supported universally by web browsers.

You might find it difficult to distinguish colors in the Web Safe RGB Color palette. I'd like to see the Color palette present these colors in a more accessible way, but for now, I'll have to add that to my wish list for Illustrator 11. An easier way to view and assign web-safe colors is to view a special swatch palette buried in Illustrator. To access that palette, choose Window | Swatch Libraries | Web, and use the swatch palette that appears to assign browser-safe colors.

Even with browser-safe colors, there is variation between how colors look on Macs and PCs. You can preview how colors will look on either the Macintosh or Windows operating system by choosing View | Proof Setup, and then choosing either Macintosh RGB or Windows RGB.

What if you've already created an illustration and assigned CMYK coloring to it? Or, what if you need both a hardcopy CMYK version of your artwork and a web version? Well, you'll be OK. You'll want to save two versions of your artwork: one for the Web, and one for CMYK printing.

To convert CMYK colors to RGB, choose Filter | Colors | Convert To RGB. Just remember to save a separate version of your file with CMYK colors if necessary.

DEFINING A WEB-SIZED ARTBOARD

You can size your artboard to match the width of a typical web page. But what is a typical web page width? There isn't one, but web artists have to have a page width in mind when they are designing.

Web page width is measured not in inches, meters, or picas, but in *pixels*: those tiny dots that make up the unit of measurement for monitors. The increasing availability of large monitors has opened up a wide range of potential page widths for web pages. Still, I'm going to go out on a limb here to advise that, in general, it's most helpful to envision an 800-pixel-wide web page.

Whatever page width you determine to be your target, you can define the artboard to match that size.

To Change ARTBOARD SIZE FOR TYPICAL WEB PAGE WIDTHS

1 Choose File | Document Setup.

2 In the Document Setup dialog box, choose one of the preset web page widths, as shown next. Or choose Custom in the Size drop-down list, choose Pixels in the Units drop-down list, and enter values in the Width and Height boxes.

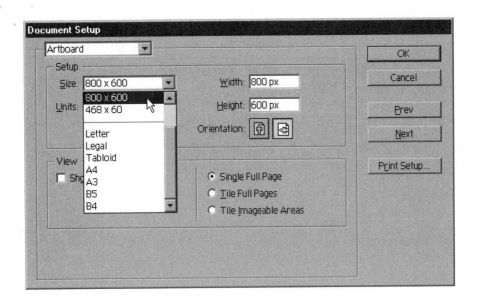

3 Click OK to close the Document Setup dialog box, and assign a web-sized artboard to your document.

PREVIEWING RASTERS

You can change your Illustrator display to simulate the rough edges and grainy resolution of raster images. Ouch! Why would you want to make your graphics look uglier like that? The reason is to simulate how they will look on a web page, and then adjust your objects so they are more web-compatible.

To convert your display to simulate a web page, choose View | Pixel Preview. You'll note changes in your image. For example, gradient fills might appear more banded (instead of as even gradation from one color to another). Edges of curves might look more like small steps. And transparency effects might look less subtle and intricate.

If you're preparing images for the Web, it's best to see these changes before you send your image to a web site, so you can adapt and adjust your file as necessary.

OFF TO THE WEB

As you already learned, the two main file formats for the Web are GIF and JPEG. The PNG file format is a variation on GIF that has minor improvements, but it is somewhat less widely interpreted by web browsers. The driving force behind the PNG format is not technical innovation, but some long-lost copyright disputes. And any advantages PNG might have over GIF do not change the fact that it's not universally accepted.

What are the differences between GIF (and PNG) and JPEG? The very short version is that GIF (and PNG) support transparency (as shown in the top portion of the following illustration), and JPEG handles complex colors better (as shown in the bottom half).

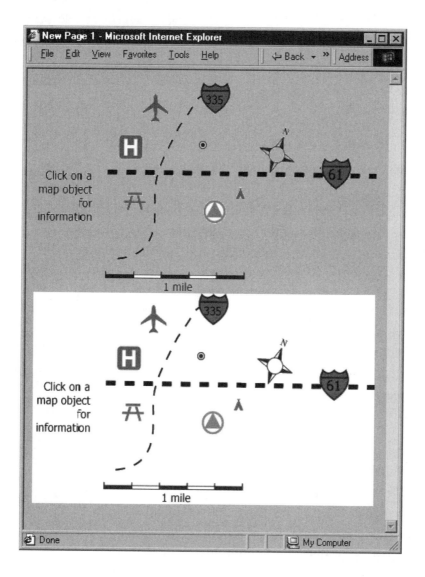

JPEG format is usually used for photographs. The JPEG format supports more colors than the GIF format. And JPEG provides compression options that allow you to reduce file size (although with the price that image quality decreases with file size).

The best news is that Illustrator's features for saving web graphics provide a really easy way to test images in both formats before you export to a web-compatible graphic format.

To save a file as a GIF (or PNG) or JPEG image, choose File | Save For Web. The Image appears in the Save For Web dialog box.

> **NOTE** Here, the term *transparency* means something completely different than when we talk about transparency/opacity as an effect in Illustrator. Transparent web graphics do not employ the same kind of finely tuned opacity/transparency settings allowed for Illustrator effects. Instead, "transparency" applies to only one color, and is applied completely—making the one color disappear.

The most powerful way to experiment with file options is to choose the 4-Up tab in the Save For Web dialog box. The upper-left window of the four display windows shows your original illustration. You can click any of the other display windows to apply and preview different file attributes. You can, for example, experiment with both GIF and JPEG export options at the same time, and keep both options visible. This setup allows you to compare and contrast different web export options, and choose the one that looks best.

The Save For Web dialog box preview menu (a pop-out menu that works like palette menus) lets you define which download speed you expect most visitors to use when they see your graphics on the Web. Selecting a speed from this menu, as shown in the illustration on the right, lets Illustrator calculate download time for your images depending on which file format and other attributes you select.

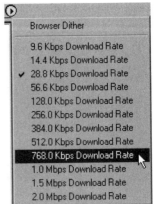

You can resize an image as you export it by selecting the Image Size tab in the Save For Web dialog box. Here, you can define size by entering values in the Width and Height boxes. Keep the Constrain Proportions check box selected to keep your height-to-width ratio unchanged as you resize. Or, you can use the Percentage box to resize an image as you export it. To trim the exported illustration to only that portion within the artboard, choose the Clip To Artboard check box.

The Image Size tab of the Save For Web dialog box also includes the Anti-Alias check box. Anti-aliasing helps smooth out jagged edges that often result when you convert a vector image to raster art. The Save For Web dialog box is shown here.

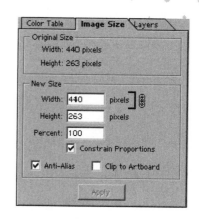

Use the Hand tool in the toolbox in the upper-left corner of the Save For Web dialog box to move images around within preview windows. Once you have experimented with different export settings and previewed how they will look, you can save to your defined export settings. To do that, click the Save button in the Save For Web dialog box. The Save Optimized As dialog box appears, and the settings you defined already are incorporated into how the file will be exported. Navigate to the folder to which you'll save the file, assign a file-name, and click Save in the Save Optimized As dialog box to export the image to a new file format.

EXPORTING GIFS (AND PNGS)

Once you have opened the Save For Web dialog box (choose File | Save For Web), you can configure the dialog box for GIF export by choosing GIF from the Optimized File Format drop-down list, as shown on the right.

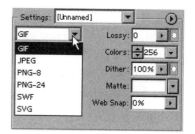

The Settings drop-down list in the Save For Web dialog box lists many different GIF file options. You can experiment with any of these settings and test the effect in the selected preview window.

To export your image with the browser-safe color palette, choose Web from the Color Reduction Algorithm drop-down list in the Settings area of the Save For Web dialog box. A new color palette will appear in the Color Table area with the web-safe colors needed to display your image. If not all 216 browser-safe colors are required, Illustrator will create a restricted palette that will reduce the size of your GIF file.

To assign transparency to your image, choose one of the four display windows, and click the Transparency check box in the Save For Web dialog box. The Matte drop-down list provides options for tinting the transparent color.

Increasing the value of the Lossy slider decreases file quality and increases download time. You can see the changes reflected in the preview window.

Interlaced images fade in as they download into a web site. Instead of appearing in strips, from top to bottom, the entire image is visible in low resolution at first, and then fills in more detail as the entire file downloads. You can add interlacing to GIF images (but not JPEG) by clicking the Interlaced check box in the Save For Web dialog box.

Dithering generates colors not available from the limited 216 color web-safe set of colors by mixing pixels of different colors—like red and blue to make purple. The Dither slider allows you to experiment with different percentages of dithering for your illustration, and the Specify The Dither Algorithm drop-down list allows you to experiment with different dithering techniques. Dithering sometimes produces inaccurate coloring. If your illustration includes many colors, the JPEG format may handle those colors better than applying dithering to a GIF image. You can see the effect of your dithering settings right in the selected preview window of the Save For Web dialog box.

Exporting JPEGs

To export your image to JPEG format, choose one of the preview windows in the Save For Web dialog box (choose File | Save For Web), and then choose JPEG from the Optimized File Format drop-down list.

The Compression Quality drop-down list and Quality slider do the same thing: they allow you to use more or less compression. More compression produces faster download times. (Check the listed download time in your preview window as you adjust compression.) But more compression also reduces quality. When deciding how much compression to assign to a JPEG image, assess both the appearance of your image in the preview window and the resulting download time.

The Progressive check box causes JPEGs to download in a way similar to interlacing for GIF images. Instead of appearing in strips, the image appears first as a low-resolution image, and then later as the fully resolved version.

You can use the Matte drop-down list in the Save For Web dialog box to change a JPEG image background color. The Blur slider literally causes a JPEG to become blurry, and it has limited usefulness in diffusing jagged edges in images.

The ICC Profile check box creates and embeds a monitor profile with your exported image. This profile is not widely supported enough to be useful in exporting for web display.

EXPORTING TO WEB-FRIENDLY VECTOR FORMATS

The process of exporting an Illustrator image to the SWF and SVG vector formats is very similar to exporting to the JPEG and GIF raster formats. You do it all in the Save For Web dialog box (choose File | Save For Web). You can experiment with different settings and preview the results before you export.

The Image Size tab in the Save For Web dialog box works with SWF and SVG files, as does the download speed calculator.

You'll find fewer options when you export to SWF and SVG than you have to confront when you export to JPEG or GIF. That's good. There are fewer options because there is less to convert. Your scalable, smooth, small-file-sized vector images retain most of their Illustrator qualities when you export to SWF and SVG.

SAVING AS SWF IMAGES

SWF files can be viewed with any web browser that has the Flash (aka Shockwave) Player. They can also be opened in Flash and used by Flash developers. Other vector graphic programs also support the SWF format.

When you choose SWF from the Optimized File Format drop-down list, you can select the Read Only check box to keep people from opening the file in Flash and editing it.

The Curve Quality slider defines image quality for exported SWF files. Higher values on the Curve Quality slider create smoother curves and take longer to download. You can preview quality and download time as you experiment with curve quality.

The Type Of Export list allows you to export the entire image as a single SWF image, or to create a separate SWF frame for each layer in your image. In effect, you can create simple Flash animations by exporting layers to frames. When you do, each layer becomes a separate frame in a Flash movie. This strategy is most useful when you (or someone else) are going to edit the exported images in Flash.

USING SVG FORMAT

Partly because Adobe is associated with and promoting the SVG format, the Save For Web dialog box provides more options for exporting to SVG than to the Macromedia-based SWF format. The options available when you select SVG from the Optimized File Format drop-down menu are shown in the next illustration.

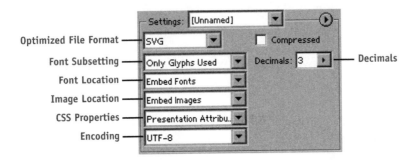

The Font Subsetting options allow you to attach fonts if necessary. The Only Glyphs Used option includes only characters necessary for the file, and is sufficient for most web uses.

The Font Location options allow you to embed fonts, which is the best way to make sure the fonts are available in the viewed version of your image on the Web. Similarly, you should almost always choose Embed Images from the Image Location list so your images don't get lost or disassociated from your file.

As long as you are exporting to SVG, you might as well stick with the default Presentation Attributes setting in the CSS Properties list.

The Decimals setting defines image quality—higher settings create better images and slower download times.

CREATING HTML WEB PAGES IN ILLUSTRATOR

Illustrator provides minimal options for saving a document as an HTML web page. If you are serious about creating web pages, you'll need to take up HTML, or use Illustrator in conjunction with a web design program like Dreamweaver,

FrontPage (for Windows only), or GoLive. In particular, Illustrator does not provide the ability to save text as HTML text. So when you export your document as an HTML page, all text is converted to images.

Because Illustrator is not much of a functional web page design program, I'll provide just a brief overview of how to generate web pages. The key feature and concept to understand is *slicing*. Slicing has a lot of different meanings in web graphic design, but here I'm talking about the Illustrator feature of allowing you to designate individually exportable objects within a single document. For example, say your illustration has a photo, a map, and a logo. You can elect to make each of these elements into a slice. Then, when you export to web graphics, you can export the photo as a JPEG image, the map as an SWF file, and the logo as a GIF image.

If you do not do any slicing, you can still convert an Illustrator element into an HTML page. But the page will just have one graphic file that includes all objects on the page.

To Create A SLICE

1 Select an object or objects on the artboard.

2 Choose Object | Slice | Make. The document will appear "sliced" into rectangular pieces as needed to define a slice for your selected object, as shown in Figure 15-2.

FIGURE 15-2
The text *Moose Lake* has been defined as a slice.

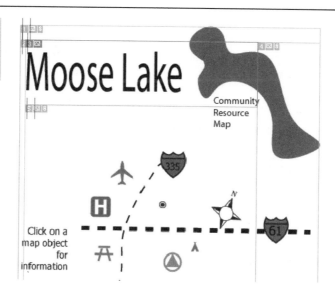

3 Continue to select objects on your page, and make them into slices. Create a new slice for each object you want to manage independently when you save the image to a web page.

Another technique for defining slices is to create a grid on your page using guides, and then generate slices based on those guides.

To Generate SLICES FROM GUIDES

1 Choose View | Show Rulers to display rulers.

2 Click and drag from either the horizontal or vertical ruler to place guides on the artboard.

3 After you place guides on the artboard, choose Object | Slice | Create From Guides to generate slices from the grid you defined with horizontal and/or vertical guides.

Again, it's not necessary to create slices before saving an Illustrator document to HTML. And, unfortunately, there is no option for saving text slices as HTML text, which means you can't really create very functional web pages—even simple ones—from Illustrator. But you can at least break up the images on your generated web page into smaller images, allowing the page to load more efficiently.

To Save AN ILLUSTRATOR DOCUMENT AS AN HTML PAGE

1 Choose File | Save For Web.

2 If you have sliced objects on your page, choose the Slice tool from the Save For Web dialog box toolbox (in the upper-left corner of the dialog box), and select one of the sliced objects.

3 Define specific image export attributes for the selected slice (if you created slices).

4 Define additional specific export attributes for other slices.

5 After you've defined your web export settings for each slice in the Save For Web dialog box, click Save.

6 In the Save Optimized As dialog box, choose HTML And Images in the Save As Type drop-down list, as shown next.

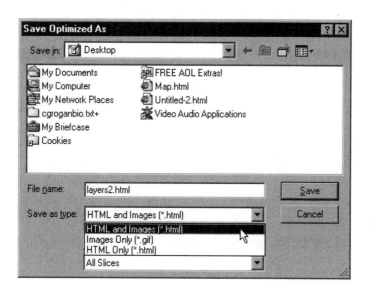

7 Navigate to a file folder, and enter a filename in the Save Optimized As dialog box.

8 Click the Output Settings button in the Save Optimized As dialog box. The Output Settings dialog box opens.

9 Use the Prev and Next buttons to move to different pages in the Output Settings dialog box. The options define some aspects of how HTML code is generated, and mainly define how filenames will be created for different graphic files in your HTML document. If you are familiar with HTML and file-naming conventions for your operating system, feel free to change these settings, but the defaults are fine. Click OK to close the Output Settings dialog box.

10 Click Save to save your file. If you are replacing an earlier version of your HTML page (or there is a different HTML page with the filename you selected), the Replace Files dialog box appears. You can deselect the check box(es) next to file(s) that you don't want to replace. Then click Replace.

The web page you generate using the export options in Illustrator will have images embedded within it. You can open it in an HTML editor for further refinement.

SAVING PDF FILES

The Portable Document Format (PDF) file format is supported on the Web and in hardcopy printing. That's what's so cool about it. To view (and print) PDF files on the Web, visitors to a web site must have the PDF viewer, but that's available free from Adobe, and it's easy to get.

Illustrator provides different settings options for exporting to PDF format. But, in general, you can choose between two groups of settings: one for hardcopy output, and one for screen (including web) output. The hardcopy output options allow the file to be opened and edited, and generate thumbnails for display in operating system file managers. They compress files using the Zip file format for faster downloading.

Screen (including web) options use other compression features appropriate for web downloading, and do not generate thumbnails. All of these options are customizable using check boxes and radio buttons. So, for instance, if you don't want thumbnails when you generate a hardcopy PDF file, you can deselect that option.

To Save AN ILLUSTRATOR DRAWING AS A PDF FILE

1 Choose File | Save As, and choose Adobe PDF as the file type.

2 Enter a filename, and navigate to a folder to which you'll save the PDF file.

3 Click Save. The Adobe PDF Format Options dialog box opens.

4 The Options Set drop-down list provides three choices: Default, Screen Optimized, or Custom. Use Screen Optimized for output destined for the Web, and use Default for files you are sending to hardcopy output. You can customize any of the options as needed by choosing either General or Compression from the drop-down menu at the top of the Adobe PDF Format Options dialog box. Use the radio buttons and check boxes to alter standard PDF export settings for web or hardcopy output.

5 Click OK to save the file.

SUMMARY

More and more, illustrators are designing artwork for the Web. The basic challenge is that the Web displays artwork with a limited set of colors, a grainy, low-resolution monitor, and for the most part, without scalable graphics.

Illustrator helps solve this challenge with the Save For Web dialog box. Here, you can experiment with different file formats, tweak how coloring is managed, and even assign different attributes to different "slices" (selected areas) of an illustration.

ON THE VIRTUAL CLASSROOM CD In Lesson 11, "Saving for the Web," I'll show you how to use Illustrator's Slice tool to create sections of your illustration that can be exported to distinct graphic files. And I'll show you how to use the powerful features in the Save For Web dialog box to fine-tune your illustration for export to GIF or JPEG format.

16

Working Smart

There was a time when you had to do practically everything from scratch when working with a vector-based program such as Illustrator. All that has changed, however. Illustrator now contains many tools that help you automate your work. There's built-in textures and styles, actions, templates, and even data-driven templates that you can use to speed up the process of creating artwork.

USING STYLES

Using Illustrator's built-in styles is a great way to save time when you create artwork.

Styles are a named set of appearance attributes that you can apply to objects in your artwork. The styles don't actually affect your artwork; rather, they affect its appearance.

In other words, a style is *linked* to an object. If the linked style is changed in some way, that change affects the appearance of every object to which the style is applied.

OPENING THE STYLES PALETTE

A dozen preset styles are built into Illustrator 10. You can see them by opening the Styles palette (choose Window | Styles). The present styles in the Styles palette are shown here.

> **NOTE** A shortcut for opening the Styles palette is pressing SHIFT-F5. This is a toggle that will open the palette if it's not visible and close it if it is visible.

With the Styles palette open, you can view the available styles by clicking and dragging the scroll bar. Depending on the current size of the palette, all of the styles may be visible without the need to scroll.

In the Styles palette, you'll see small thumbnails of what the applied style will look like when applied to an object. Preset styles include Caution Tape, Star Burst, and Blue Goo.

You can read the whimsical names of the available styles by hovering the mouse pointer over a style in the Styles palette. After a short pause, the name of the style will appear.

APPLYING STYLES

You can apply styles to an object, a group of objects, a sublayer, or a layer. Keep in mind that when you apply a style to a group, sublayer, or layer, that style will be applied to all of the objects therein.

Applying styles can save you a great deal of time. A style can store dozens of attributes (including effects, stroke and fill settings, and transparency settings), so applying a style serves as a shortcut for individually applying a whole set of styles to objects one by one.

APPLYING A STYLE TO AN OBJECT

To apply a style to an object or group of objects, the object or group must be selected. You can select an object by clicking it with the Selection tool. In the following illustration, I'm applying the Rustic Pen style to one of the objects.

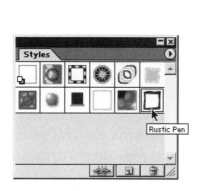

If your objects are grouped, you can select all of the grouped objects by clicking one of them with the Selection tool. Even if the objects you want to apply a style to are not grouped, you can select them all using the Selection tool. To do so, you can click and drag around the objects you want selected, or you can press COMMAND/CTRL and click them. To select different objects in this manner, simply press COMMAND/CTRL and click the objects you wish to apply a style to.

If the objects you wish to apply a style to reside on a layer or sublayer, you can target the layer or sublayer, as demonstrated in Chapter 13. To refresh your memory, simply click the Target icon (the small round icon to the right of a

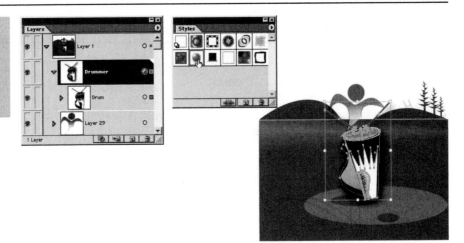

FIGURE 16-1

By selecting a layer in the Layers palette, you can apply a style to each object on the layer.

layer's name in the Layers palette). Doing so will "target" all of the objects on that layer or sublayer. Applying a style will then affect all objects on that layer. In Figure 16-1, I'm applying the Blue Goo style to an entire layer.

CREATING NEW STYLES

Styles are useful as a time-saving technique. But they are also a creativity tool. You can define your own styles, save them, and then apply them to add continuity and theme to an illustration.

Styles can contain any number of colors, fills, strokes, patterns, etc. This means you can create some fairly complex styles. You can also create simple styles such as fills and drop shadows, too. Even then, you'll find that creating a style will end up saving you plenty of time in the long run.

To Create A STYLE BY USING THE EASIEST METHOD

1 Create an object, whether it's a line or a shape.

2 Apply to the object whatever fill, stroke, color, etc., you want in your style.

3 With the object selected, click the New Style button in the Styles palette, as shown next. Doing so will automatically create your new style.

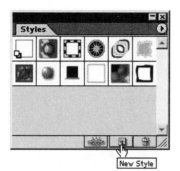

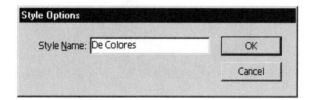

4 Double-click the icon for your new style, and enter a name for your style in the Style Options dialog box, as shown here.

5 Click OK in the Style Options dialog box to save the style.

UNLINKING STYLES

As I already mentioned, styles are linked to objects in your artwork rather than permanently applied to them.

> NOTE If you ever want to change the name of a style, double-click its icon in the Styles palette, and the Style Options dialog box will open.

You can break the link between an object, or set of objects, and its styles. Doing so does not remove the appearance of the style. Instead, it makes the changes you applied via the style permanent changes to the object. (Of course, you can always select Edit | Undo to undo this change, but the changes are permanent in that they are no longer linked to the style. And if a style is changed, changes to that style will not affect an unlinked object.

To Unlink A STYLE FROM AN OBJECT OR SET OF OBJECTS

1 Select the object or objects.

2 Click the Break Link To Style button in the Styles palette, as shown here.

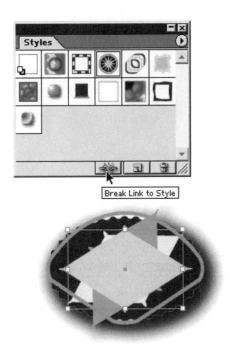

If you no longer need a particular style, you can delete it. Deleting a style breaks the link to objects that have had the style applied, but it does not remove or change the appearance of those objects. To delete a style, drag it onto the Delete Style (trashcan) button at the bottom of the Styles palette.

CHANGING A STYLE

Like with styles that are applied with a word processor, a desktop publisher, or web-supported style sheets, Illustrator styles are changeable. After you create a style, you can later edit its appearance, and the changes will be applied automatically to every object to which the style is linked.

You can edit styles using a combination of the Styles and Appearance palettes.

To Edit AN EXISTING STYLE

1 Deselect any selected objects (choose Select | Deselect) so that you look at and edit only the attributes of a style.

2 Select the style by clicking its icon in the Styles palette.

3 View the Appearance palette (choose Window | Appearance). Here, you'll see all the attributes assigned to your style, as shown in Figure 16-2.

4 In the Appearance palette, double-click any of the attributes of the selected style to open the appropriate palette. For example, if you click Opacity, the Transparency palette opens, and you can change the opacity/transparency setting for the style.

> **NOTE** Other changeable style attributes include the stroke or fill.

5 With the changes made, select Redefine Style *"Style Name"* from the Appearance palette menu, as shown here.

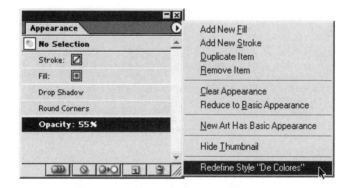

FIGURE 16-2
The Appearance palette reveals that the De Colores style has no stroke, a gradient fill, drop shadows, round corners, and default transparency.

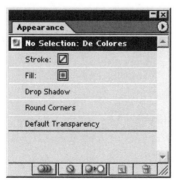

Remember, changing a style affects the appearance of any objects to which the style has been applied.

NOTE Styles are saved along with your artwork when saved to a file.

CHOOSING STYLES FROM THE MENU

You can select a limited number of styles from the Effects menu. For example, you can choose to add a drop shadow effect to an object or a group of objects.

To Apply A STYLE FROM THE MENU

1 Select the object or objects you want to apply the style to.

2 Choose Effects | Stylize.

3 Choose the style you want to apply to the objects.

NOTE Some styles may ask you to make choices from various dialog boxes. Make the appropriate choice and/or change the settings as you wish and click OK to continue. The chosen style will be applied to the selected artwork.

USING ACTIONS

Using an action is like applying a set of commands to the chosen artwork. In other applications, this process is referred to as creating a macro. When you apply an *action,* it's as if you applied a series of steps against a piece of artwork. The beauty of it, though, is that all you need to do is click the mouse a couple times to have all the work done for you.

Even better, though, is that you can create your own actions and share them with others. Using an action is as simple as selecting it from the Actions palette.

To view the Actions palette if it's not already open, choose Window | Actions. This is a toggle, so if the palette is not visible, it will be displayed; if it is visible, it will be hidden.

The Actions palette includes sets of steps that apply formatting changes to a selected object, like rotation or simplifying paths. Other actions allow you to perform file operations, like exporting a selected object to a web-friendly JPEG image. The Actions palette is shown next.

If you expand an action (click the triangle next to it so that the triangle is pointing down), you can see all the tasks that action will perform. For example, the action I've selected in Figure 16-3 will save the selected object as a GIF image, with transparency (the background color hidden) and no interlacing (it won't phase in, but instead will appear all at once in a browser). And it even figures out a folder to which to save the file on my hard disk. Wow! That not only saves me a bunch of work, but it also helps me make some sound decisions about the best file attributes to export my selected image for the Web.

NOTE Some of the default actions require a selection to be made. This is usually reflected by the fact that the word *selection* is displayed parenthetically after the action's name. Also, actions cannot be undone easily by selecting Edit | Undo because some actions may perform many steps.

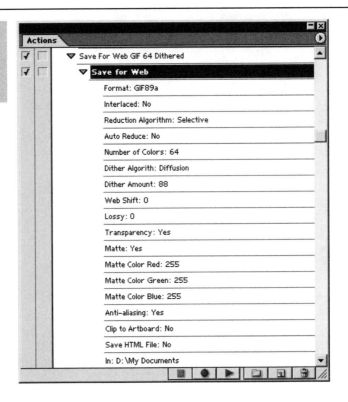

FIGURE 16-3
The Save For Web action saves selected artwork as a web-friendly GIF file.

To apply an action, simply click the action's name in the Actions palette and then click the Play button in the Actions palette, at the bottom of the palette.

CREATING AN ACTION

Creating an action can be an elaborate process. How elaborate depends on what you're trying to accomplish. Something like creating rounded rectangle buttons for a web page can be done without too much effort. Of course, the more elaborate the effort in the beginning, the more work your action will save you in the long run.

In the following steps, I'll illustrate how actions work with a simple example. The action you define will create a simple rounded rectangle button that you can use on a web page.

To Create AN ACTION FROM SCRATCH

1 Click the Create New Action button at the bottom of the Actions palette, as shown next. It resembles a page with its lower-left corner bent upwards.

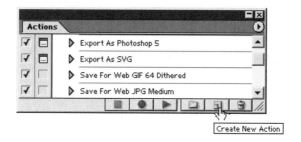

2 The New Action dialog box appears. Enter a name for your action and choose a set where it will reside. It's safe to leave it at the default, Default Actions, if you wish. (I'll explain what sets are and how to create them in the section "Saving an Action" later in this chapter.)

3 Click the Record button in the New Action dialog box, as shown here, to start recording the steps to create your action.

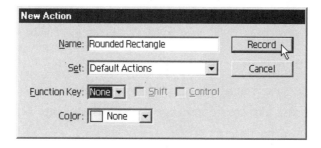

4 Select the Rounded Rectangle tool and draw a rounded rectangle somewhere on the artboard.

5 Select the Gradient tool and set the gradient to a white-to-black linear gradient in the Gradient palette. (See Chapter 11 for more information on how to accomplish this task.) Drag the Gradient tool from the left side of the rectangle to the right side to fill the object with the gradient.

6 Choose Edit | Copy.

7 Choose Edit | Paste In Front to duplicate the object.

8 Choose Object | Transform | Scale, and enter 90 percent in the Scale window under Uniform.

9 Choose Object | Transform | Rotate, and enter 180 degrees in the Angle box.

10 Click the Stop Playing/Recording button at the bottom of the Actions palette.

Voila! You've just created your first action. To see it in *action* (sorry—pun intended), select the objects you created and press DELETE to clear the artboard. Then select your action in the Actions palette and click the Play button. If everything worked right, the action should create a rounded rectangle button for you.

DELETING ACTIONS

If you have an action that you have no further use for, you can delete it by selecting it in the Actions palette and clicking the small trashcan icon in the Actions palette.

Alternatively, you can drag-and-drop the action from the palette onto the trashcan icon, or you can select the action and choose Delete from the Actions palette menu.

SAVING AN ACTION

To save an action, you must create it in a new set. You can create a new set when you first create an action, or you can create a set by clicking the Create New Set button at the bottom of the Actions palette.

With a set created, choose Save Actions from the Actions palette menu. The Save Set To: dialog box will open. From within that dialog box, you can choose a location for your action set and give it a filename.

SHARING ACTIONS

Any set of actions that you've saved can be shared with other files or with other Illustrator artists.

To share a set of actions, simply locate the file that you saved the set to and copy that file onto a disk, e-mail it to someone, or place it on the Web for others to share.

Action sets are saved with the extension .atn, and the files are cross-platform compatible. That is, actions created on a PC should work on a Mac, and vice versa.

USING SWATCHES TO SAVE TIME AND WORK

In Chapters 11 and 14, I've touched on the use of *swatches* to store customized patterns (Chapter 11) and special fill colors (Chapter 14). Here, I want to focus on how you can save time by building up a collection of swatches, including color, gradient, and pattern swatches, to use and reuse as you create your artwork.

The Swatches palette is fairly simple to work with. If it is not visible, simply choose Window | Swatches (which works as a toggle). The buttons at the bottom of the palette (from the left) offer these options: Show All Swatches, Show Color Swatches, Show Gradient Swatches, Show Pattern Swatches, Create A New Swatch, and Delete Swatches.

ORGANIZING SWATCHES

After you've created a swatch, Illustrator assigns it a default name. You can rename the swatch by double-clicking its thumbnail. The Swatch Options dialog box opens, as shown here, enabling you to rename the swatch.

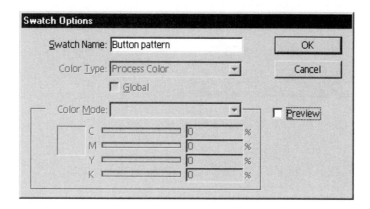

To delete a swatch that you've created, select the swatch's thumbnail in the Swatches palette and either drag-and-drop it onto the trashcan icon, or simply click the trashcan icon with the thumbnail selected.

Note that, unlike when a style is deleted, deleting a swatch has no affect on objects that have had the swatch applied to them.

USING SYMBOLS

Like swatches and styles, *symbols* are a great time-saver. They can be especially helpful when you need to add clipart-like images to your artwork.

Symbols, like styles, can be updated throughout an illustration. So, for example, if your organization's logo changes midway through an art project, you can instantly update that object throughout an illustration if the logo was saved as a symbol. In this sense, symbols in Illustrator are similar to symbols in Macromedia's Flash and other programs that use stored, editable symbol objects.

The Symbols palette displays all of the currently available symbols. At the bottom of the palette are several buttons that help you control and use the available symbols. They are identified in the following illustration.

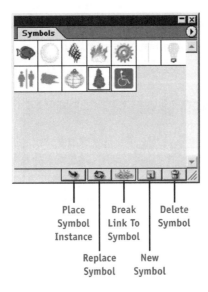

ADDING, REPLACING, AND EDITING SYMBOLS

You can easily add existing symbols to any open file. To add a symbol to your artwork, select the symbol you want from the Symbols palette and click the Place Symbol Instance button at the bottom of the Symbols palette.

You can also perform a kind of search-and-replace procedure using symbols, where you substitute one symbol for another throughout an illustration.

To Replace AN EXISTING SYMBOL IN YOUR ARTWORK

1 Select the symbol object using the Selection tool.

2 Select the new symbol you want to use in the Symbols palette.

3 Click the Replace Symbol button at the bottom of the Symbols palette.

Breaking a link to a symbol removes the link between the symbol and the object. The object then becomes a series of editable objects that were used to create the symbol.

To Break THE LINK TO A SYMBOL

1 Select the symbol object using the Selection tool.

2 Click the Break Link To Symbol button at the bottom of the Symbols palette.

CREATING OR DELETING SYMBOLS

You can create your own symbols, which can be handy when you want to create multiple instances of objects and preserve objects for later use.

To Create A NEW SYMBOL

1 Create an object or group of objects.

2 Select the object or objects with the Selection tool.

3 Click the New Symbol button at the bottom of the Symbols palette.

You can remove any symbols you no longer need. To delete an existing symbol, simply select the symbol in the Symbols palette and click the Delete Symbol button at the bottom of the Symbols palette.

SUMMARY

Styles, actions, swatches, and symbols are all different ways to save time and avoid boring, repetitive activity while creating artwork in Illustrator.

Styles are sets of attributes, like stroke, fill, transparency, and so on, that can be applied all at once to any object.

Actions are recorded steps that can be used for anything from applying a complex set of filters to an object to saving a selected object as a web-compatible GIF image. Illustrator comes with a nice list of carefully defined, useful actions, and it's worthwhile to check them out and use them as needed.

Swatches can save you time by storing commonly used colors. If your client provides you with a set of defined colors for his or her project, stash them in the Swatches palette to save time in designing the project.

Finally, symbols are graphic objects that can be placed in artwork. What's special about them is that they can be easily updated or replaced throughout an illustration.

ON THE VIRTUAL CLASSROOM CD In Lesson 12, "Styles," I'll demonstrate how to work more efficiently by defining and applying styles, actions, and symbols.

Index

LEARN FROM THE EXPERTS!

MASTER GRAPHICS SOFTWARE QUICKLY AND EASILY WITH MORE VIDEO LESSONS FROM BRAINSVILLE

CD Extras use the same easy-to-follow video presentation style as the CD included with this book. Each **CD Extra** is over an hour in length, with the author appearing on video throughout the entire presentation.

Adobe Premiere 6 CD Extra with Bonnie Blake

Bonnie shows you how to use edit tools, apply motion settings, use transitions, batch capture, create rolling titles, apply audio effects, and more!

Flash 5 CD Extra with Doug Sahlin

Create movie clips, gradients, motion paths, and special effects, animate multiple objects, use ActionScripts, and more…guided by a Flash expert.

Dreamweaver 4 CD Extra with Robert Fuller

Learn how to create styles, tables, links, Flash elements, and more from author and Web designer Robert Fuller.

Web Design CD Extra

Speed Web site development and improve design with Laurie's lessons on design tools, HTML basics, tables and frames, Web site critiques, and much more.

```
Name: Brainsville
Project: CD Extras
```